How to Use

Macromedia®

Dreamweaver® MX and Fireworks® MX

First Edition

Lon Coley

que®

201 W. 103rd Street
Indianapolis, Indiana 46290

How to Use Macromedia® Dreamweaver® MX and Fireworks® MX

Copyright © 2003 by Que Publishing

International Standard Book Number: 0-7897-2725-0

Library of Congress Catalog Card Number: 2001099409

Printed in the United States of America

First Printing: September 2002

05   04   03   02   4   3   2   1

Trademarks

Warning and Disclaimer

Executive Editor
Candace Hall

Acquisitions Editor
Kate Small

Development Editor
Maryann Steinhart

Managing Editor
Thomas F. Hayes

Project Editor
Tonya Simpson

Copy Editor
Mike Dietsch

Indexer
Kelly Castell

Proofreader
Benjamin Berg

Technical Editor
Jason Cranford Teague

Team Coordinator
Cindy Teeters

Interior Designer
Anne Jones

Cover Designer
Anne Jones

Page Layout
Ayanna Lacey

Contents at a Glance

Contents

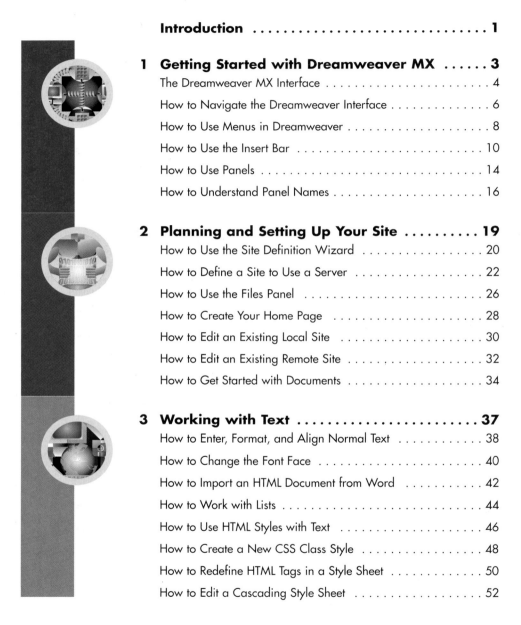

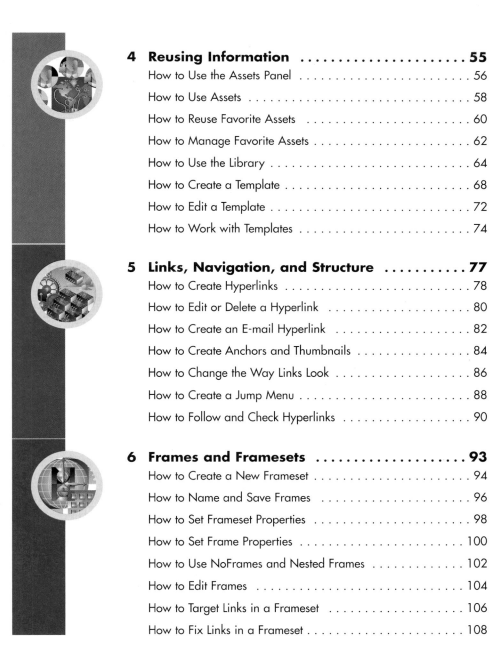

v

About the Author

Lon Coley (LonColey@ariadne-webdesign.co.uk) is an information-technology professional specializing in Internet solutions and the Internet in education. More details than can be put here are available at http://www.ariadne-webdesign.co.uk.

She has been active professionally within the Internet sector for five years, working with companies and colleges looking to understand and expand into the Internet in the modern working environment.

Although she designs Web sites for clients, her experience and expertise mean that she now mainly consults and troubleshoots for companies and colleges of all sizes that are looking to improve and develop their Internet presence or that feel they have sites that don't do their organizations justice.

A firm believer that anyone can build a Web site with the right tools and training, Lon often works with companies that want to develop their own Web sites but think they need an expert to call on when they are struggling. She also assists companies that need professional guidance about new technologies and avoiding common pitfalls when developing their existing sites.

An experienced teacher and trainer, Lon writes and develops dedicated customized training courses for both business and education. These courses cover the whole Macromedia and Microsoft product families and are always prepared with the individual client in mind. This way, Lon can guarantee the needs of the client are addressed and met in full. She has written or contributed to a variety of titles, including *How to Use Dreamweaver 4 and Fireworks 4, Flash Site Workshop,* and *Special Edition Using Flash MX.*

Dedication

To the one I love—always and forever.

Acknowledgments

Thanks to everyone at Que for their help and support in getting this book to print, but special thanks to Kate and Jeff for being themselves and always being there when I needed help, support, or even a reminder about deadlines!

Thanks to my family for giving me the time and space to work and for their never-ending support and patience. Special thanks to my son Jon for putting up with me being grumpy and busy too much of the time.

We Want to Hear from You!

As the reader of this book, *you* are our most important critic and commentator. We value your opinion and want to know what we're doing right, what we could do better, what areas you'd like to see us publish in, and any other words of wisdom you're willing to pass our way.

As an executive editor for Que, I welcome your comments. You can email or write me directly to let me know what you did or didn't like about this book—as well as what we can do to make our books better.

Please note that I cannot help you with technical problems related to the *topic* of this book. We do have a User Services group, however, where I will forward specific technical questions related to the book.

When you write, please be sure to include this book's title and author as well as your name, email address, and phone number. I will carefully review your comments and share them with the author and editors who worked on the book.

Email: feedback@quepublishing.com

Mail: Candace Hall
Que Publishing
201 West 103rd Street
Indianapolis, IN 46290 USA

For more information about this book or another Que title, visit our Web site at www.quepublishing.com. Type the ISBN (excluding hyphens) or the title of a book in the Search field to find the page you're looking for.

The Complete Visual Reference

Each chapter of this book is made up of a series of short, instructional tasks, designed to help you understand all the information that you need to get the most out of your computer hardware and software.

 Click: Click the left mouse button once.

 Double-click: Click the left mouse button twice in rapid succession.

 Right-click: Click the right mouse button once.

 Drag: Click and hold the left mouse button, position the mouse pointer, and release.

Pointer Arrow: Highlights an item on the screen you need to point to or focus on in the step or task.

 Selection: Highlights the area onscreen discussed in the step or task.

 **Type:** Click once where indicated and begin typing to enter your text or data.

 **Drag and Drop:** Point to the starting place or object. Hold down the mouse button (right or left per instructions), move the mouse to the new location, and then release the button.

Each task includes a series of easy-to-understand steps designed to guide you through the procedure.

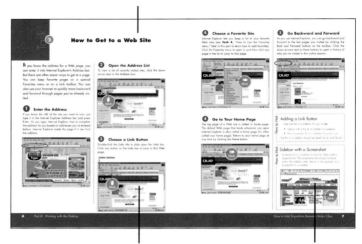

Each step is fully illustrated to show you how it looks onscreen.

Extra hints that tell you how to accomplish a goal are provided in most tasks.

 Key icons: Clearly indicate which key combinations to use.

Menus and items you click are shown in **bold**. Words in *italic* are defined in more detail in the glossary. Information you type is in a `special font`.

Introduction

"Anyone can design a Web site"—A statement I have used many times in the last few years, teaching and educating people about the concepts and skills needed for Web site design, development, and application building.

Dreamweaver and Fireworks make this statement easy to justify and prove.

The two pieces of software work seamlessly together, offering the user a complete tool for Internet design. From basic sites and graphics to totally dynamic interactive sites, it is all at your fingertips.

What Are Dreamweaver MX and Fireworks MX?

Good question—and not one easily answered in a couple of sentences. Let's start with Dreamweaver.

Macromedia's Dreamweaver MX

Since its first release, Macromedia Dreamweaver has led the way in professional Web design; this latest release only enhances that position. For beginners to Web design in general, and Dreamweaver in particular, Dreamweaver MX is certainly the best and most powerful tool available.

From static HTML to dynamic database-driven Web sites, Dreamweaver MX has it all. You work in a visual design-based way, or use the built-in code editing features to work by hand if that is what you prefer. Dreamweaver MX enables you to edit the HTML, work with CSS, handle text files, and do just about any other task you can think of.

You actually don't need to learn any code—simply use the Dreamweaver visual interface to lay out, design, and create professional-looking Web pages without ever needing to touch the code. You can edit existing pages made in other applications, safe in the knowledge that Dreamweaver will leave your code alone. You can even use Dreamweaver to tidy up the messy code other applications create.

This book covers only the more basic parts of what Dreamweaver can do—of course, I introduce some of the more technical elements, but only briefly. Even so, I hope that once you have mastered the basic tasks in this book you'll feel confident enough to move on in your learning and tackle bigger and better Web design and development projects.

Macromedia's Fireworks MX

Now, what about Fireworks? When Fireworks was first released, it was unlike any other design application on the market. The main difference between Fireworks and the applications already in the marketplace is that Fireworks was designed to create and edit Web graphics and animations and to meet the needs of Web designers and developers, without the constraints of worrying about printed media. It's a simple difference, but it remains the main feature of Fireworks.

This latest version of Fireworks has many new and enhanced features. One of the most obvious is much better integration with other Macromedia applications—not just Dreamweaver, but also Flash, Freehand, Director, and Generator. This improved integration makes Fireworks a hugely powerful and must-have application for anyone wanting to create Web graphics.

Unlike other applications that are designed to work with either bitmap images (described using dots) or vector graphics (described using lines and curves), Fireworks enables you to work in either mode and has a huge array of tools to create new graphics or edit existing ones.

Fireworks also lets you work directly from within Dreamweaver to create or edit a graphic on-the-fly. Dreamweaver remembers the Fireworks source file that is in use and lets you launch and edit the image at any time.

You can create buttons, imagemaps, and pop-up menus in Fireworks and then export them into Dreamweaver, complete with the entire HTML required for them to work immediately.

Although Dreamweaver and Fireworks can be used as standalone products, they work best together, and this book will help you get started with both applications in a task-based environment that lets you set the pace.

Who Should Use the Software?

In reality, the answer to this could or should be everyone, but the applications are best suited to those who not only want to create wonderful Web sites, but also want to control the way their sites look.

From the user-friendly interfaces that Macromedia has made even better in this latest release of its titles to the ever-present user control, there is something for everyone in both Dreamweaver MX and Fireworks MX.

Whatever your level of knowledge or skill, you can use these applications to create Web sites with the content and design you want. As your skill grows you can start to use more and more of the features offered by both Dreamweaver MX and Fireworks MX.

Stunning visuals combined with excellent layout will always make for successful Web pages—and Dreamweaver and Fireworks give you the power to create both, simply and easily.

I hope you enjoy the book and have fun learning.

—Lon Coley

Task

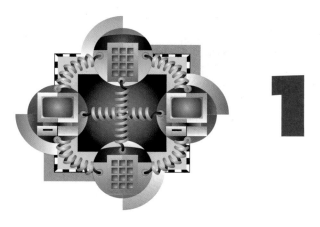

Getting Started with Dreamweaver MX

The software is out of the box, it's all nicely installed, and you are raring to go, so let's get started. Assuming that you have followed the default installation instructions, you can open the application by selecting **Start**, **Programs** (**All Programs** on Windows XP), **Macromedia Dreamweaver MX**, **Dreamweaver MX**.

Despite all the high-end technical things Dreamweaver can do, it's still an excellent HTML editor, site manager, and authoring program, combined in one easy-to-use interface. The HTML editor is where you can input page content and change the HTML code (the main language that actually tells the browser how your page is supposed to look); the site manager lets you see all the files in your Web site at a glance and generate reports in a couple of clicks; and the authoring side of Dreamweaver lets you add scripts, animations, and plug-ins wherever and whenever you want them.

Once open, the workspace might look confusing, especially if you haven't used Dreamweaver before. Even if you have seen or used previous versions, the new-look interface is very different.

Let's begin by showing you around the workspace, introducing some of the Macromedia terminology, and generally giving you a feel of the software. When you know your way around, you'll find it much easier to use the program effectively. You'll also find it much easier to understand Fireworks when you start using it later in the book. Macromedia's new integration features mean that you can switch between the applications and not get lost, because the interfaces look so similar.

The tasks in this part of the book introduce you to the various areas of the Dreamweaver workspace. Some of these you'll use almost daily and others less often. You still need to know what they all do. They're all discussed in more detail as we work through the book.

Once you have had a chance to read through the tasks in this part, the terminology should start making sense and it should be easier than ever to find your way around and get started.

Before we jump into the first task, take a look at the next two pages, which provide a basic "roadmap" to the Dreamweaver MX interface.

The Dreamweaver MX Interface

When you open Dreamweaver (choose **Start**, **Programs**, **Macromedia Dreamweaver MX**, **Dreamweaver MX**), you see its standard interface. Here's a rundown of its basic areas.

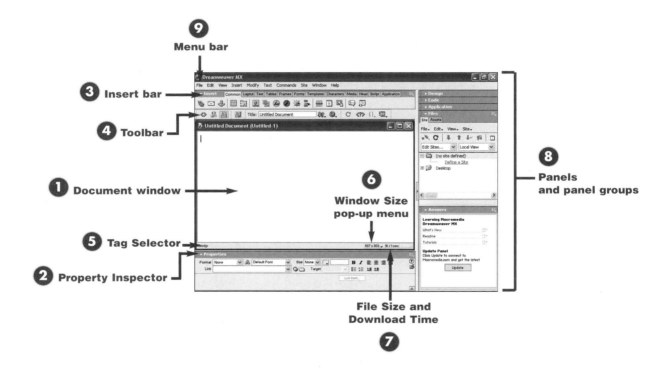

1 **Document window:** This is your main working area, where you create and edit files. You can work either in Design View, Code View, or a split screen.

2 **Property Inspector:** Here's where you'll see the properties for any object or text selected in the document window. The information displayed in the Property Inspector changes depending on the selection at the time.

3 **Insert bar:** The Insert bar is jam-packed with buttons, options, and tabs to enable you to insert page content into your documents and sites. Each tab contains different buttons to insert different topic-oriented objects.

4 **Toolbar:** The Toolbar buttons in Dreamweaver let you control the way you view your document, preview your pages in browsers, and access reference information.

5 **Tag Selector:** The Tag Selector enables you to select any tag in the document and highlights the selected content in the document window.

6 **Window Size pop-up menu:** Dreamweaver has some preset window sizes that let you change the document size. This enables you to see how the layout works at different screen sizes—an important part of Web design.

7 **File Size and Download Time:** This shows you the size of your file (including images and other media) and the estimated time it will take for the file to be downloaded into a browser at different connection speeds.

8 **Panels and panel groups:** All down the right side of the screen are panels and panel groups (a panel group is a collection of panels grouped together under one title bar). These can be hidden, expanded, and moved to suit your requirements.

9 **Menu bar:** Just like any application, Dreamweaver has a menu bar at the top. This gives you access to standard menu commands, and lets you open and close windows and open and save files in much the same way as any other application.

How-to Hint

Mac OS X Users

New in OS X is the application menu, which appears in bold at the far left side of the Menu bar. The application menu uses the name of the running application (in this case Dreamweaver or Fireworks) and contains application-specific options: About Macromedia Dreamweaver MX, Preferences, Services (disabled in Dreamweaver), Show Dreamweaver, Hide Other Applications, Show All, and Quit Dreamweaver.

The Preferences option is also available in the Edit menu, but Quit is available only from this menu.

How to Navigate the Dreamweaver Interface

Okay, we've had a quick look around the user interface, so now let's look at some of those areas in more detail. (One great thing about Macromedia is that the terminology you learn and use here will be the same in Fireworks as well; this makes the learning curve easier for everyone.) We'll start by creating, naming, and saving a new document.

1 Create a New Document

From the **File** menu, choose **New** to open the New Document dialog box.

2 Select a Document Category

The New Document dialog box lets you choose from many document types. We'll look at the most common options as we work through the book, but for now let's concentrate on HTML pages. Select **Basic Page** from the **Category** column (it should be selected by default).

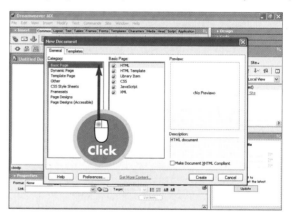

3 Select a Document Type

Click **HTML** in the **Basic Page** column. (We'll examine other options later). Click **Create** to continue.

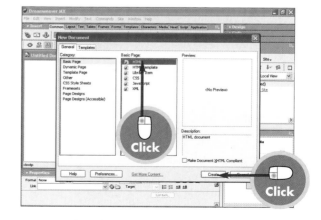

4 Look at the Document Window

The dialog box closes, and you are presented with a blank, new document ready and waiting for you to add your content.

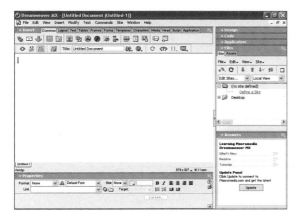

5 Add Some Text

Type a few words into the document window, just so you can see how it works. Pretty simple really—what you type appears onscreen just like a word processor.

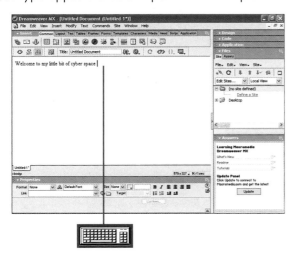

6 Name the File

All Web pages need a title. The Toolbar has a box called **Title.** By default, it says **untitled document.** To add a page title, type in the **Title** box. In this case, you could type `Welcome to my first ever Web page with Dreamweaver`. Even though the title box is small, you can keep typing. When you're finished, the screen refreshes and your title appears in the title bar at the top of the application.

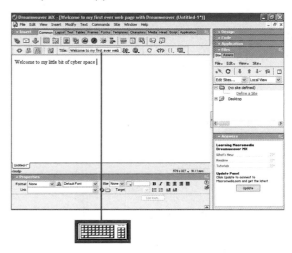

7 Save the File

Saving a file in Dreamweaver is easy. From the **File** menu, select **Save**, and browse to the location you want to save your file. Type a name for the file in the **File name** box, and click **Save** to continue.

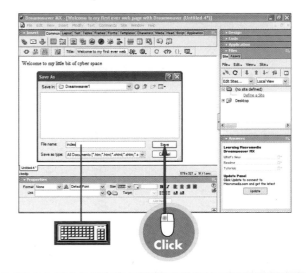

How to Use Menus in Dreamweaver

Like almost any computer application, Dreamweaver has a menu bar to help you get the most from it. I don't know if you've ever thought about the names of menus, but almost universally they are there to help you. Dreamweaver is no exception. The **File** menu, for example, lets you work with files—opening them, saving them, previewing them, and so on. In this task, we'll look at some of the more common menu commands in Dreamweaver, starting with the **File** menu.

❶ The File and Edit Menus

The **File** menu contains commands relating to your files. Standard file commands include **Open** and **Save**. The **Edit** menu contains commands that you'll find useful when editing a document: **Cut**, **Copy**, and **Paste** appear in this menu, as well as some Dreamweaver-specific items such as **Select Parent Tag** and **Select Child**.

❷ The View and Insert Menus

The **View** menu lets you change the way you see the document window. Use its options to display gridlines, borders, and rulers, as well as the head content and meta tags for your file. The **Insert** menu enables you to add images, tables, horizontal lines, and more to your page.

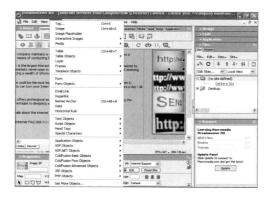

❸ The Modify and Text Menus

The **Modify** menu lets you change the elements you have already inserted on the page. You use it to change the appearance of tables, links, and so on. The **Text** menu contains all the options you will ever need to make your text appear the way you want it—including indents, fonts, styles, and sizes.

The Commands and Site Menus

The **Commands** menu lets you perform some advanced options, such as cleaning up HTML imported from Microsoft Word and choosing preset color schemes. You use the **Site** menu to manage all the pages in your Web site, to check the links across an entire site, and to define a new site.

The Window and Help Menus

Use the **Window** menu to display and hide all the Dreamweaver panels and windows. Click a panel name to display that panel; click again to hide it. Use the **Help** menu to locate everything you need to know about Dreamweaver and to access local and online help quickly and easily.

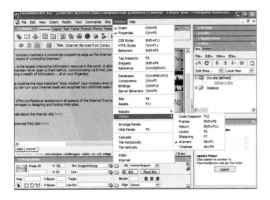

Show More Panels

The panels that are open by default are often all that you need in Dreamweaver, but the **Window** menu lets you access those panels used less often.

View Context Menus

Perhaps the most forgotten type of menu is the context menu, which gives you options based on the selected text or image. Right-click an object in the document window (Ctrl+click on a Macintosh) to open the context menu for that object. This example shows the context menu for the selected image.

How-to Hint

Helpful Menu Names

When you first start using Dreamweaver, the mass of different views, options, and menus can be quite intimidating. One way to avoid the confusion is to use the menus. Each menu is named to help you find commands in that category: File commands are in the **File** menu, and so on. If you are struggling to locate the right option in the toolbars or panels, use the menus until you become more confident with the panels and inspectors.

How to Use the Insert Bar

The Insert bar enables you to insert and control all types of page elements, from tables and layers to adding media and almost everything else you want in your Web pages. The Insert bar is divided into categories—you can easily switch between categories simply by choosing the appropriate tab on the Insert bar.

1 Open and Close the Insert Bar

By default, the Insert bar is open and accessible at all times, but you can close it simply by clicking the down arrow next to the word **Insert**. Reopen it by clicking the arrow a second time.

Click to close Insert bar

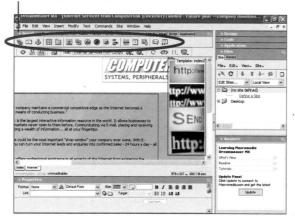

2 Insert an Object

Inserting an object is simply a case of selecting the button you want on the Insert bar. Moving your mouse over the buttons displays tooltips to help you.

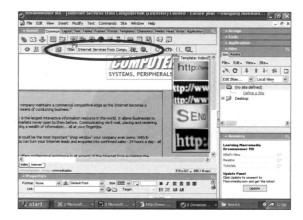

3 Complete the Dialog Box

Many of the options from the Insert bar open dialog boxes. Here you see the Select Image Source dialog box that enables you to select an image to insert.

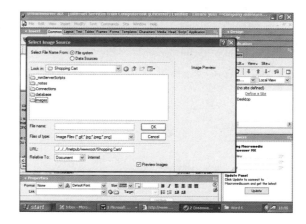

④ The Common Tab

The Insert bar's **Common** tab has buttons for inserting the most commonly used page elements, such as tables, layers, images, and so forth.

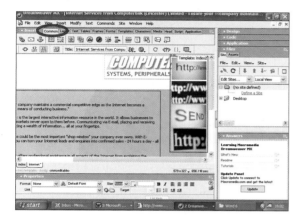

⑤ The Layout Tab

The **Layout** tab enables you to insert layout tables and cells into your documents. You can easily switch between layout and standard view. Layout view enables you to lay out your page before you start thinking about adding content; standard view is much more about laying out and adding content as you go.

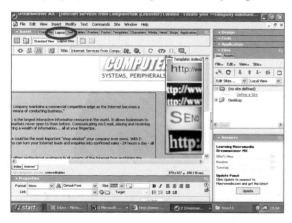

⑥ The Text Tab

The **Text** tab inserts some specific HTML tags used for formatting text.

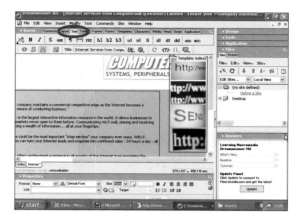

⑦ The Tables Tab

From the **Tables** tab you can insert complete tables or simply add table-specific HTML tags.

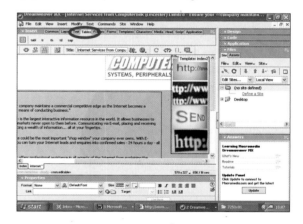

⑧ The Frames Tab

The **Frames** tab enables you to insert preset frame options or add frames to existing frame-based Web sites.

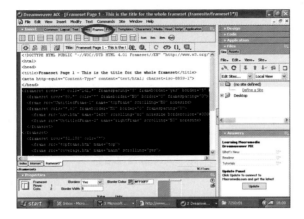

⑨ The Forms Tab

The **Forms** tab contains all the elements for creating forms in your Web site. Each of the possible form page elements is accessible at the click of a button.

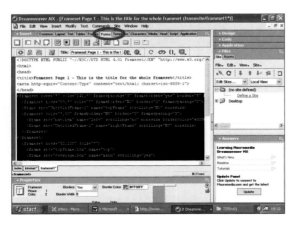

⑩ The Templates Tab

The **Templates** tab lets you add regions into your templates. In Dreamweaver, a template is a predesigned page that lets you lock areas, creating consistency between pages because you change only the required content on each page. You can also update all pages at once based on a template.

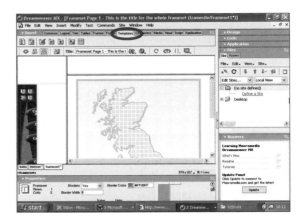

⑪ The Characters Tab

Use the **Characters** tab to insert symbol-based characters such as ©, ®, ⇔, ¥, and the pound sterling symbol that do not appear on your keyboard into your Web pages just by selecting the appropriate button.

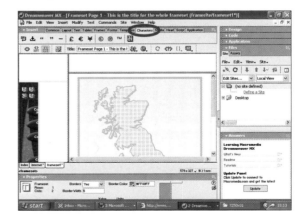

12 The Media Tab

You use the **Media** tab options to insert Flash movies, Java applets, and Active X controls into your Web pages.

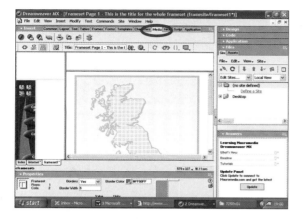

13 The Head Tab

From the **Head** tab you can easily add meta content (specific tags for keywords, content, and descriptions that define your pages to search engines and other content regulators) and other tags that sit in the head section of your page.

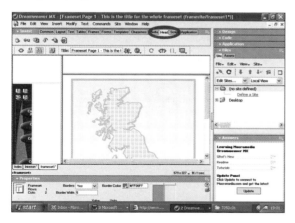

14 The Script Tab

Use the **Script** tab options to insert scripts into your Web page or to add server-side includes, both of which we will look at later in the book.

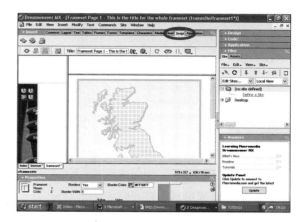

15 The Application Tab

The **Application** tab enables you to add dynamic content—such as recordsets from databases—to your Web page.

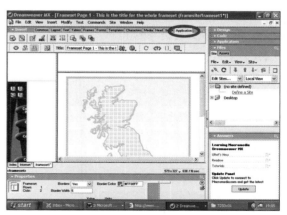

How to Use Panels

As you've already seen, the Dreamweaver interface is made up of many different panels. All of these are designed to make your experience of using the application as straightforward as possible. Many panels are visible when the application launches, and these are the ones you're likely to use most often. Panel groups are made up of similar items that are often used at similar times; they can be opened, closed, moved, or expanded at any time.

❶ Expand a Panel Group

To expand a panel group to make the contents visible, click the arrow in the panel's title bar. Clicking the arrow a second time toggles the action, closing the panel. Note that on a Mac a panel group is resized using the **Window Resize** button at the bottom right of the panel group.

❷ Select a Panel Inside a Group

After a panel group is expanded, you can select the panel you want to work with by clicking the desired tab at the top of the panel group.

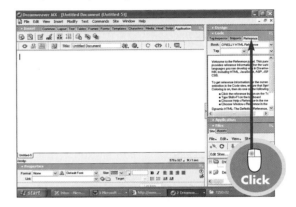

❸ Undock a Panel Group

By default, the panel groups are docked to the left of the screen. You can undock (and redock) a panel by grabbing it and pulling it away from the left (or back to the left). Click and hold the **Panel Grabber** (the dotted area) until the cursor changes as shown, then simply pull the panel group away.

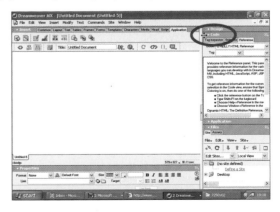

4 View the Panel Options

Most panels have an options menu that changes depending on the panel you have selected. Simply click the down arrow at the top right of a panel to view its menu options.

5 Close a Panel Group

You can close a panel group at any time by selecting **Close Panel Group** from the panel's menu. This closes the panel group completely.

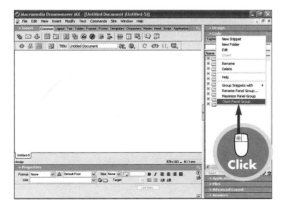

6 Open a Panel Group

To reopen a panel group that has been closed completely, you must select the group or panel you want from the **Window** menu. (When you select a panel, the panel group it is within opens.)

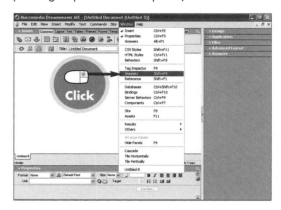

7 Hide All Panels

You can hide all panel groups on the screen to increase the document window area by clicking the expander arrow on the right of the document window.

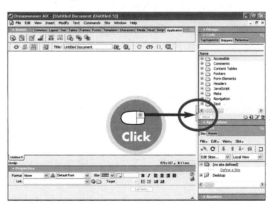

How to Understand Panel Names

You've seen how the panel groups fit together in the workspace and how to open and close them, but what do the names actually mean? In this task, we'll look at the most common panels and explain a little about what they are used for.

① CSS Styles Panel

Located in the Design panel group, the CSS Styles panel is used to create and edit Cascading Style Sheets (CSS), which enable you to format and update complete sites quickly and easily.

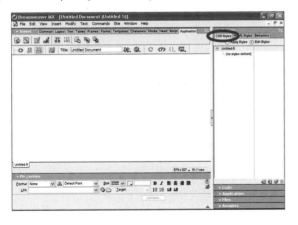

② HTML Styles Panel

Also inside the Design panel group, the HTML Styles panel is used to add quick and easy formatting to text in your documents.

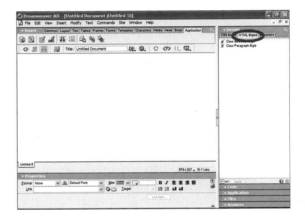

③ Behaviors Panel

The last panel in the Design panel group is the Behaviors panel, which is used to add behaviors to your page elements. Dreamweaver behaviors are pieces of JavaScript that let you add interaction to your pages easily.

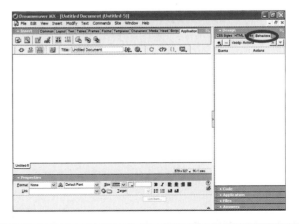

④ The Code Panel Group

The Tag Inspector enables you to change tags within a property sheet and shows possible attributes for a selected tag. The Snippets panel provides sections of code you can use to create elements such as tables, page footers, and comments. The Reference panel supplies HTML tag and CSS reference information, and much more.

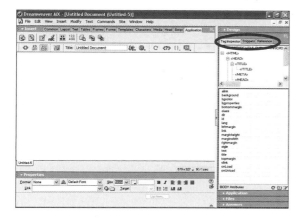

⑤ The Application Panel Group

The Databases, Bindings, Components, and Server Behaviors panels make up the Application panel group, and are all used when working with dynamic page content. From setting up a connection onward, dynamic content is controlled from these panels.

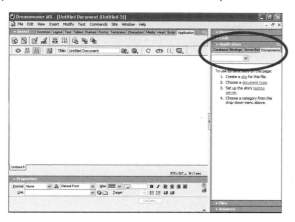

⑥ The Files Panel Group

The Site and Assets panels are located in the Files panel group. From the Site panel, you can define sites and view all local and remote files that are part of your Web site. The Assets panel offers a quick and easy way to see all site assets (elements)—such as sound files, colors and images—in a convenient location.

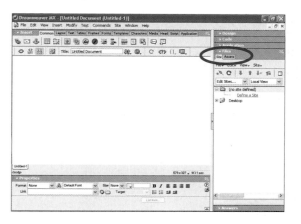

⑦ The Answers Panel

This is a new feature in Dreamweaver MX that, assuming you have an active Internet connection, enables you to access information and tutorials by clicking the link you want. The **Update** option downloads the latest Dreamweaver information from Macromedia directly into the panel.

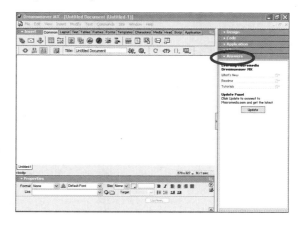

Task

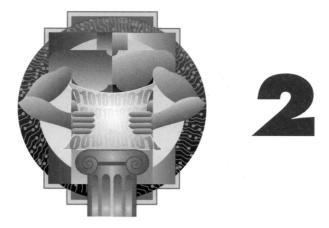

Planning and Setting Up Your Site

You've looked around Dreamweaver and are familiar with the names for everything and where all the tools and panels are located. Before we start creating a Web site, though, let's take a minute to explain a couple more words. Everyone knows what a Web page is—it's what you look at on the Internet. But what makes a Web site? In simple terms, a Web site is a group of Web pages that are linked together and reside at the same Web address (**http://www.yourdomain.com**, for example).

A good Web site should be informative, easy to use, accurate, and up to date. Its information should be well organized and relevant—don't claim to have a Web site on a certain topic and then fill it with other stuff just because your service provider says you can use 50MB.

In Dreamweaver, the word site can refer to either the storage location of the files and other elements that come together to create a Web site, or the Web site itself.

Spend some time considering what your site will be about, who you want to visit it, and what (if any) objectives the site has. You could just jump in and start creating pages in Dreamweaver, but it's far better to plan your site first. (There are complete books, theories, and papers about planning Web sites. We can't discuss them here, but you should avail yourself of these resources.) Many Web designers still use a pen and paper to draw a rough plan of how the finished site should look; other designers create a complete mockup using graphics applications such as Fireworks. (Everyone has different ways of working through the planning stage; however, by the end of this book you should feel confident enough to plan your second Web site in Fireworks.)

When you have your plan, a Dreamweaver site gives you somewhere to store all the information you want to use, as well as a structure in which to work. You can also check on the status of the site as a whole rather than checking every single page. Dreamweaver lets you edit a site that you've created in another application, even if it's already on the Internet.

This part of the book looks at the various options available to get you started with sites. You'll need to identify which tasks are appropriate for you.

How to Use the Site Definition Wizard

When you create a Web site using Dreamweaver, you must define the site before you can do any other work on the site. Although there's no limit to the number of sites you can create in Dreamweaver, each site must have a unique name and a folder on your local machine where its files are stored.

If you're new to Dreamweaver, I recommend that you use the Site Definition Wizard, which guides you through the process of creating a site with the minimum of fuss and time.

❶ Open the Site Definition Dialog Box

Using the Site Definition Wizard makes creating a site a nice, straightforward process. From the **File** menu, choose **Site**, **New Site**.

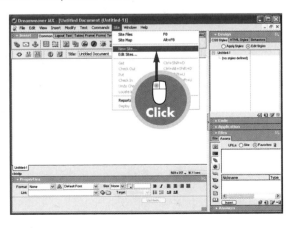

❷ Open the Basic Screen

In the Site Definition dialog box, click the **Basic** tab. The screen changes to a much friendlier-looking screen, complete with a text box prompting you to name the site.

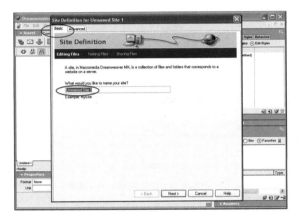

❸ Name the Site

In the text box, type a name for your Web site. This is for your use only and can be a nice friendly name; I'm naming mine **MyFirstSite**. Click **Next** to continue.

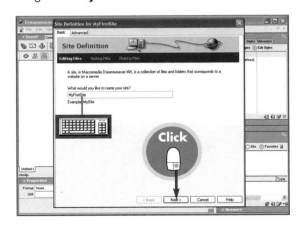

4 No Server Yet

Click the **No, I do not want to use a server technology** radio button (we'll look at servers a little later), and click **Next** to continue.

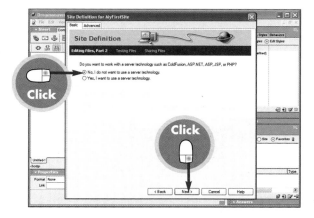

5 Where Are You Working?

From the three options available, choose **Edit local copies on my machine, then upload to server when ready**. This option allows you to create, edit, and delete files on your local machine without affecting anyone else. (We'll look at the other options later in this part.) Click the folder icon to continue.

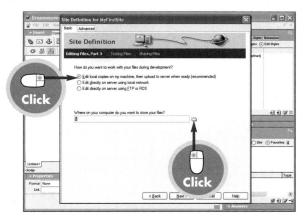

6 Choose a Folder

Use the Choose Local Root Folder dialog box to select a folder to use for MyFirstSite. (If necessary, you can create a new folder.) When you have selected a folder, click **Open**, then **Select** to return to the Site Definition dialog box.

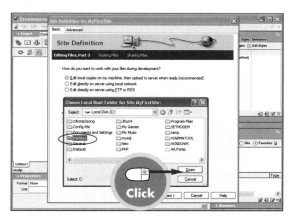

7 All Done For Now

Click the **Next** button to continue; then click **Next** again to bypass the remote information (see Task 3). The dialog box displays the information you have completed. Assuming this is all accurate, click **Done** and click **OK** to let Dreamweaver create a cache. (The cache keeps track of all the files in your site and makes site management far easier.)

How to Define a Site to Use a Server

In Task 1, we set up a quick, simple site—ideal for those of you keen to get in there and start creating files. However, if you're using a Web server or an application server, you need additional settings. In this task we'll look at the Advanced tab of the Site Definition dialog box and create a site that uses additional technologies. If you want to learn more about Web servers and application servers, check out Parts 19 and 20 of this book.

1 Open the Site Definition Dialog Box

From the **Site** menu choose **Site**, **New Site** to open the Site Definition dialog box. Be sure you have the **Basic** tab selected.

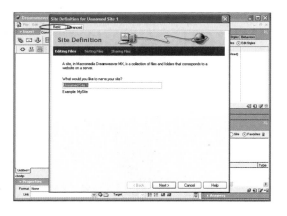

2 Name the Site

Type a name for the site. This is for your use only, so it can be anything you want as long as the name is unique. I am naming this site **ServerSite1**. Click **Next** to continue.

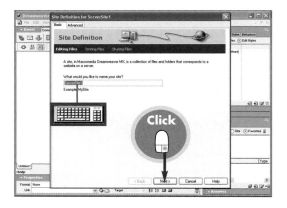

3 Choose a Server Technology

If you're planning to work with dynamic sites, click the **Yes, I want to use a server technology** radio button, and choose the technology from the **Which server technology?** drop-down list. Click **Next** to continue.

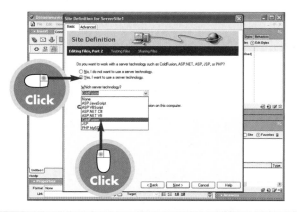

4 Choose How You Work

From the four radio buttons, choose the option that most fits your working setup. I work with a server on my local machine and test on that server, so I've chosen the top radio button.

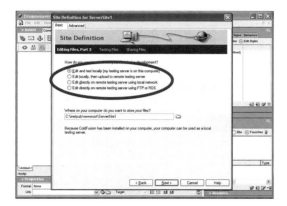

5 Choose a Storage Location

With a local server, Dreamweaver automatically suggests a storage location (using PWS or IIS, this will be in the Inetpub directory). If you are working with any other option, browse to where you will store your files. Click **Next** to continue.

6 Set the Testing URL

To test server-based pages, Dreamweaver needs to know the location of the files in the format of a Web address. If the address is not automatically entered, type it in. You might need to check with your network administrator for this information.

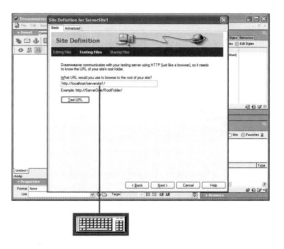

7 Test the URL

Click the **Test URL** button to check that the communication works okay. You should see the screen shown here. If you see an error message, check the URL you entered in the previous step, or check with your network administrator. Click **OK** to close the alert box.

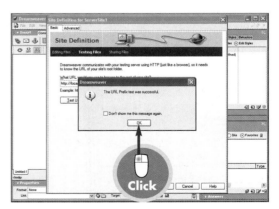

8 Remote Information

Depending on your work setup, you might need to copy files to a network location such as a shared server or your network Web server. If so, check the **Yes, I want to use a remote server** radio button. If not, click the **No** radio button. If you transfer files directly to the Internet, click **No.** If you clicked No, jump to Step 12.

9 Choose Your Connection Type

From the **How do you connect to your remote server?** drop-down menu, choose how you connect to the remote server. Next, use the File icon to browse to your storage area on the server. Click **Next** to continue.

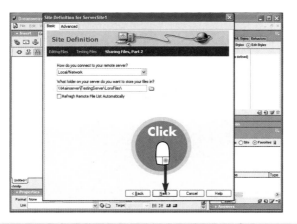

10 Check In and Out

Document check in and check out control whether multiple users can edit files at the same time. Assuming you're on a network, you need to find out network policy. To be safe, choose not to set this up now. Click **Next** to continue. (If you find later that you need to use check in/out, it's covered in the final task of Part 22, "Project Management.")

11 All Done

Click **Done** to continue. You don't need to configure an Internet connection because you transfer files to a remote folder on your network. Dreamweaver finishes creating the site and cache, including creating folders, if needed. If you've completed Task 2 through this step, you don't need to follow steps 12–14; continue to Task 3.

⑫ Choose Remote Information

Click the **Advanced** tab of the Site Definition dialog box, and choose **Remote Info** from the **Category** list.

⑬ Choose Your Connection Type

From the **Access** drop-down list, choose **FTP**. This is how the files will be transferred to the Internet. As soon as you choose FTP, the screen refreshes with the other options you need to configure.

⑭ Complete the Dialog Boxes

Complete the rest of the fields with your connection information, which will have been supplied by your Internet service provider or Web hosting company. Click **OK** to continue and allow Dreamweaver to finish creating the site and cache, including folders if needed.

How to Use the Files Panel

In Dreamweaver MX on a Windows system, site files are visible within the integrated workspace at all times, and you can expand this view as required. When you close the Site Definition dialog box, you return to the Dreamweaver interface and little appears to have changed. However, Dreamweaver now knows that you've created the structure where you intend to keep the files for a Web site, and the files you create can be stored correctly with accurate links at all times. In this task we look more closely at the Files panel and some of the available options.

❶ Locate the Files Panel

If you cannot already see the Files panel group in Dreamweaver, select it by choosing **Site**, **Site Files**, or by pressing the **F8** key on your keyboard.

❷ Understand the View

There are two tabs at the top of the Files panel group: **Site** and **Assets** (we'll deal with **Assets** throughout the book). Ensure that the **Site** tab is selected.

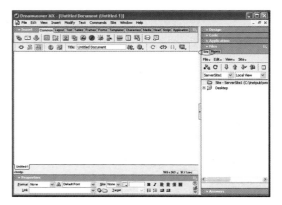

❸ Use the Site Selector

The Site Selector (which is accessed by clicking the down arrow at the side of the site name) allows you to view the files for different sites that you have created. Clicking the down arrow shows you all current sites or lets you open the Site Definition dialog box to edit or create a site definition.

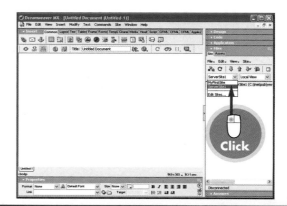

④ Expand to Full Screen View

Click the **Expand/Collapse** button to see the site files in full-screen view.

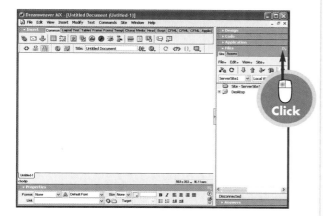

⑤ Examine the Expanded View

You can see all your local files in the list view as before, or click the **Site Map** button to see the structure of your site. I'm using an existing local site as an example here. Until you've created files, your view will be empty.

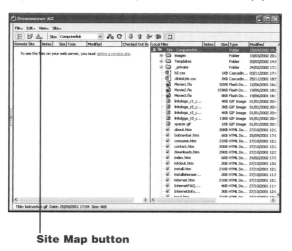

Site Map button

⑥ View the Site Map

Here we can see the site map for a completed site. This view shows how the pages are linked together. The + (plus sign) next to a page indicates that there are further links to be seen. Click the **+** to expand the view and see linked pages. The sign changes to a **–** once the view is expanded.

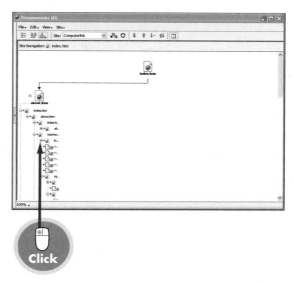

How to Hint

More About the Files Panel

As you can see, the Site panel in the Files panel group controls many views. We have only touched on the basics to get you started, but don't worry— we'll be dipping in and out of these views throughout the book. Part 22, "Project Management," covers this in much more detail and takes you through uploading your files to the Internet.

How to Create Your Home Page

For your site map to work for you, you obviously need some pages—more specifically, you need a home page. A home page is what visitors see first after they type in your Web site address. Most Web hosts require this page to have a particular name, usually `index.htm(l)` or `default.htm(l)`. Check with your hosting company or ISP to find out what your file needs to be called. Once you have a file with the correct name, which we'll create in just a minute, you need to tell Dreamweaver where it is on your hard drive.

❶ Close the Expanded Files Panel

If the Files panel is still expanded to full screen, close it now by clicking the **Expand/Collapse** button.

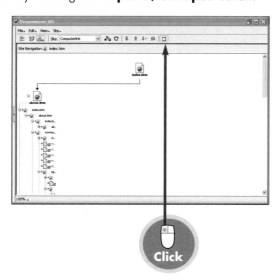

❷ Save a Blank Document

When you opened Dreamweaver, a blank document was automatically created. For now, we'll simply save this page without any content and set it as the home page. Click once anywhere inside the document, and then select **Save** from the **File** menu.

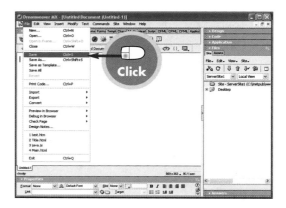

❸ Browse to the Save Location

Browse to the folder in which you chose to store your local files in either Task 1 or 2. In the File name box, type **index** or the name given to you by your hosting company for your home page.

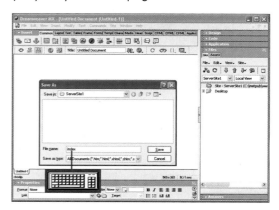

4 Save the File

You don't need to change the file type or add a file extension. Dreamweaver automatically makes the file an **.htm(l)** page and adds the extension for you. Simply click **Save** to continue.

6 Set the Home Page

Right-click the **index.htm** file in the Site panel to open the context menu, and choose **Set as Home Page**. Dreamweaver now knows that this is the starting point for your site.

5 Refresh the Site Files View

Although you've saved the page, the Site panel does not yet show the page in the site. Click the **Refresh** button to update the file list for your site.

How-to Hint

Check Your Home Page

To check that the file is correctly recognized as the home page, expand the Site panel and click the **Site Map** button. Your index.htm file should display in the middle of the screen. If not, repeat Step 5 of this task to set it.

File Extensions

For the purpose of creating your files, .htm and .html are one and the same thing. By default, Windows operating systems only add a three-letter file extension when you create a document.

How to Edit an Existing Local Site

Dreamweaver enables you to work on files that have already been created on your local hard drive and treat them as a Dreamweaver site. This is useful if you are moving to Dreamweaver from another application, have created pages by hand in the past, or have taken over the job from someone else.

Anything created that is specific to another application might not work in Dreamweaver, so be careful! For example, Dreamweaver doesn't support FrontPage components, so if someone has created pages using FrontPage, you must take care that you do not lose functionality. Macromedia's Web site (www.macromedia.com) has a great article about migrating from FrontPage to Dreamweaver.

❶ Open the Site Definition Dialog Box

From the **Site** menu choose **New Site** to open the Site Definition dialog box.

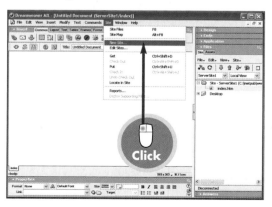

❷ Choose to Define a New Site

Even though the pages have been created, your site is treated as new in Dreamweaver. Click the **Advanced** tab in the Site Definition dialog box.

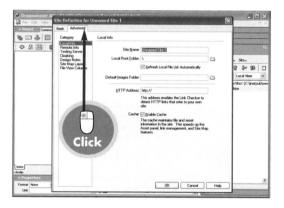

❸ Name the Site and Find the Files

Give the existing site a name, and then click the folder icon next to the **Local Root Folder** field. Browse to the location that holds the existing files.

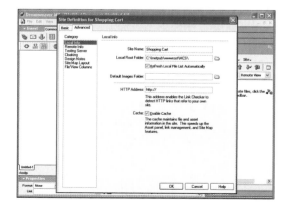

4 Set the Images Folder

If the existing site has an images folder, select that as well. If not, you can safely leave the **Default Images Folder** field blank. The **Refresh Local File List Automatically** option (below the **Local Root Folder** field) is selected by default. This option tells Dreamweaver to refresh the listing of local files whenever you copy something into the site.

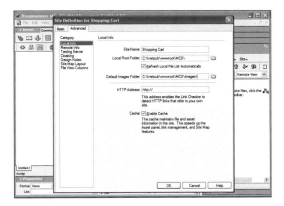

5 Create the Cache

Click **OK** in the dialog box, and then click **OK** in the information box to allow Dreamweaver to build the site cache—this may take a minute or two depending on the size of the site. Dreamweaver scans all the files in the specified folder to build the site.

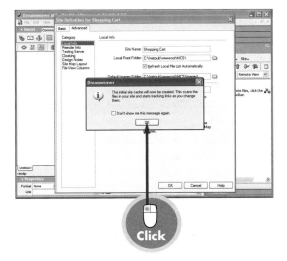

6 View the Site Files

Dreamweaver automatically opens the site you have created, and the files are visible in the Site panel (located in the Files panel group).

7 Open a Page

You can open any page from the Site panel. Simply double-click the page you want to open, and it will appear in the document window ready for editing.

How to Edit an Existing Remote Site

Dreamweaver not only enables you to create and manage your local files, but lets you directly connect with the remote server so you can copy a complete site from the Internet to your hard drive for editing. If you're taking over a site from someone else, for example, just copy the whole site directly to your hard drive. You can copy just the bits you need to work on, but because you must ensure that you have the same structure set up locally to hold the files, it's easier to import the whole site once.

1 Create a Folder to Hold the Content

On your hard drive, create a new folder to contain the files you download from the Internet (remote) site. If you are using a server, create your new folder in the default location for server files—that is, `Inetpub\wwwroot\foldername`.

2 Define a New Site in Dreamweaver

Click **Site**, **New Site** to open the Site Definition dialog box. Name the site, and then browse to the new local folder to hold the files. Complete the **HTTP Address** box with the location of the existing Web site.

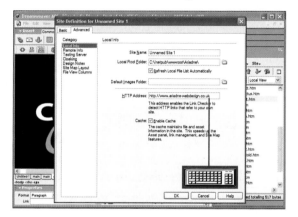

3 Complete the Remote Info

From the Category list on the left, select **Remote Info**. We need to tell Dreamweaver where to get the files.

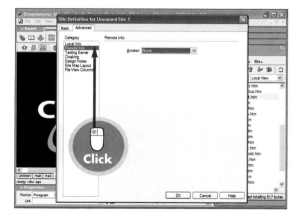

4 Choose the Connection Type

How you connect to the remote server is controlled by the **Access** selection. In most cases this will be **FTP** (File Transfer Protocol), so select this from the **Access** drop-down menu. The rest of the screen fills with the options you need to complete. (If you use a connection other than FTP, select the appropriate option.)

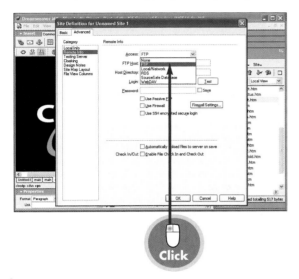

5 Complete the Dialog Box

Using the information supplied by either your ISP or whoever you are taking the site over from, complete the connection information in the Remote Info dialog box. Click **OK** twice, and then click **Done** to continue.

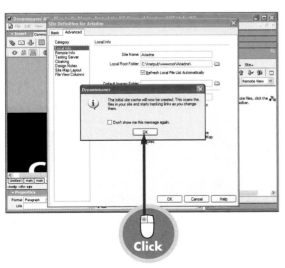

6 Connect to the Remote Server

Expand the Files panel to full screen as you did in Task 2, Step 4, and click the **Connect** button on the toolbar. If you are behind a firewall and have any problems connecting, check the settings you put in the **Remote Info** screen on the **Advanced** tab of the Site Definition dialog box, and try checking the **Use Passive FTP** option.

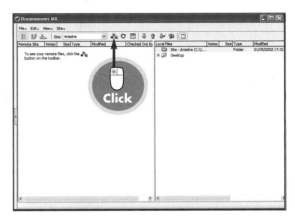

7 Download the Files

Select the root folder of the remote site (usually called `webroot`, `htmldocs`, or something similar), and then click the **Get Files** button on the toolbar. Dreamweaver will download the files to the folder you specified on your hard drive. This can take a while depending on the size of the site.

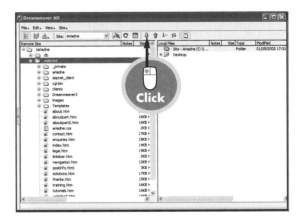

How to Get Started with Documents

You now have a newly created site on your local drive that contains a single empty home page, an existing site that Dreamweaver is ready to work with, or a complete site imported from the Internet. Now all you need to do is create or edit some Web pages.

Open the site you created in Task 1 or Task 2 (Site1). Dreamweaver lets you create many different document types, and we'll look at some of the others as we work through the book, but for now we'll stick to HTML.

① Open the `index.htm` File

Double-click the file named `index.htm` in the Files panel to open it into the document window. This is a nice simple HTML file with no content. The title bar displays the site name and filename for you.

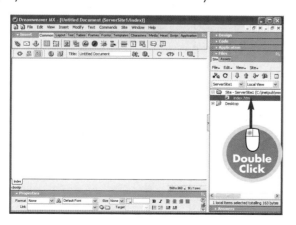

② Edit the Page Properties

From the **Modify** menu, choose **Page Properties** to open the Page Properties dialog box.

③ Give the Page a Title

Every Web page needs a title, which is always displayed in the title bar of the browser. In the **Title** box, give your page a meaningful name—avoid names like Welcome and Home Page.

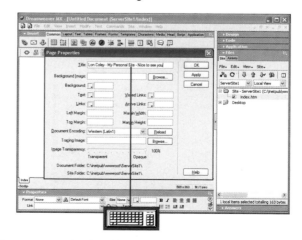

④ Apply the Title

Click the **Apply** button in the dialog box—Dreamweaver immediately applies the title to the page and it becomes visible in the document window. Click **OK** to close the dialog box.

Title bar

⑤ Save the Page with the Title

Note that the Dreamweaver title bar shows the filename as Site1/index*. The * indicates that a change has been made since the file was last saved. From the **File** menu, choose **Save** to save the file with the title.

How to Hint

More About Page Properties

Don't worry that we ignored link colors or the rest of the page properties. We'll be looking at link colors and how to set them in the next part, "Working with Text."

The rest of the page properties will be addressed as we go through the book in sections about layout, design, and images, to mention only three.

Task

Working with Text

Now that you have a solid understanding of the basics of Dreamweaver, let's get you started with text—one of the most important features of any Web page.

Text might seem like an obvious element in a Web page—you type, it appears, and that's that. Well, actually there's a bit more to it. Text can be formatted in only a limited number of fonts—those that are recognized by almost all computers—so forget about twirly, elaborate text. That stuff is very difficult to read on a screen, anyway.

When it's neatly aligned on a page, text can enhance the page, but be careful not to mix too many sizes and colors on the same page. Not only is that hard on the eyes, but it can make your site look confusing and distract those trying to read your sales information or product details. Use the bold, italic, and underline formatting options only when required.

Remember that most Web page text is going to be seen on a screen. Let your eyes guide you to use the font size that looks right for the job. Text that is too big can spoil even the best-planned Web site.

Text can be typed straight into a page or can be inserted into a layer or table cell. In fact, you can add text to your page anywhere you want it to be.

Formatting text can be done in different ways as well. You can select some text and apply a formatting command, such as bold; you can format text with HTML styles, which control only the text to which they are applied; or you can use Cascading Style Sheets (CSS), which can be saved as external files and applied to a complete page or even an entire Web site. If you change the style sheet, you update all the pages in your site in one fell swoop—how's that for a time-saving plan?

Dreamweaver allows you to create three types of styles: custom CSS styles, also known as class styles, that enable you to format any block of text; HTML tag styles, which redefine the formatting for chosen tags (h5, for example); and CSS Selector styles, which enable you to redefine combinations of tags.

There's more about using style sheets in Part 21, "All About CSS."

How to Enter, Format, and Align Normal Text

Normal text is just that: text that is typed in as plain text, not for use as a heading or a list. This task shows how to enter some text in a Dreamweaver document and then perform some basic formatting and alignment on it.

1 Enter Several Lines of Text

Start by typing something simple, such as **Welcome to my Web site**. To start a new line of text with blank space between the lines, press **Enter**, which inserts an HTML <p> paragraph tag that provides space between lines. To start a new line without inserting space, press **Shift+Enter**, which inserts the HTML <br> break tag. The new line stays in the same paragraph as the previous one but on a new line.

2 Change the Color of Text

By default, the text you type appears black. To change the color and other formatting options, be sure that the Properties Inspector is displayed (choose it from the **Window** menu if it isn't). Select the text and use the color picker from the Properties Inspector to choose a color.

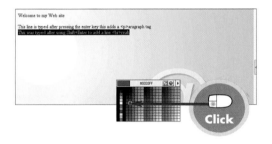

3 Set a Specific Font Size

Text in HTML can be specified in seven standard sizes, which more or less equate to standard point sizes: Size 1 is 8 points, size 2 is 10 points, and so on. To set a font size, select the text you want to affect, click the down arrow next to the **Size** field in the Properties Inspector, and pick a number from 1 to 7.

4 Set a Relative Font Size

By default, the text you type is size 3, the BASEFONT size. You can also set your text to be bigger or smaller relative to the default size by using the numbers preceded by a + or in the **Size** list.

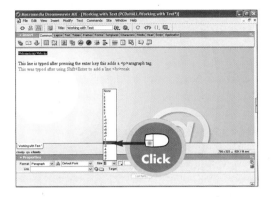

5 Make Text Bold, Italic, or Underlined

You can make the text on your page bold or italic by selecting the text you want to affect and clicking the **Bold** or **Italic** button in the Properties Inspector. To underline text, select the text and choose **Text**, **Underline** from the menu bar. Be careful when applying the underline attribute to text: most Web site visitors expect underlined text to be a hyperlink.

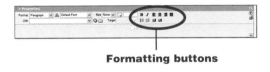

Formatting buttons

Head for Headings

How-to Hint

Task 1 concentrated on normal text; however, if you want your text as a heading, just select the heading size you want from the **Format** drop-down menu in the Properties Inspector and, presto! It's done. Just remember that when working with headings, h1 is the biggest and h6 is the smallest. We will look at headings a little more later in this Part when we examine CSS (Cascading Style Sheets).

6 Align Some Text

When doing any kind of text formatting, you must first select the text you want to affect. For this step, select the text you want to center on the page and click the **Align Center** button in the Properties Inspector. To left-align text, click the **Align Left** button; to right-align, click the **Align Right** button.

7 Indent or Outdent Text

To indent text from the left margin, select the text you want to indent and click the **Text Indent** button in the Properties Inspector. Click the button again to indent the text even more. You can outdent text (that is, remove an indent) by selecting the indented text and clicking the **Text Outdent** button on the Properties Inspector.

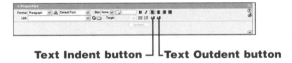

Text Indent button — └**Text Outdent button**

How-to Hint

It Just Isn't Justified

Did you notice that there is no "justify" option in the Text menu or in the Properties Inspector? This is a deliberate omission because most older browsers can't display justified text. The only way to add justified text is by using Cascading Style Sheets, which are discussed later in this Part and again in Part 21, "All About CSS." Note, however, that Cascading Style Sheets are interpreted consistently only by browsers of version 4.0 and later. Even those browsers might not display pages formatted with CSS as you might expect. Check your pages in several versions of each browser.

How to Change the Font Face

In most browsers, the default text font is Times (unless the viewer has changed the settings). Although you can choose a different font for your page, remember that it should be one that almost all Macs and PCs have installed. Instead of selecting a single font, you select a group of similar fonts (such as Arial, Helvetica, and sans serif). This instructs the browser to display the text using Arial first. If that font isn't installed (which it won't be on most Macs), the browser looks for Helvetica, and so on. If none of these fonts is available, the browser uses its default font, usually Times.

❶ See What's Available

You can see the font options that ship with Dreamweaver by choosing **Text**, **Font** or by clicking the **Font** menu in the Properties Inspector. The options appear in the submenu. To apply any of these font combinations to the currently selected text, choose the option from the menu. If you select the font before you begin typing, the new font is applied to the text you type.

❷ Change the Font Combinations

If the font you want to use is not in the list, you can create your own font combination. Choose **Text**, **Font**, **Edit Font List**. The Edit Font List dialog box opens.

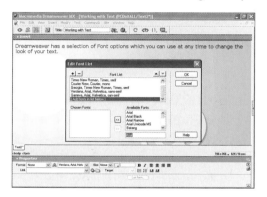

❸ Create the Combination You Want

From the **Available Fonts** list, select the first font you want to include on your page, and then click the **<<** button to move it to the **Chosen Fonts** list. Choose fonts that are common to most computers. Normally, a font combination contains three or four fonts: a PC font or two, a similar Mac font, and a font family.

4 Add a Font Family

After you have chosen the specific fonts you want, you should specify a font family. Any browser that can't display the specific fonts you have picked will display a font from the family you specify last in your list. For example, if all the specific fonts you selected are sans serif, choose the sans serif family. When you are finished, click **OK**.

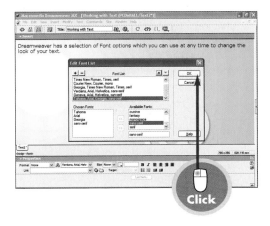

5 Edit a Font Combination

To edit the fonts in a particular font combination, choose **Text**, **Font**, **Edit Font List** to display the Edit Font List dialog box. To remove a font, choose its combination from the Font List at the top, select the font in the **Chosen Fonts** list, and click the **>>** button. Select from the **Available Fonts** list and click the **<<** button to add a font to the combination.

6 Reorder the Font Combinations

You can reorder the way font combinations appear in the **Font List** in the Edit Font List dialog box and in the **Text**, **Font** submenu. In the **Font List** at the top of the dialog box, select the combination you want to move and use the up and down arrows to change the order of this entry in the list.

How to Hint

What Is a Font Family?

The term *font family* is a generic name for a group of similar fonts. Most computers and browsers acknowledge the following font families: cursive, fantasy, monospace, sans serif, and serif. If a browser cannot display any of the specific fonts you have chosen (as when the font is not installed on the user's computer), the browser displays the text using the default font associated with the font family. For example, on most computers, the default font for the monospace font family is Courier.

Remember that Mac computers and Windows systems have different fonts available. To add a font from a different operating system, type the font name into the field below the Available Fonts list Edit Font List dialog box and click the **<<** button to add it.

How to Import an HTML Document from Word

Being able to use previously created documents from Microsoft Word can save you a lot of time retyping information. However, if you don't import the Word file into Dreamweaver correctly, you can cause yourself a lot of trouble. Documents saved in Word in HTML format can have a lot of spurious and unnecessary tags. Dreamweaver can clean up the file for you. Be sure you keep a copy of the original file in .DOC format; after Dreamweaver has cleaned up the HTML version, Word might not be able to open it.

① Import the File

Choose **File**, **New**, **HTML Document** to open a blank document into which you will import the Word document. Then choose **File**, **Import**, **Import Word HTML** to open the Select Word HTML File to Import dialog box. Navigate to the Word file that you saved in HTML format (it has the .htm extension) and click **Open**. The file opens in the document window with the Clean Up Word HTML dialog box open in front.

② Clean Up the HTML

Dreamweaver is going to go through the document and remove a series of HTML tags that complicate the formatting of the document. All the kinds of potential trouble spots that Dreamweaver will look for and fix are marked with a check mark in the dialog box. Click the **Detailed** tab to open the second page of the dialog box.

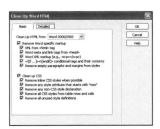

③ Check the Advanced Options

The **Detailed** tab lists all the specific tags that Dreamweaver intends to remove. These HTML tag descriptions are unlikely to mean much to you at this stage, so don't worry about them. In general, you want Dreamweaver to fix all potential problems with the HTML code that Word created, so leave all these options selected.

4 Start the Cleanup Process

You should not have to select the version of Word that created this HTML file; Dreamweaver detects and displays the appropriate version of Word in the list box at the top of the page. Click **OK** to accept the settings and start the clean-up process.

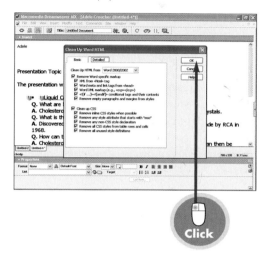

5 Review the Changes

When it's done, Dreamweaver displays a screen showing you what tags have been removed from the Word HTML document. Click **OK** to continue.

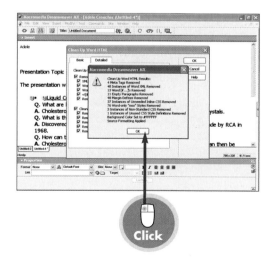

6 Save the File

The document now has none of the unnecessary tags, but all the original formatting (such as italics and bold) is retained. Choose **File**, **Save As** to save the document into your site folder as a Dreamweaver file.

How to Hint

Advanced Options

However good a word processor Microsoft Word might be, it sure isn't great as an HTML editor. The Clean Up Word HTML utility is a lifesaver if you do a lot of your typing in Word and then want to use those documents in Dreamweaver. To make sure that the cleaned-up file fits in with the rest of your site, you can set a background color as part of the clean-up process by selecting the **Set background color** option on the **Basic** tab of the dialog box. If you don't set one, the background color is automatically set to white.

How to Work with Lists

In HTML documents, lists come in various shapes and sizes: bulleted lists, numbered lists, and definition lists. (In a definition list, you have a word on the left and its definition on the following line, slightly indented.) As you might guess, Dreamweaver makes it easy to format all these kinds of lists.

① Create a New List

On the Properties Inspector, click either the **Bulleted List** (unordered list) button or the **Numbered List** button. A bullet or number appears in the document at the insertion point. Type the first list item and press **Enter (Return)**; a new bullet or number is added to the list. Continue until you complete your list. To end the list, press **Enter (Return)** twice; the cursor returns to the normal alignment without a bullet or number.

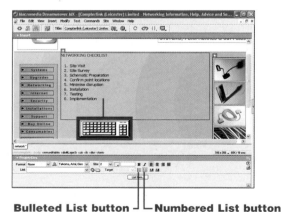

Bulleted List button ⌐⌐ **Numbered List button**

② Create a List from Existing Text

You can turn text that already exists into a bulleted or numbered list. Each paragraph of text becomes a separate item in the list. Select the text you want to turn into a list, and click the appropriate button in the Properties Inspector. The text is formatted into the list type you chose.

③ Create a Definition List

To create a definition list, first type the items: Type the term to be defined, press **Enter**, and then type the definition or meaning on the next line. Select your list, and choose **Text**, **List**, **Definition List** to format the text accordingly. In this example, the definition list format is used to list the titles of some company officers and the names of the people who hold those offices.

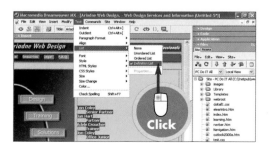

④ Remove List Formatting

If you change your mind about the formatting you've applied to a list, you can unformat the text. Select the text that you've formatted as a list and click the button in the Properties Inspector that was used to apply the list formatting in the first place. If it's a definition list, choose **Text**, **List**, **None**, and the list formatting is removed from the text.

⑤ Create a Nested List

A *nested list* is one in which certain items are *subpoints* under the main numbers or bullets. To create a nested list, select the items to be in the sublist and click the **Text Indent** button in the Properties Inspector.

⑥ Edit List Properties

Select a single item in the list and click the **List Item** button in the Properties Inspector to display the List Properties dialog box. From the **List Type** drop-down list, select the type of list item you want to work with. If you're working with a bulleted list, choose the bullet you prefer.

⑦ Change the Numbers

If you want your numbered list to start at a number other than 1, select a list item and open the List Properties dialog box and type the number you want the list to start at in the **Start Count** field.

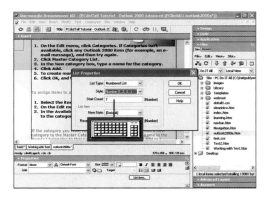

How to Hint

More About Numbers

You can even change numbers within a numbered list. For example, items can be numbered 1, 2, 3, and can then start back at 1. Select the paragraph at which you want to reset the count and specify the number to which you want to reset the count in the **Reset Count To** box.

You also can change the numbers to be letters or numerals: Simply use the **Style** drop-down list to select the style that best suits your document.

⑤ How to Use HTML Styles with Text

Although they are being used less and less in favor of Cascading Style Sheets (see Task 6), HTML styles are still a necessary part of Web design, because older browsers (Version 3 and earlier) offer little or no support for CSS but do support HTML styles. HTML styles enable you to save a particular formatting style, such as the font, bold, and alignment, and use it again and again in your document or site. HTML styles do not update automatically, so if you manually change an HTML style after it has been added to a Web page, you must reapply it to your text.

❶ Show the HTML Styles Panel

Open a document that has text to be formatted. From the **Window** menu choose **HTML Styles** to open the HTML Styles panel.

❷ Open the Define HTML Style Dialog

Click the **New Style** button in the HTML Styles panel to open the Define HTML Style dialog box.

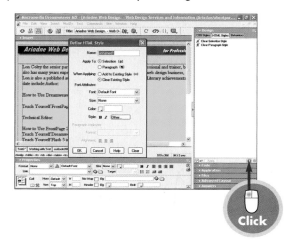

❸ Select the Font, Color, and Size

Use the dialog box to select a font group, color, and size for the text to be formatted using the HTML style.

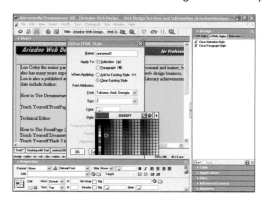

④ Name the Style

In the **Name** field, type a name for the style you have created. I have called mine **mystyle1**, but you can use any name that is appropriate. Click **OK** to continue. Your new HTML style will appear in the HTML Styles panel.

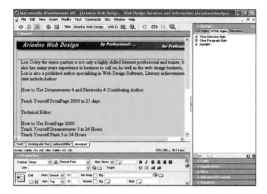

⑤ Select The Text

Select some (or all) of the text in your document that you want to format with the style you have created.

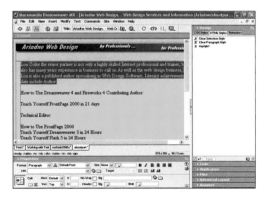

⑥ Apply the Style

With the text selected, click the style name in the HTML Styles panel to apply the style. The text is immediately formatted to your selection.

Click

Clear the Style Formatting

You can clear the formatting you applied by selecting the text again and choosing **Clear Selection Style** or **Clear Paragraph Style** in the HTML Styles panel.

Delete a Style from the Panel

You can delete an HTML style that you no longer want by selecting it in the HTML Styles panel and then clicking the **Trash Can** icon located at the very bottom right of the panel. This delete action cannot be undone, so be careful when using it.

Edit a Style

You can edit an HTML style by double-clicking the style name in the HTML Styles panel. The dialog box opens and you can edit anything in the dialog box: Just remember that you will need to reapply the style to existing instances in the text because HTML styles do not update automatically.

How to Create a New CSS Class Style

The main thing to remember about CSS is that *cascading* means they are hierarchical—an inline style overrides both embedded and linked styles and an embedded style overrides a linked style. In this task we'll create a class style called class1 that can be used over and over again.

1 Show the CSS Styles Panel

From the **Window** menu choose **CSS Styles** to open the CSS Styles panel; then click the **New CSS Style** button to open the New CSS Style dialog box.

2 Name the Style

In the **Name** field of the dialog box type the name `.class1` for this style. Class style names must begin with a period (if you forget the period, Dreamweaver will add it for you). Be sure that **Make Custom Style (Class)** is selected.

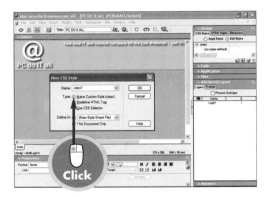

3 Choose New File

In the **Define in** field, select **(New Style Sheet File).** Click **OK** to continue and open the Save Style Sheet File As dialog box.

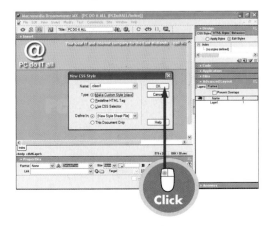

4 Name and Save the File

Browse to the folder for your Web site (**Site1**), type a name for the style sheet—I am calling mine **style1**. Click **Save** to continue and open the CSS Style Definition dialog box.

5 Define the Style

Select **Type** from the **Category** list on the left, and then use the options on the right to choose the **Font**, **Size**, and **Color** you want for **style1** (or whatever you named your style sheet). Click **OK** to continue.

6 View the CSS Styles Panel

The CSS Styles panel in Dreamweaver updates to show the new style sheet we created and the class **.class1** inside it. I have expanded the panel here so that you can see the complete class inside the style sheet.

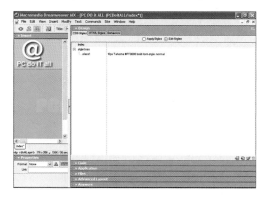

7 Apply the Style

Select the text in your document to which you want the style to apply. Select the **Apply Styles** radio button at the top of the CSS Styles panel, and then click the **class1** entry.

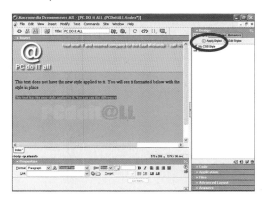

How to Redefine HTML Tags in a Style Sheet

Cascading Style Sheets (CSS) allow you complete control over formatting options. You can use CSS to format all your text as well as the complete page or site. You can create style sheets externally and link them into Dreamweaver. The "cascading" part of the name comes from the fact that the styles you create can cascade through your entire site. For this task, create a new page, add a small amount of text, and use the Properties Inspector to format part of the text as a Heading 5.

1 Create a Style Sheet

Open the CSS Styles panel and click the **New Style** button at the bottom of the panel to open the New CSS Style dialog box.

2 Select the Type of Style

We are going to redefine some HTML tags so that the styles we create will update the properties for the HTML tags in any pages that use the style sheet. In the New CSS Style dialog box, enable the **Redefine HTML Tag** option. From the Tag drop-down menu, choose **h5** as the tag to be redefined. Click **OK** to continue.

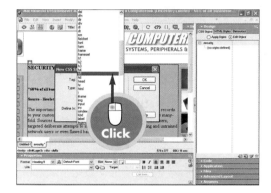

3 Name and Save the File

The Save Style Sheet File As dialog box opens. Name the file (**h5style** or **h5define** is appropriate) and navigate to select your site folder as the **Save in** location. Click **Save** to continue.

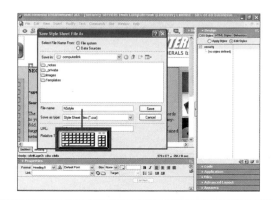

4 Redefine the HTML Tag

In the CSS Style Definition dialog box that opens, select the **Font**, **Size**, **Color**, and any other attributes you want to apply to all the text formatted with the **h5** tag in your file. Click **OK** to continue.

5 See the Effect

In the document window, you should be able to see immediately that all the h5 tags in the file have been updated to reflect the properties we defined in Step 4. In this example, there is now one very green line of italic text.

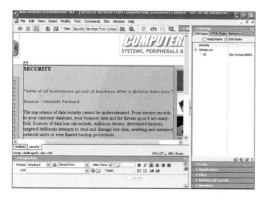

How to Hint

Don't Apply HTML Formatting to CSS

When you use CSS style sheets, you just type the text and then apply the appropriate style; the style sheet does the rest. Don't apply HTML formatting tags to text that's been formatted with CSS, or you will override the style sheet. Any text formatted without using the style sheet won't be updated if you amend the style sheet.

Why Use a Linked Sheet?

Linking a style sheet to your page gives you more flexibility than setting up a separate style sheet for each page. If you link the same style sheet to several pages, you can update the style sheet and watch the changes affect all the pages linked to that style sheet.

Import a Style Sheet

If someone else has developed a style sheet that you want to use, it's easy to import that external style sheet to your site. CSS files are simply text files that hold the formatting options for your pages. If you want to use someone else's CSS, start by putting that file in your site folder on your hard drive. Now you can link your page to that file from the CSS Styles panel: Click the **Edit Style** button, select the **Link** radio button, and browse to the location of the CSS file you want to link to. Click **Done** to link the file.

How to Edit a Cascading Style Sheet

In the previous task, you created a very basic style sheet (it has only one style: Heading 5). In this task, you learn to edit the style sheet so that it contains more styles, and to modify the existing style. When you're finished modifying the style sheet, be sure you save the sheet. Now all the updated styles will be applied to all the pages linked to this style sheet.

1 Open the Style Sheet

Open the CSS Styles panel if not already showing and open the file from the previous task. Select the style sheet called **h5style** and click the **Edit Style Sheet** button at the bottom of the palette. The dialog box for h5style.css opens.

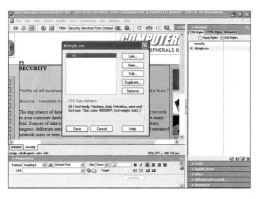

2 Edit the H5 Formatting

Select the **h5** tag in the **h5style.css** dialog box, and then click **Edit** to open the CSS Style Definition dialog box.

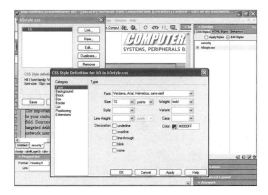

3 Make Some Changes

In the definition dialog box, select **Type** in the **Category** list, and change the **Font**, **Color**, or **Size** of the h5 tag. When you finish, click **Apply** and then **OK**. The h5 tag in your document is immediately updated.

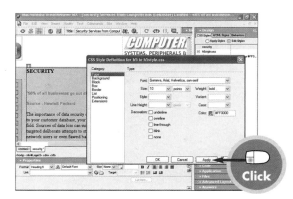

Click

④ Add More Styles

With the **h5style.css** dialog box still open, click **New** to add a style for a different tag. The New CSS Style dialog box opens to let you select a new tag to redefine.

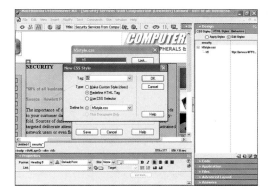

⑤ Choose the Formatting

Here I redefine the **p** tag. Complete the dialog box with the settings you want for paragraph text. When you finish, click **OK**, and then click **Save** to update the style sheet. This figure shows some paragraph text added after I updated the style sheet.

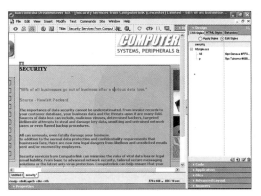

⑥ Apply the Style Sheet to Another Document

Open another page in your Web, or create a new file and add some text. We'll now apply the **h5style** to the new page. From the **Text** menu, choose **CSS Styles**, **Attach Style Sheet**. Select the **h5style.css** file and click **OK**.

Click

⑦ View the Result

The **h5style.css** file is immediately attached to the second file and the text in the document is updated automatically.

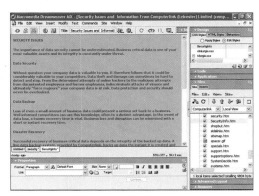

Task

4

Reusing Information

Most likely, you are coming to realize that Dreamweaver is a wonderful application. As you work to develop meaningful information for your Web sites, you'll appreciate that Dreamweaver lets you use that information more than once. Dreamweaver MX and Fireworks MX make reusing information easier than ever with the use of assets, templates, and the library. I introduce reusing information here to make sure you know how to use these elements as soon as you need them.

The Assets panel lets you organize and display all the different elements in your site. You can drag images, URLs, colors, and other elements contained by your site from the Assets panel directly onto the page where you are working. This resource center complements the existing libraries and templates and will benefit both new and experienced users.

In Dreamweaver, assets refer to all the elements that make up a Web site. Images, movies, and animations are all assets of your site, as are the colors and URLs that you use in your site's creation. Dreamweaver stores all the element information in the Assets panel, giving you a single resource for locating and reusing them in your site.

By using the site cache feature, Dreamweaver knows where all the files are within your site. They are categorized based on either the HTML code (in the case of a URL or color) or the file extension (such as .gif).

Templates and libraries make reusing information a straightforward process. The Library facility is ideal for reusing single images, tables, or layers that you want to use in more than one page but want to create only once. Templates enable you to create a complete page layout and use it for as many pages as you want, with a minimum of fuss.

All the Dreamweaver elements discussed in the following tasks are designed to make your life easier when creating both single pages and multiple-page sites.

In this Part of the book we add assets to the site we created earlier but also look at using assets in an existing site.

How to Use the Assets Panel

When the Assets panel is open, it displays different categories of elements included in your site. The most important thing is to remember that assets relate to the whole site, not just the current document: Images, URLs, colors, and movies are all assets. You can display elements in the different categories independently (for example, you can show a list of all the images you have used in your site). Being able to arrange and display the elements used by your Web site is the first step in reusing that information. Initially in this task I am working with a completed site to ensure that there are already assets available. In a new or nearly new site, you won't have assets yet.

① Show the Assets Panel

Click the **Assets** tab in the Files panel group to display the Assets panel. If the Files panel group is not visible, choose **Site Files** from the **Site** menu, and then select the **Assets** tab. Alternatively, you can press the **F11** key on your keyboard.

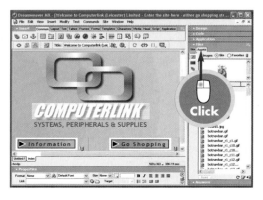

② Create a Cache

For the Assets panel to work, you must have the site cache enabled. If it has not been enabled, Dreamweaver prompts you to refresh the local files before the assets can be displayed. Click the **Refresh** icon to continue and see the site assets.

③ View the Category Types

Dreamweaver defines assets as the different elements that make up the site. The Assets panel categorizes the assets for your site by type, and each category has an icon to identify it. These icons appear on the right side of the Assets panel. From top to bottom, they are **Images**, **Colors**, **URL Link**, **Flash**, **Shockwave**, **Movies**, **Scripts**, **Templates**, and **Library**.

④ Show Assets in a Category

To see the assets in your site for any category, click the appropriate category icon. You can reorganize the list of assets alphabetically by name or according to size, file type, or value. Click the **Images** category icon and then click the **Type** column heading to reorganize the list according to image types. (I've expanded the panel to make this more visible.)

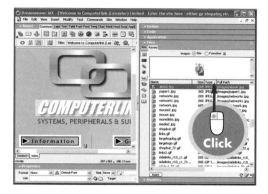

⑤ Preview an Asset

To preview an asset, select it and look in the Preview pane at the top of the Assets panel.

Preview pane

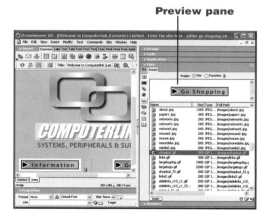

⑥ Find an Asset You Have Used

Dreamweaver can display a particular asset in the Site Files window, showing you which folder contains the asset file. Right-click (**Command+click** on a Macintosh) the asset name in the Assets panel to display the context menu. Choose **Locate in Site** from the menu to open the Site window with the selected asset highlighted. Note that this feature does not find the HTML files containing the asset.

How-to Hint

Can't Find Colors?

You can't use the **Locate in Site** option to find either colors or Web site addresses. These items are HTML references and do not exist as objects in their own right.

Embedded or Linked?

When you insert an image into a Web page, it's embedded into the page. The HTML code tells you the name and source of the file, which is then called into your page from that location. Updating or modifying the image changes the page without your having to reedit or save the page at all.

Linked assets, on the other hand, are library items and templates. This means that the completed page shows the actual contents of the asset rather than calling it in by a reference.

How to Use Assets

After you create them, you can use assets in as many different sites as you want. To use the current site's assets in another site, just copy them to the other site. (Of course, the other site must be defined already.) Inserting assets into your current document is as easy as selecting them from the Assets panel and clicking to insert them.

❶ Copy an Asset to Another Site

You can copy an asset in the current site to another site. In the Assets panel, select the asset you want to use in the other site and right-click it (**Command+click** on a Macintosh) to open the context menu. Choose **Copy to Site**, and then choose the site to which you want to copy the asset from the submenu that appears.

❷ Copy Multiple Assets

To copy multiple assets to another site, click to select the first asset, and hold down the **Shift** key as you click other contiguous entries. (Press and hold the **Ctrl** key as you click to select separate entries; Mac users have just the **Shift** key option.) Right-click a selected asset and choose **Copy to Site** from the context menu; select the site to which you want to copy the selected assets.

❸ Choose an Asset to Insert

To insert an asset on the current page, first click to position the insertion point in the document window. Then, in the Assets panel, click the icon for the category of the asset you want to use. Select the asset you want to insert and preview it in the window at the top of the panel.

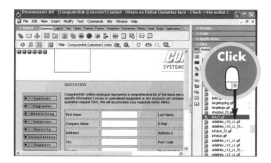

④ Insert the Asset

Click the **Insert** button at the bottom of the Assets panel. The selected asset appears in the document window at the insertion point.

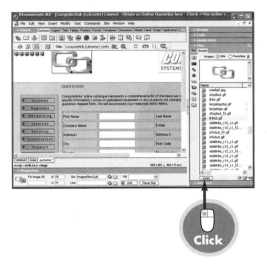

⑤ Choose a Template

You can use a template to format an entire page. In this example, we apply a template to a new blank page. (You learn more about templates later in this part.) Click the **Templates** category icon in the Assets panel and choose the template you want to use for the current document. Click **Apply**.

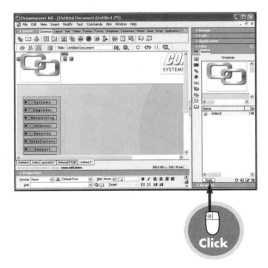

⑥ Apply a Color to Text

Your site's assets include all the colors you've already used in your site. You can apply these colors to text and other elements on the page. In the document window, select the text for which you want to change the color. In the Assets panel, click the **Colors** category icon, select the desired color from the list, and click **Apply**. (The hexadecimal code—that horrible set of numbers and letters with the # in front—displays in the preview pane in the color it represents.)

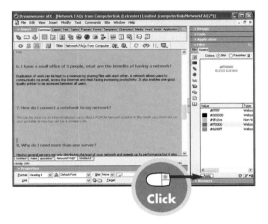

⑦ Insert a Link

Your site's assets include all the hyperlinks—internal, external, and mailto: hyperlinks—within the current site. In the document window, select the text or image you want to use as a link. In the Assets panel, click the **URL Link** category icon and then choose the URL to which you want to link. Click **Apply** to add this link to the selected text or image.

URL Link category icon

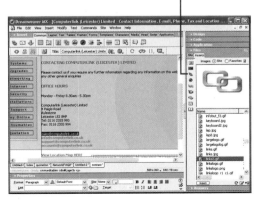

How to Reuse Favorite Assets

Some of the assets you create for your site might be things you'll reuse. You can save some of your favorite assets into a special group so that they're easy to locate and use. Each category in the Assets panel can be further divided into lists of Site assets and Favorites. (The radio buttons at the top of the panel determine which list you are viewing.) You can even give your favorite assets nicknames to make them easier to find.

① Add to Favorites

In the Assets panel, click the appropriate category icon, and then select the asset you want to save as a favorite. Click the **Add to Favorites** icon in the bottom-right corner of the panel. The selected asset is saved into your Favorites list for the current category. A message confirms the entry.

Add to Favorites icon

② Look at the Favorites

The message box that Dreamweaver displays tells you to switch to **Favorites** view to see the favorites for the category you are in. Click **OK** to continue and see the Favorites view.

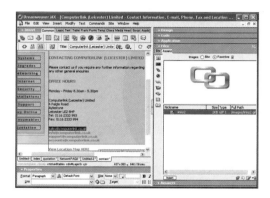

③ Switch Views

You can view the assets in a category in one of two ways: **Site view** (shows all the assets in the selected category for the entire site) or **Favorites view** (shows only the assets that you have specifically identified as favorites in the selected category). Click the radio button for the view you want.

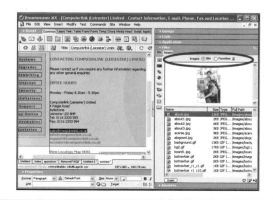

4 Give a Favorite Asset a Nickname

By default, Dreamweaver displays your assets according to their filenames. In Favorites view, each asset has a nickname, which by default is the filename minus the file extension. You can change this nickname to anything you want—click the name of an asset, and the name bar becomes editable.

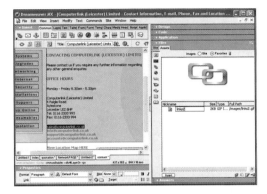

5 Select the Nickname

Type the nickname you want to give this asset and press **Enter**. The new nickname appears in the Nickname column of the Assets panel. This can be handy if you want colors as favorites—you can name them blue, red, and so forth instead of seeing the hexadecimal code.

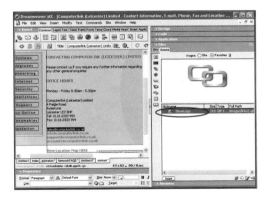

Deleting Assets Is Easy

In previous tasks, we looked at what assets are and how to create them. In most cases, you can't delete assets because they're part of your site. You can, however, delete those assets that you specifically create (that is, library items and templates). Simply select the item you want to delete in the Assets panel and click the **Trash Can** icon at the bottom of the panel. The asset is removed—but any page already created using that asset is left intact.

How to Manage Favorite Assets

It's easy to manage the lists of favorite assets presented in the Assets panel. You can add and remove assets to and from the Favorites categories. Managing your assets makes managing the whole site a lot easier and is a good habit to get into from the start.

1 Group Your Favorites

You can create subgroups within the Favorites view for any category. For example, if your list of favorite images is getting too long or has files from different parts of your site, you can divide the list into smaller groups. To create a new group for your favorites in a particular category, switch to Favorites view by clicking the **Favorites** radio button.

2 Create a New Favorites Group

Click the **New Favorites Group** icon at the bottom of the panel. A new folder icon is added; its text box is selected and ready for you to name the folder. Type a name for this folder and press the **Enter** key. The folder icon remains next to the text, so you can easily see that this isn't an individual asset.

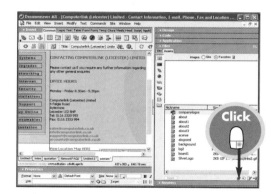

3 Add Assets to the Group

Select the assets you want to add to the new group and drag them into the group (folder) you created in Step 2. You can drag the assets individually, or select multiple assets using **Shift+Click** or **Ctrl+Click**.

④ Remove an Asset from Favorites

To remove an asset from your Favorites list or from a group you have created, select the asset you want to remove, and then click the **Remove from Favorites** icon at the bottom of the panel. The asset is removed from your Favorites list, but can still be found in the Site list for that category.

View Differences

One of the advantages of the Favorites view is that you can add certain elements (such as library items, templates, colors, and URLs) to the list that you have not yet used in your site. You can do this only in Favorites view because the Site view is created from the cache and contains only those elements that Dreamweaver finds in your directories.

If you have decided on certain elements to use in your site but haven't yet placed them in the site structure, you'll find it handy later to go ahead and add these elements to your Favorites now.

⑤ Create a New Favorite Color

Whenever you use a color in your site, it becomes part of the site's assets. You can't add unused colors in the Assets panel's normal view, but you can in Favorites view. To add colors to your site's Favorites list, click the **Colors** category icon and click the **New Color** icon at the bottom of the panel. Use the color picker to choose a new color to add to your list.

Colors category icon

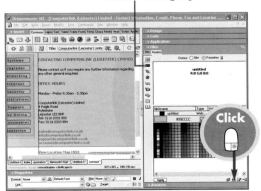

How to Use the Library

The Library stores elements, such as text and images from your Web pages that you are likely to reuse in your site, or that might need to be updated frequently. If, after you have inserted a library item onto several pages in your site, you then edit and save the original library item, all the pages that contain the library item are automatically updated. If you just used the Assets panel to insert an item onto your pages, you'd have to update each instance of the item when it changed. The Library makes the process of keeping your site up to date much simpler.

① Select the Element to Add

In the main document window, select the page element that you want to use as a library item. In this example, I selected an image to save to the Library.

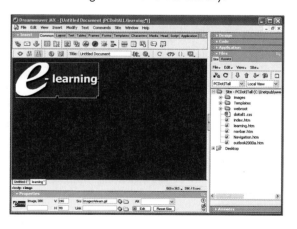

② Open the Library

Choose **Window**, **Assets** to display the Assets panel if it isn't already onscreen. Click the **Library** category icon to open the Library.

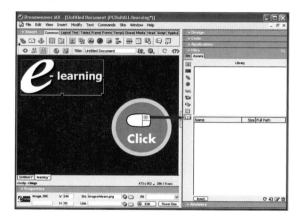

③ Add the Library Item

Drag the selected element from the document window and drop it into the Library window. Give the element a useful name in the Library by typing into the name box.

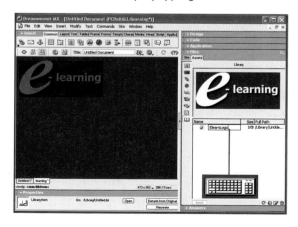

④ Choose the Location for a Library Item

When you add a library item to your page, Dreamweaver records a reference to the original library file so that it can update the item on the page if the original item is changed. To insert a library item on the page, click in the document window to position the insertion point where you want the item to appear.

⑤ Insert the Library Item

In the Assets panel, click the **Library** icon to open the Library. From the list of items in the Library, select the one you want to insert. Click the **Insert** button at the bottom of the panel to place the selected item in the current document.

Library icon

Click

⑥ Rename a Library Item

You can rename any item in the Library. Select the item you want to rename by clicking it, waiting a moment, and clicking the item a second time. (Note that this is not a double-click.) A box surrounds the name, indicating that you can edit it. Type a new name for the item and press **Enter** (or click away from the panel). The new name is accepted.

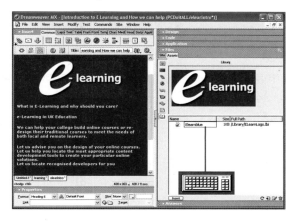

⑦ Select a Library Item to Edit

You can edit any library item whenever you choose. To open the item in a window appropriate for editing, simply double-click the item in the Library. The item opens on a blank screen. The title bar indicates it's a library item.

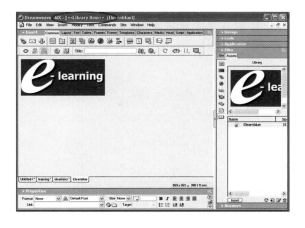

(8) Edit the Library Item

From this screen, you can edit a text or table item as a library item file, or choose how to edit the image file by right-clicking the image to open the context menu. If the **Edit with Fireworks** option is available, select it. Otherwise, choose **Edit With**, and then choose the application you want to use from the submenu.

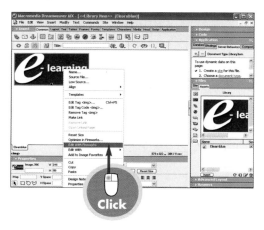

(9) Edit a Library Item

In this example, the file from the previous step is opened in Fireworks MX and being edited. (Note that the Fireworks document window shows you are working from Dreamweaver.) Make changes to the file using all the editing powers of the application you have invoked.

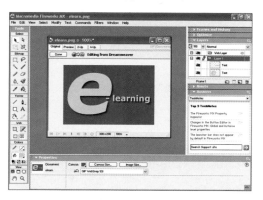

(10) Save the Changes

When you have finished editing the library item, save the changes you have made. In Fireworks, just click the **Done** button. Dreamweaver immediately prompts you to update both the .lbi files and pages where the item appears.

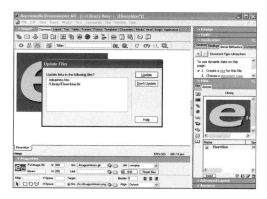

(11) Delete an Item from the Library

You can remove an item from the Library at any time. This doesn't remove the element from any page on which you have inserted it. In the Library category of the Assets panel, choose the item you want to delete, and click the **Trash Can** icon at the bottom of the panel.

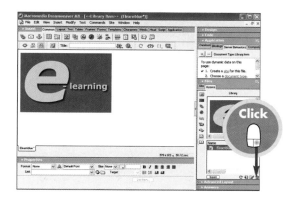

⑫ Are You Sure?

Dreamweaver prompts you to confirm that you want to delete this item. Click **Yes** to delete the item from the Library.

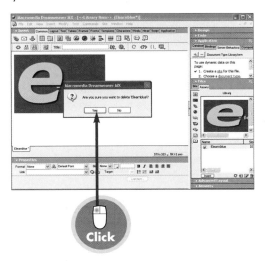

Click

<small>How to Hint</small>

Visibility and Colors

When you use library items in your pages, Dreamweaver can highlight them on the page for you. Choose **View**, **Visual Aids**, **Invisible Elements** to turn on this feature.

You can change the highlight color Dreamweaver uses to show the library items by opening the Preferences dialog box. Choose **Edit**, **Preferences** to open the dialog box and, in the **Highlighting Options** section, use the color picker to select the color you want Dreamweaver to use to highlight your library items.

Still There?

After you delete a library item from the Assets panel, you won't be able to insert it from the Library again. However, all pages that use the item are unaffected by the removal of the entry from the Library. Removing an item from the Library does not delete that item from your existing pages.

How to Create a Template

Templates are great tools when you want several pages to have the same look and feel without having to create the same content over and over again. You can create a template from scratch or save an existing page as a template. A template file has the extension .dwt. In creating a template, you specify locked regions (areas that will remain static) and editable regions (areas that can change from page to page). When you create a new page from a template, you can alter only the editable content. If you edit the actual template file, you can change anything you want. When you change the underlying template, you can update all the pages you created from that template in one easy step.

① Create a New Template

If it isn't onscreen already, display the Assets panel by clicking the **Assets** tab in the Files panel. Click the **Templates** category icon to see a list of all the templates in your site. (Your list will probably be empty if this is your first time working with templates.) Click the **New Template** icon at the bottom of the panel.

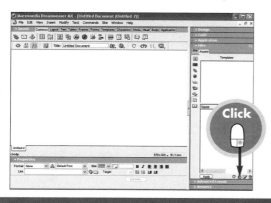

② Name the Template

The new template appears in the panel. While it is still selected, type a meaningful name for this new template and press **Enter**.

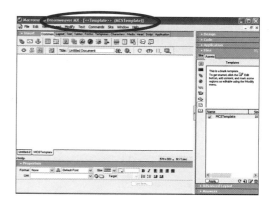

③ Open the Template to Add Content

In the Assets panel, double-click the template you just created. The .dwt file opens so that you can add content to it. Initially, the page is completely blank.

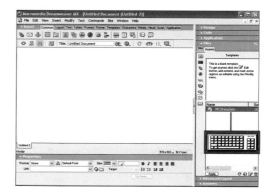

4   Add Content to Be Locked

Create the page as you would any other page, inserting a background, links, and so on. At this stage, add only the content that you want to be the same on all pages; leave all the other areas of the page blank.

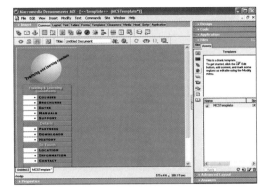

5   Add Editable Content

Complete the page by adding content or placeholders that will be changed on each page that uses the template. These areas will become the editable regions. For now, the text and images you insert here can be anything at all; they are merely placeholders. In this example, I've added a title image and some irrelevant text.

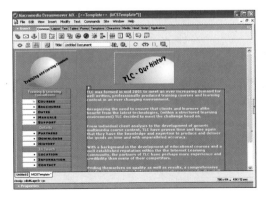

6   Create Editable Regions

Decide which areas of the template page will be editable. (In this example, they're the title image and the text.) Select the first editable region and choose **Insert**, **Template Objects**, **Editable Region** to open the New Editable Region dialog box.

Selected region

Click

7   Name the Editable Region

In the dialog box, type a name that will identify this particular region. In this example, I made the main content area editable region, so I have assigned it the name **ContentArea**. Click **OK** to continue.

Click

8 Create and Name the Other Regions

Repeat Steps 7 and 8 to create each of the rest of your editable regions. There is no limit to the number of these you can have in a template.

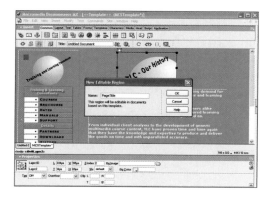

9 Save the Template

Choose **File**, **Save** to save the file with the editable regions in place.

10 Use the Template

To use the template as the basis for a new page in your site, choose **File**, **New** and click the **Templates** tab. In the Templates For column, select the site your template is for. Dreamweaver shows you all templates for your site. Select the template you have just created and click **Create**.

11 View the New Page

When the new page opens, it looks exactly as the template did when you saved it. The new page file is called **untitled-*** and has the template name visible in the upper-right corner of the page.

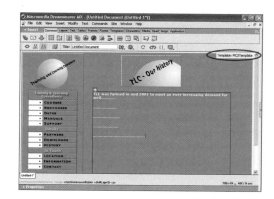

Edit and Save

You can change only the regions you made editable. The rest of the page is locked and displays a no-entry sign if you attempt to change anything. When the page is complete, save it as you normally would, remembering to add a page title.

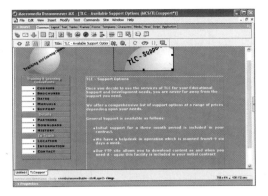

How to Hint

Using Existing Pages as Templates

If you have a page or pages with the main content in place, you can save these pages as templates without affecting the original page. Simply follow Steps 6 and 7 of this task to create the editable regions, and then choose **File**, **Save As Template** to save the file as a template into the current (or any other) site. The template file then appears in your list of templates, and you can use it to create new pages as described in Steps 10 and 11.

Setting Preferences

You can use the Preferences dialog box to change the way Dreamweaver highlights the editable regions on your templates. These editable regions are visible only in Dreamweaver and are highlighted to make them obvious to you when you are working. They're not visible to site visitors when the page is saved as an HTML file.

Choose **Edit**, **Preferences** to open the Preferences dialog box. In the Highlighting area, choose **Editable Regions**. Use the color picker to set the color you want Dreamweaver to use to highlight the editable regions on your templates.

How to Edit a Template

When you create a page based on a template, you can change only the editable regions. If you want to change any other areas of the page, you must edit the template itself. Doing this allows you to remove and add editable regions and change static areas, if that's what you want to do. When you create a new page from a template, Dreamweaver provides the **Update Page when Template Changes** option. If you enable this option, the changes you make to the template (a new background, navigation buttons, and so on) are all transferred into the existing pages.

① Open the Template

Open the Assets panel and click the **Templates** category icon to see a list of all the templates for your site. Locate the template you want to edit and double-click it to open the template in a new document window with the Template name visible in the title bar.

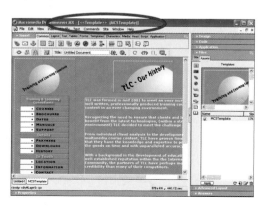

② Add New Content

Add some new content in the template. In this case, I'm adding a new image. I want an image to appear on every page, and I'll make this region editable in the next step so it can be a different image.

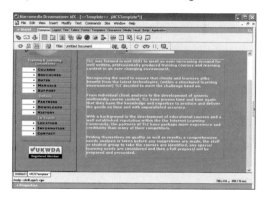

③ Make a New Editable Region

Choose **Insert**, **Template Objects**, **Editable Region**. In the **Name** field in the dialog box, type a unique name for this new editable region. Click **OK**. You can create new editable regions anywhere on a template. I made an image an editable region so I can change or delete the image on pages created from the template.

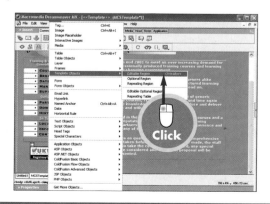

④ Identify the Region

The new editable region should be highlighted onscreen. If you don't see the highlighted area, be sure the **Invisible Elements** option is enabled. (Choose **View**, **Visual Aids**, **Invisible Elements** to turn on this feature.)

⑤ Removing an Editable Region

When you remove an editable region from the template, the content remains intact, but that part of the page becomes locked, and you can't change the content on pages based on this template. Select the editable region you want to lock by clicking on that region's name tag. Then choose **Modify**, **Templates**, **Remove Template Markup**.

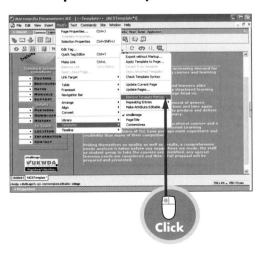

⑥ Save the Template

Choose **File**, **Save** to save the template with the changes you made. You're prompted to update all pages based on the template. You can choose either **Update** or **Don't Update**. Choosing **Update** modifies all the pages you already created using this template to reflect the changes you just made.

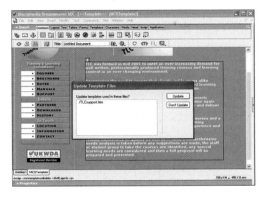

Optional Template Regions

Dreamweaver allows you to mark certain regions in your templates as optional. You then have the choice in the template-based pages as to whether these areas are hidden or visible in individual pages.

Repeating Regions in Templates

Repeating regions (**Insert**, **Template Objects**, **Repeating Region**) is a great new addition in Dreamweaver MX. For example, you can add a table in the underlying template, make the table row a repeating region, then in the page based on the template you can add instances of the row to expand the size of the table as required. For the repeating region to be editable, you must mark the region as not only repeating but also editable.

How to Work with Templates

As you have seen, creating a template is not difficult; all you do is create the bare bones of a page. This task explains how to apply the templates you have created and use them to create document pages for your Web site. You can use a template to create a brand-new page (just start typing and inserting images into the already created editable regions), or you can use a template to reformat an existing page. Applying a template to an existing page has inherent risks and can produce some strange results until you fully understand the options.

1 Create a New Document from a Template

To create a new page from an existing template, choose **File**, **New** and select the **Templates** tab. Choose the site you are working with in the Templates For section, and select your template. Click **Create** to continue and start working.

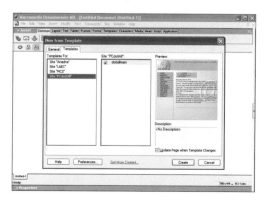

2 Apply a Template to an Existing Document

You can apply a template to a document you've already started to create. This isn't the ideal way to use templates, and getting it right can be tricky. Open the existing document to which you would like to apply a template. In this example, I've opened a page with a little text and a background color.

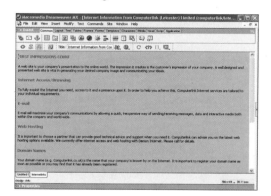

3 Apply the Template

Choose **Modify**, **Templates**, **Apply Template to Page** to open the Select Template dialog box. The dialog box defaults to showing templates for the current site, although you can change this using the drop-down menu.

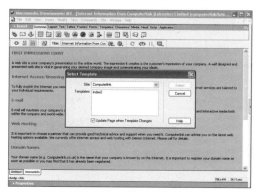

④ Choose a Template

From the list of available templates, choose the template you want to apply to the open document. Click **Select** to continue. The Inconsistent Region Names dialog box opens.

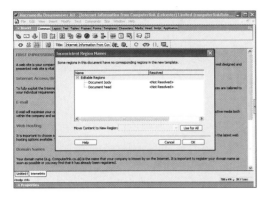

⑤ Decide What to Do with Current Content

This is where things get a little complicated! Dreamweaver knows that you already have content on the page and that you must decide what to do with it. Select one of the editable regions listed.

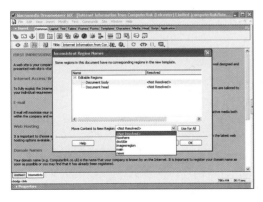

⑥ Choose a Region

From the options in the drop-down menu, choose which editable region in the template should hold the content. The Resolved column updates to show where the content will be held. Repeat these steps for all unplaced content.

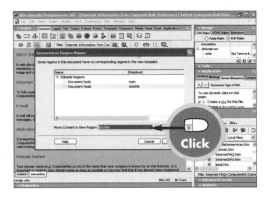

⑦ Edit As Required

The result from the previous step might not be what you expected, but it's still better than retyping the content you wanted to use. In this example, I would fix up the page by deleting unnecessary table cells and removing unnecessary formatting.

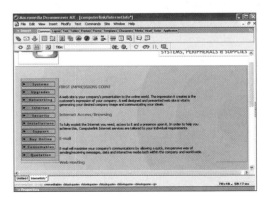

Task

Links, Navigation, and Structure

Hyperlinks are what make the Internet the information superhighway. Before the Internet, most things we looked at, read, or watched were called linear media, designed to start at the beginning and work through until the end in a straight line. The Internet introduced us to the concept of *hypermedia*—being able to move around in the order we want, when we want, and how we want. The previous restrictions were removed, giving the Internet user control over the sites and pages they looked at.

Being able to move from page to page and site to site is possible only by the use of hyperlinks. Hyperlinks are the way visitors move between different Web pages. You know you are over a hyperlink on a Web page because the mouse pointer changes to a hand with one finger pointing upward. When you click a hyperlink, a new page loads into your browser. The new page can be from the same site (an internal hyperlink) or from an entirely different site (an external hyperlink). There are many different ways to set up the links on your Web page: You can use text, images, or even "jump menus" and navigation bars. Navigation bars will be covered a little later in the book—once we have some images to use!

Making sure that there is a logical and structured route through your site is vital to a successful Web site, however big or small. Personally, I still resort to planning with a pen and paper before creating the links. In terms of your site, one useful rule of thumb is to have links to major site sections on all pages and then links to subsections on relevant pages in the site. Commonly this is achieved using navigation bars or jump menus. We will look at both of these here, although there is a lot more navigation information in Part 10, "Navigation in Fireworks."

The tasks in this part of the book start you out by creating a simple hyperlink from one page of your site to another. As you work through these tasks, you will learn how to create links wherever and however you want—and not just links to other pages. You'll also learn to create e-mail links, the easiest way to let site visitors contact you.

How to Create Hyperlinks

Hyperlinks come in many shapes and sizes, but there are only two real types of hyperlinks: internal and external. Internal hyperlinks link from one page of your site to another page in your site; external hyperlinks link from one page of your site to another site entirely. Dreamweaver enables you to create hyperlinks by simply pointing to files within your site, by typing URLs directly into the Property Inspector, and even by cutting and pasting from a browser window. Once you know the options, you can decide which best suits you.

1 Select the Text

You can make a link out of any text on the page. First, select the text you want to turn into the link. Next, in the Property Inspector, click the folder icon to the right of the **Link** field. The Select File dialog box opens.

2 Create the Link

Browse to the file to which you want the selected text to link. The file should be in the same site folder as the current page. Choose the file and click **OK**. The selected text changes to blue and is underlined, indicating that it is now a link. The **Link** box in the Property Inspector now contains the filename of the linked page.

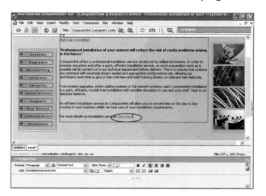

3 Point to the File

Dreamweaver enables you to simply point at a file in your local site to create a link. Again, select the text to use as a link in the document window.

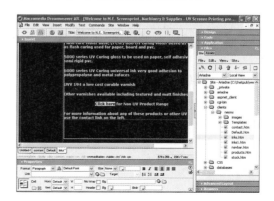

④ Select the File

Simply click and hold the **Point to File** icon in the Property Inspector and drag to the file to which you're linking in the site listing.

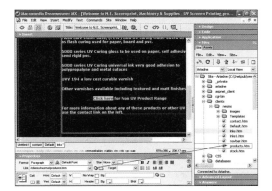

⑤ Use an Image As a Link

You can also use an image as a hyperlink. Select the image that you want to use. Access the Select File dialog box as you did in Step 1, browse to the file to which you want to link, select it, and click **OK** to create the link.

Click

⑥ Create an External Hyperlink

The process for creating an external link is very simple. Select the text or image that you want to use as the link and, in the **Link** field in the Property Inspector, type the URL (don't forget the **http://**) of the page to which you want to link.

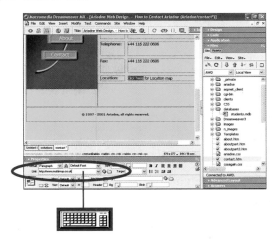

Relative Links

When selecting a file to which to link with an internal hyperlink, you can choose whether the link is relative to the file to the root of the Web site. Document-relative links are the most appropriate for internal links, and Dreamweaver adds any local path information that is required.

In document-relative paths, you can ignore the part of the URL that is the same (that is, the `http://www.yourdomain.com/` part).

How to Edit or Delete a Hyperlink

At some point in your work creating and maintaining Web pages, you'll have to change hyperlink information. For example, the URL to an external Web site might change, a link to an e-mail address might change, or you might discover that the link you set up was wrong to begin with! This task explains how you can change the information associated with the link—or even delete the link entirely.

① Locate the Link to Change

Find and select the text or image that contains the link you want to change. Look for the Link box in the Property Inspector. The current URL for the selected link appears there.

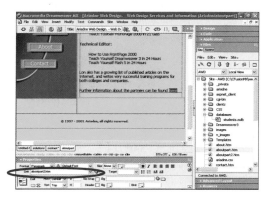

② Change the Link Information

In the Link box, type the updated link information, or select a different file to which to link. If you want to delete the link (without deleting the text or image from the page), just clear the Link box of all address information. The link is now updated or removed.

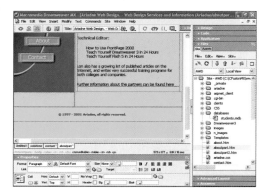

③ Use Find and Replace

If a link appears several times in your page or throughout your site, you can use Find and Replace options to locate the link and change it. Choose **Edit**, **Find and Replace**; in the Replace dialog box, select **Source Code** from the **Search For** drop-down list, and type or paste the current (incorrect) link details into the text box.

④ Enter the New Details

In the **Replace With** field, type the correct link details, or leave the field empty if you want to remove the link altogether. From the **Find In** drop-down list, choose whether you want to search the current document or an entire site or folder. Click **Replace All** and click **Yes** when prompted to make the changes.

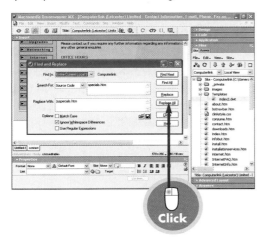

⑥ Choose a File or Type a URL

In the Select File dialog box, either select the local file to which you want the link to refer or, in the URL box, change the URL as necessary to correct the link information. Click **OK** to make the change.

⑤ Use the Context Menu

If you don't want to make changes directly in the Property Inspector, you can use the context menu. Select the text or image that contains the link you want to modify, and right-click it (Ctrl+click for Mac users) to open the context menu. Choose **Remove Link** to eliminate the link completely or **Change Link** to make changes to the link. The Select File dialog box opens.

How to Hint

Look in the HTML Source Code

Remember that the text that appears on the Web page is not usually the same as the hyperlink itself (for example, the page might display a link that reads Lon's Great Web Site, but the actual hyperlink is to http://www.pcdoitall.co.uk). The most important thing to remember is that changing the text on the page does not affect the actual hyperlink; you must remember to change both the text and the link information when necessary. The link information appears in the Property Inspector, but many times you can't see the link onscreen. To look for the link information, you must check the HTML source code, and the **Find and Replace** option is the best way to do that. If you can't remember how to use these features, refer to Part 3, "Working with Text."

How to Create an E-mail Hyperlink

E-mail hyperlinks are one of the mainstays of any successful Web site. When a visitor clicks the e-mail link, his default e-mail application opens to a new mail message, and the e-mail address you've specified is already completed in the **To** field. Dreamweaver makes it easy to create e-mail links, as shown in this task.

1 Select the Text or Choose a Location

Decide where on the page you want the e-mail link to appear. Either select the text you want to use or click to position the insertion point on the page.

2 Use the Menus

Choose **Insert**, **Email Link** to open the Email Link dialog box. In the **Text** box, type the text that will contain the e-mail link (if you selected text in Step 1, the **Text** field is already filled in); in the **E-Mail** box, type the e-mail address to link to. Click **OK**.

3 Use the Property Inspector

Instead of the menus, you can enter the e-mail link information in the Property Inspector. Select the text or image to be used as the link. In the Property Inspector's **Link** field, type `mailto:` and then the e-mail address you want to link to (be sure there is no space between the colon and the e-mail address you type).

4 Use the Insert Bar

An alternative way to create an e-mail link is to use the Insert bar (if not showing, select **Window**, **Insert**). Select the **Common** tab, and click the **Insert E-mail Link** button. The **Email Link** dialog box opens; type the text and e-mail address to link to, and click **OK**.

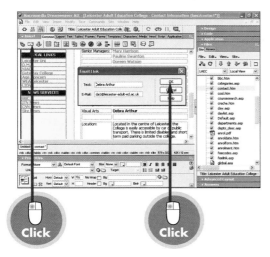

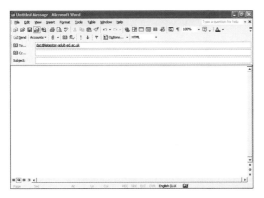

5 Test the Link

Choose **File**, **Preview in Browser** to open the page in the default browser. Click the e-mail link; your default e-mail application should open to a blank document. Check the e-mail address that appears in the **To** field.

How to Create Anchors and Thumbnails

You can set up an anchor on a page so that you can hyperlink directly to that point on the page. Anchors are often used to enable people to jump back to the top of a page from somewhere farther down the page. (You cannot jump to anchors on other sites.) A thumbnail image is a smaller version of a graphic that, when clicked, opens to a larger version of the same image (see Part 9, "Working with Images in Fireworks," for details about resizing images). To complete this task you need two copies of an image: one at full size, and one smaller version to act as the thumbnail.

1 Create an Anchor

Before you can link to a specific point in a document, you must create the anchor. Open the page to which you want to add an anchor point, and click in the document where you want the anchor. On the **Common** tab of the Insert bar, click the **Named Anchor** button to open the Named Anchor dialog box.

Named Anchor button

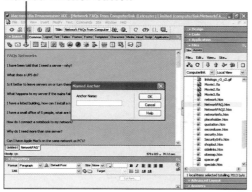

2 Name the Anchor

Type a name for the anchor you're creating and click **OK**. For a link back to the top of the page, a good name is **Top**. For more about naming links, see the hints at the end of this task.

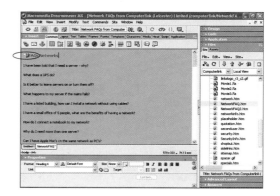

3 Link to the Anchor

To link to the anchor you just created, select the text you want to use as a link. (If you just created an anchor at the top of the page, for example, insert the text **Back to the top** somewhere else on the page as the link to the top of the page.) In the **Link** field in the Property Inspector, type *#anchorname* (for example, type **#Top**).

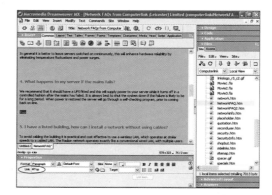

④ Insert the Small Image

If you want to show a thumbnail image on your page that links to a larger image, choose **Insert**, **Image**. Browse to the small image you want to insert and click **OK**. The image appears on your page. Save the page.

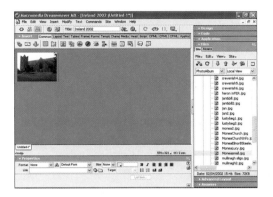

⑤ Create the Link

Select the image you just inserted. In the Property Inspector, click the folder icon next to the **Link** field to open the Select File dialog box. Browse to the full-sized image file, select it, and click **OK**.

⑥ Test the Link

Save the page and prepare to preview the page: Choose **File**, **Preview in Browser**. When the page opens in the browser, click the thumbnail image; the full-sized version of the image appears in a new page. Use your navigation buttons to return to the previous page.

How to Hint

Use Point to File

The **Point to File** icon on the Property Inspector is a handy tool that helps with creating links. When you drag the **Point to File** icon over the named anchor you just created, the name of the anchor automatically fills in the **Link** box in the Property Inspector. Simply let go of the mouse when the icon is over the anchor, and the link will be complete.

Use the Menus or Keyboard to Create Anchors

You can also create anchors by choosing **Insert**, **Named Anchor** or by pressing **Ctrl+Alt+A** (Windows users) or **Cmd+Option+A** (Mac users).

Naming Anchors

For a link back to the top of the page, a good anchor name is Top; if you're creating an anchor to a particular section in a long, text-filled page, make the anchor name similar to the title of the section. The anchor icon appears in the document window. If you don't see the icon, open the **View** menu and be sure the **Invisible Elements** option is enabled.

How to Change the Way Links Look

Links must be highly visible to site visitors. By default, Dreamweaver formats links as underlined, blue text so that the links stand out from the rest of the page. You can make changes to the default settings for links, as explained in this task.

❶ See the Defaults

Open a new page in Dreamweaver and create a simple link to another page in your site. Notice the link on the page: The text is blue and underlined. This is the default setting for links; you didn't format the link like that, the HTML standards did. Furthermore, the standards automatically change the color of the link to red as you click it and to purple after you've visited the linked page.

❷ Choose Your Colors

To change the colors of the links on your page, choose **Modify**, **Page Properties** to open the Page Properties dialog box. Use the color picker to select new colors for the **Links**, **Visited Links**, and **Active Links** options.

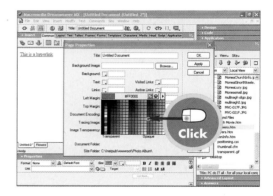

❸ Check That the Colors Work

You don't want any of your three link colors to disappear against the background color of the page or image, so preview the page in a browser to be sure you can see all of them. If you use an image as a link, any border you place around it takes on the link colors you've specified.

4 Use a Color Scheme

Dreamweaver color schemes allow you use a preset combination of text and link colors designed to work well together. To see the color scheme options, choose **Commands**, **Set Color Scheme** to open the Set Color Scheme Command dialog box. Select from the **Background** and **Text and Links** lists and preview these combinations. Click **OK** when you've found a color combination you like.

5 Make Links Stand Out

If your links still don't look obvious enough on the page, try making the link text bold. Select the link text and click the **Bold** button in the Property Inspector.

How to Hint

Links with Style

Be sure your link colors are significantly different from the color of text on the page. You don't want visitors to miss vital information because they didn't notice that a link was there. You can create links using styles, which remove the underline formatting in certain browsers. Part 11, "Working with Layers," describes styles in detail.

Think Background Colors—and Not Just Page Backgrounds

When you change link colors, be sure you check the page in a browser. Don't forget that the link color changes after you've visited the link; there are far too many Web sites on which links disappear after they've been clicked because the creator forgot to check the colors. You will have to think about link colors when you change background colors on different parts of the same page. (Tables and layers make it possible to separate the page into areas that can have different background colors.)

Image Border

To add a border to an image, select it, and type the number of pixels thick that you want the border to be in the **Border** box in the Property Inspector.

How to Create a Jump Menu

Jump menus are common on the Internet, although you might not recognize the term. A jump menu is a drop-down menu that contains hyperlinks to other pages or sites; select the link you want and "jump" to that page or site. Technically, a jump menu is a form element generated by Dreamweaver using behaviors. Great, I hear you cry, both of these are topics yet to be covered in the book. That really does not matter in this task, because a jump menu is pretty much a standalone element that you can create without prior knowledge of forms (Part 12, "Behaviors and Scripts in Dreamweaver," and Part 17, "Working with Forms in Dreamweaver").

Start by opening a page to which you want to add a jump menu.

1 Show the Form Elements

From the **Insert** bar, click the **Forms** tab to see all the Form elements that Dreamweaver offers.

Jump Menu button

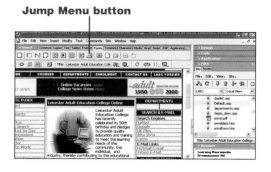

2 Select Jump Menu

On your page, click where you want the menu to appear. Then click the **Jump Menu** button on the **Forms** tab to open the Insert Jump Menu dialog box.

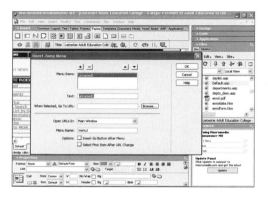

3 Add a Prompt

In the **Text** field, type a prompt for visitors so that they know this is a menu—something like "Select an area to visit." In the options at the bottom of the dialog box, click the **Select First Item After URL Change** box. This ensures that the prompt is always visible when a visitor comes to the page. (This entry is not a link.)

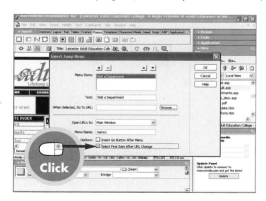

4 Add a Menu Item

Click the **+** (plus) button at the top of the dialog box to add the first menu item. In the **Text** field, type the text to appear as the link, and then click the **Browse** button next to the **When Selected, Go To URL** field. Browse to the file you want to link to, select it, and click **OK**. The filename is added into the dialog box.

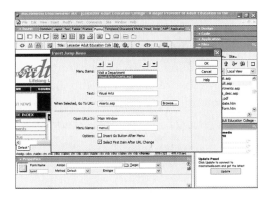

5 Add More Links

Use the **+** (plus) button to add more links to the jump menu. Repeat these steps until you have all the links you want. Click **OK** to view the menu onscreen.

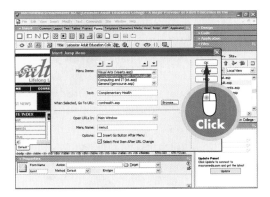

6 Edit the Menu

Once onscreen you can still edit the jump menu by adding items, removing them, or changing their order. Select the menu in the document, then, in the Property Inspector, click the **List Values** button to see the jump menu items in the List Values dialog box.

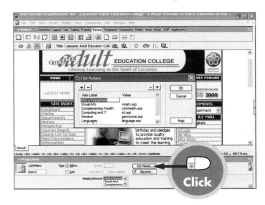

7 Make Edits

Use the **+** button to add menu items. Select an item and click the **−** button to remove it. Alternatively, you can simply click a name or link and edit it manually. Select an item and click the up or down arrow to change its position in the order of menu items.

How to Hint

Frames and Jump Menus

The next part of the book is all about frames—you can use frames in jump menus by telling your links where to open. In the Insert Jump Menu dialog box, use the **Open URLs in** drop-down menu to select a frame for the link to open in.

How to Follow and Check Hyperlinks

Checking your hyperlinks before uploading the site is not only a good idea, it's also vital if you are going to have a successful Web site. Internal links can be checked (followed) from within Dreamweaver; you check external links from a separate browser. You learn to do both in this task.

1 Follow an Internal Hyperlink

Open the page in Dreamweaver and select a link. Open the context menu by right-clicking the link (Ctrl+click for Mac users). Choose **Open Linked Page** from the context menu.

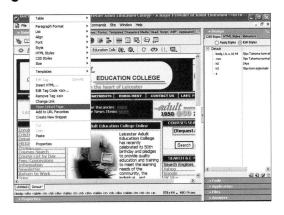

2 Open the Linked Page

The page you linked to opens for editing into the document window. This result tells you that the link is correct and that it works.

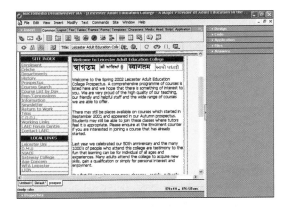

3 Check an E-mail Link

To check whether an e-mail link works, open the page in the default browser by choosing **File**, **Preview in Browser**. Click the link to make sure that the default e-mail application opens and that the correct e-mail address is inserted into the **To** field.

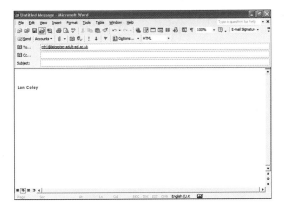

④ Check an External Hyperlink

To check an external hyperlink, you must first open the page in the default browser. Be sure you are connected to the Internet, and then click the external link. You should see the correct page in the browser window.

⑤ Check All Local Links

Dreamweaver can check the internal links in a document, folder, or site for you. Choose **File**, **Check Page**, **Check Links** to show the **Link Checker** tab in the Results panel. Use the **Show** drop-down list to select the links you want to show and check. Click the green arrow play button to choose which links to check and start the process

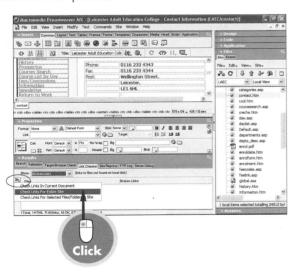

⑥ View the Results

The Results panel shows you a list of files with broken links. You can edit these pages to fix the problems. Simply double-click any filename to open it into the document window for editing.

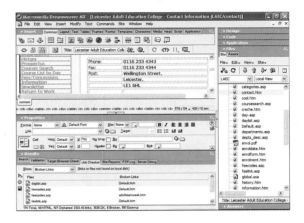

How to Hint

Checking Links

Dreamweaver can open links to local files only through the context menu. External hyperlinks and mailto: e-mail links can be checked only using the **File**, **Preview in Browser** menu option. If you use the **File**, **Check Page**, **Check Links** command, Dreamweaver creates a list of external links but cannot check whether they are still in working order.

You should always test external links manually, and on a regular basis.

Adding a Go Button

By default, the links in a jump menu are activated as soon as the user makes a selection. If you would rather have a Go button attached to your menu that the user needs to click before the link is activated, simply check the **Insert Go Button after Menu** option at the bottom of the Insert Jump Menu dialog box.

Task

Frames and Framesets

In simple terms, frames are individual Web pages held together in a set; when the browser sees them, it draws the frames together to give the impression of a single page. To use frames, you must create a *frameset*—an HTML page that holds all the size, shape, and positioning information for all the frames you want to appear together. You also must create the individual pages to be displayed as frames. It isn't as complicated as it sounds—honestly!

You have undoubtedly seen frame-based sites on the Internet. The "standard" page layout has a title frame at the top of the page, a narrow navigation frame on the left that contains the links for the page, and a contents frame where the main body of information appears. Although this is a standard use of frames, there are many alternatives.

In the standard frame-based page just described, the frameset contains three frames: three individual Web pages that are viewed together inside the frameset. The frameset is never actually displayed in the browser as a page with content—it is there to contain the information about the structure and properties of the individual frames.

Each individual frame within the frameset is an HTML page with its own content, properties, and settings. You can be as creative as you like with frames as long as you remember to check that the frames work together both visually and functionally when they all appear on the page. Each frame can have its own scrollbars if needed or can be "scroll free" and give the effect of a single page.

How to Create a New Frameset

Dreamweaver makes creating a frameset a painless task, not to mention a quick one. Making the frameset, or container, for a frame-based site is the starting point for any framed site. After the frameset is created, you can either make new pages to use within the frameset or use pages you already have.

1 Show Frame Borders

The first thing to do is to make sure you can see the borders for the frameset. The borders give you a view of how your frameset will look. Choose **View**, **Visual Aids**, **Frame Borders**. A visible line appears all around your document window. This creates your frameset.

2 See the Built-In Options

Dreamweaver comes with built-in frameset options. From the **Insert** bar, choose the **Frames** tab to see the complete selection of Dreamweaver framesets.

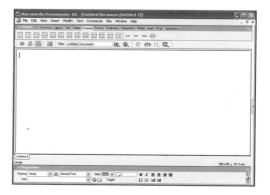

3 Make a Selection

From the options, decide which style of frameset best suits your needs. Click your selection in the panel and it will be applied immediately. I am simply creating a vertical split to have a left and right frame.

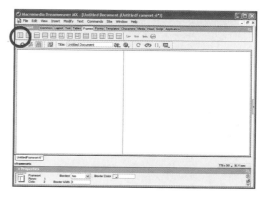

4 Add a Horizontal Split

Dreamweaver lets you add frames without starting over. Click in the right frame you created in the preceding step and choose **Modify**, **Frameset**, **Split Frame Up**, or **Split Frame Down**. The Split Frame commands give you the general layout for the frameset and the page; we'll worry about dimensions in a minute. Use both the vertical and horizontal split options to create the exact layout you want.

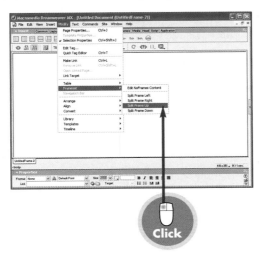

5 Create a Four-Framed Set

Here's a technique that can be employed only in a new blank page with Frame borders showing. Press and hold the **Alt** key (Mac users press **Option**) and drag from any corner of the border to create a frameset with four frames. Although four frames on a single page isn't common, this is where the term *frameset* comes from.

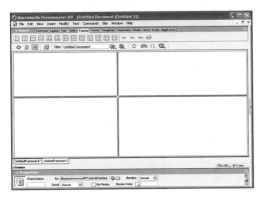

6 Delete a Frame

To delete a frame, drag the frame border all the way out of the document window.

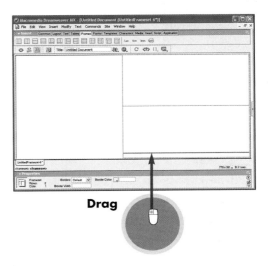

Drag

How-to Hint

Play Before Work

Before you start trying to input content into frames, be sure you understand how the frames and the frameset work. In many ways, the most important thing to understand about frames is the structure. Get the structure of your frameset right to start with, and everything else will be fine.

How to Name and Save Frames

When you create a frameset, either of your own design or a predetermined Dreamweaver frameset, you are presented with new HTML pages that must be saved individually, and also named. This task shows you how to do that quickly and easily.

1 Understand How the Framesets Work

When you select one of the predefined framesets, you create blank HTML pages in each frame. The properties of a selected frame appear in the Property Inspector.

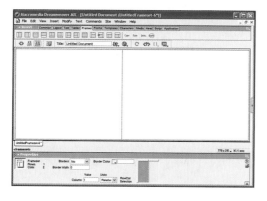

2 Name the Frames

When you start working with frames, keeping them straight can be confusing. Let's type some identifying text into our frames. I am typing **TOP**, **LEFT**, and **MAIN** as appropriate.

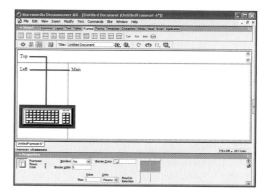

3 Save All Frames

Select **File**, **Save Frameset** to open the Save As dialog box. Type the name you want to give to this frameset (I suggest **Frameset1** as a good name for this first attempt at frames). Click **Save** to continue.

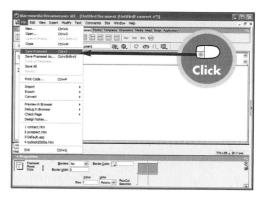

④ Save the Frame Pages

Now you need to save all the frames (HTML pages that make up the frameset). Click in the top frame and choose **Save Frame** from the **File** menu. Name the file **topframe.htm** and click **Save.**

⑤ Save All Frames

Repeat Step 4 to save each individual frame. Give them meaningful names that will help you remember what each is. Note that when you click in any frame now, its filename is displayed in the tab at the bottom of the document window.

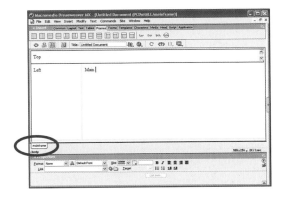

How-to Hint

Naming Frames

In Task 2 I have named the frames very simply and have included the word *frame* in the page name. This is not at all necessary, but when getting started with frames it certainly makes things easier to remember. As a general rule, however, it's a good idea to use *fr* somewhere in the filenames as an identifier. Personally, I call framesets `fr_filename` and the individual frames `frfilename`.

Pages and Frames

Normally we refer to a page as a single document that is displayed in a Web browser. When working with frames, though, the term *page* is used to describe the entire contents of the frameset. This is because it's all displayed at one time.

How to Set Frameset Properties

When you're working with frames and frame-sets, you'll want to use the Frames panel, which makes it easy to choose the frame or frameset you want to work with. After you select a frame or frameset, the properties for that item become visible in the Property Inspector. Among other things, the properties of a frame or frameset control the size of the frame, whether a scrollbar is visible, and whether the visitor can resize the frame.

1 View the Frameset Properties

Choose **Window**, **Others**, **Frames** to display the Frames panel. The Frames panel is located within the Advanced Layout panel group.

2 Select the Frameset

In the Frames panel, click the frameset border; the Properties Inspector now shows the properties of the frameset for the page.

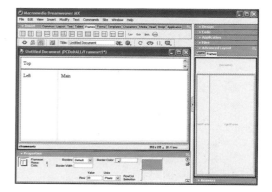

3 Set Borders for a Frameset

From the **Borders** drop-down menu in the Properties Inspector, choose whether you want to have a visible border between frames. In this example, visible borders have been turned on.

4 Set Border Properties for a Frameset

If you turned on the visible borders, you can set the size and color of the borders. In the **Border Width** field in the Properties Inspector, type the width, in pixels, for the border. Click the **Border Color** box and use the color picker to choose a color for the borders (if you know the color you want, you can simply type the hex code for that color).

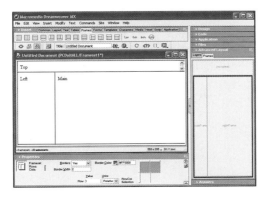

5 Set the Column Width

Use the Frames panel to set the column or row value for your frames. (Either Row or Column displays, depending on the selected frame.) You can set these values to be a relative percentage of the total frameset or a set number of pixels. This image shows the left frame with a column value of 200 pixels—notice how much wider that frame is now.

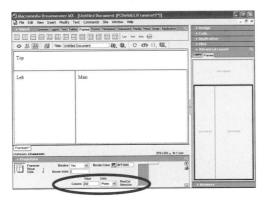

6 Give the Frameset a Title

In the Frames panel, be sure the frameset is selected (click the outside border of the frameset), and then choose **Modify**, **Page Properties**. In the Page Properties dialog box, type a title for the frameset page and click **OK**. This title appears in the title bar of the browser when the frameset is displayed.

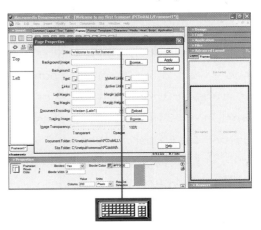

How-to Hint

Understanding the Frames Panel

The great thing about using the Frames panel is that it gives you the best possible view of your frameset. Moving between frames in the panel is easy: Just click inside the frame you are interested in. The selected frame always appears highlighted for you. Note that the frameset is highlighted by a large, thick border, and the individual frames are highlighted by a thinner line.

How to Set Frame Properties

Each frame within the frameset contains an HTML document. You can specify properties for each frame within the frameset. You can select individual frames using the Frames panel and use the Properties Inspector to change the settings. Note that any frame properties you set will override the frameset properties.

① View Frame Properties

In the Frames panel, click the frame whose properties you want to see. The Properties Inspector displays the property information for the frame you have selected.

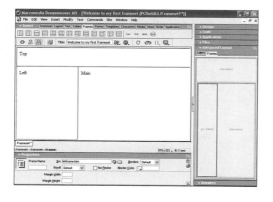

② Name the Frame

Type a relevant name (**leftFrame** in this example) for the frame in the **Frame Name** text box on the left side of the Property Inspector. This name is used for targeting hyperlinks. If you will use any scripting in your site, avoid using scripting words such as top or navigator.

③ Set Scroll Properties

From the **Scroll** drop-down menu, choose whether scrollbars will appear at the edge of the frame. For browsers to show scrollbars only when browser size requires them, select **Auto**. Select **Yes** to force scrollbars. Select **No** to never show them; you must ensure that your content never outsizes the frame because your viewers won't be able to scroll to see the content.

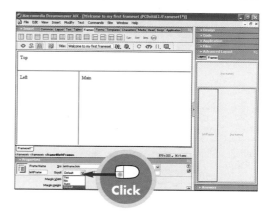

④ Set Border Properties

Setting a border color for a frame overrides any border colors you set in the frameset Properties Inspector. Use the color picker to set a new **Border Color**. You can turn off borders in the Properties Inspector for the frame only if the **Borders** option for every adjacent frame in the frameset is set to **No**.

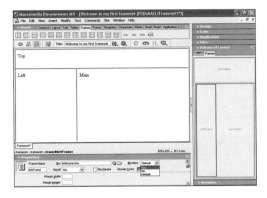

⑤ Set Resize Options

Although you can allow visitors to your site to resize frames in the browser window, this flexibility is usually not provided. You should size frames at the design stage rather than allowing visitors to resize the frames. Enable the **No Resize** box to ensure that visitors cannot change the size of the frames.

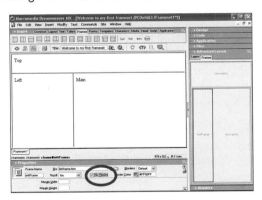

⑥ Set Margins

The margin controls set the distance between the edge of the frame and the frame contents. In the **Margin Width** and **Margin Height** fields, type the number of pixels you want for a margin. Width controls the distance from the side, and Height the top and bottom.

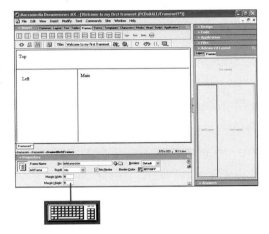

⑦ Preview the Frameset

The effect of the margin setting is visible only when the page is viewed in a browser. I set the **Margin Height** and **Width** to 100 simply to ensure that the effect is obvious. Preview the file in your browser (**File, Preview in Browser**) to see the margin in effect.

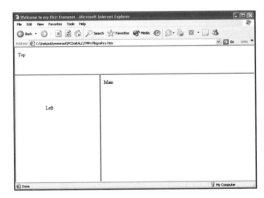

How to Use NoFrames and Nested Frames

The NoFrames option lets you control what the visitor sees if he is using a browser that cannot display frames. You also can have frames within frames (just as you can with tables). The Nested Frameset option refers to frames and framesets within frames, and simplifies your work with these more complex arrangements. As soon as you place a new frame or frames inside an existing one, you have a nested frameset, regardless of how many new frames you add. Luckily, Dreamweaver handles this for you and maintains all the code neatly, meaning that you still have only one frameset to maintain.

① See the NoFrames Content

You can modify the default message that appears to a visitor using a browser that doesn't support frames. If your page uses frames, take the time to modify the default message so that the visitor isn't frustrated at being unable to access the content of your page. To view the default message, choose **Modify**, **Frameset**, **Edit NoFrames Content**.

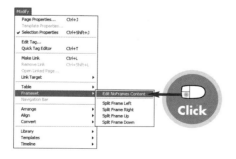

② Enter the Content

The screen refreshes to a screen that simply says NoFrames Content. You can type whatever content or instructions you want onto this page to tell visitors why they can't see your page and what they can do instead.

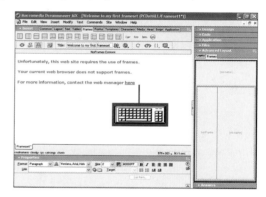

③ Return to Frames View

After you have entered the information you want to display, choose **Modify**, **Frameset**, **Edit NoFrames Content** again to return to the normal view of your frames. Note that you don't have to actually save the NoFrames message information separately because it is stored with the frameset.

4 Insert a Nested Frameset

Nested framesets are used to further divide existing frames; when used carefully, they can create interesting effects. Click inside the frame you want to hold the new frameset and use the **Frames** tab of the Insert panel to insert a new predefined frameset. In this example, we insert a new top frame in the existing top frame on the page.

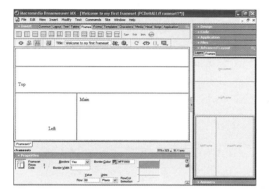

5 Format the Nested Frameset

Nested frames and framesets can be formatted in the same way as first-level frames. Open the Frames panel and click inside the new frame; use the Properties Inspector to set the properties for it.

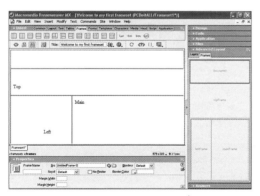

6 Save the New Layout

Choose **File**, **Save All** to save the newly created top frame. Be sure you give this new frame a unique name within the frameset.

How-to Hint

Use a Framed Page As Your Home Page

If you want to use a page formatted with a frameset as the home page for your site, you must name the frameset accordingly. To make a page the home page, the frameset must be named either **index.htm** or **default.htm**. (Your ISP will tell you which name to use.)

Saving Frames

Did you notice that when we saved the new frames page, the option we selected on the **File** menu was **Save All Frames**? Continue to use this option to save all the frames in your frameset at once. If you want to save the frameset with a different name, select the entire frameset in the Frames panel and choose **File**, **Save Frameset As**. This option is available only after you have selected the frameset.

How to Edit Frames

You can change the layout of your frameset even after you have started working on its content. Frames can be deleted or split at any time to create new frames. If you want, you can add existing HTML pages to a frame instead of using the new blank HTML pages that Dreamweaver automatically adds when you insert a frame. This task explains some of the editorial jobs you can accomplish with frames

① Delete a Frame

Deleting a frame is simple even if you have started working with the content of the frame. Select the frameset using the Frames panel. In the document window, simply drag the frame border off the page.

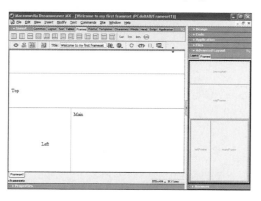

② See the Effect

The frame you dragged disappears, and the contents of the rest of the frames adjust to fill the screen. In this example, we deleted the new top frame; the contents of the lower frame adjust to fill in the gap.

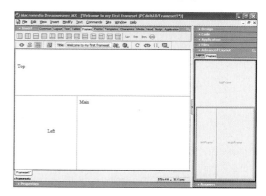

③ Split a Frame

You can split an existing frame into more than one frame. Select the frame you want to split by clicking in the Frames panel. Then, hold down the **Alt** key. (Mac users press **Option**.) In the document window, drag the frame border to split the frame.

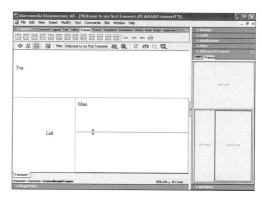

④ Change the Page to Be Displayed

You can fill a frame with a previously created document. In the Frames panel, select the frame you want to change. In the Properties Inspector, click the folder icon next to the **Src** field. In the Select HTML File dialog box, select the HTML page you want displayed in the frame, and click **OK**.

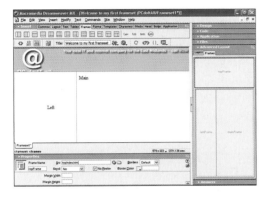

⑤ Adjust the Frame Size

If the frame is not wide or deep enough to display the contents of the page you choose, drag the frame border to widen or lengthen the frame. Alternatively, you could manually change the value in the **Value** box in the Properties Inspector.

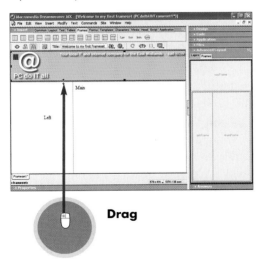

Drag

⑥ Preview the Page

Add content into all the frames, then choose **File**, **Preview in Browser** to check that the page looks how you expect. Verify that the frames contain the chosen pages in the correct places, that the scrollbars work as expected, and so on.

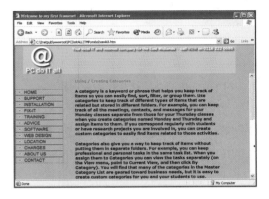

How-to Hint

Don't Forget

The pages that display in the frames are complete HTML pages in their own right and can be edited either as part of the frameset or as an individual page. To open the page away from the frameset, just open the page from the Site window.

How to Target Links in a Frameset

The way links in framesets work is unique. Get the links right, and your site will look wonderful. Get the links wrong, and it will look like your worst Web design nightmare with pages opening in the wrong places. When we looked at hyperlinks in Part 5, "Links, Navigation, and Structure," we mentioned the target options; now is the time to use those options.

❶ Get Familiar with Frame Names

Open the Frames panel for your frameset. Note the names for each frame on the page. Recall that you can change the names of the frames in the **Frame Name** field in the Properties Inspector. You'll refer to these frame names when you create your links.

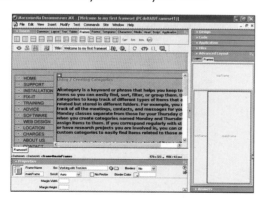

❷ Create a Hyperlink

In any frame in the document window, type a line of text or a word to use as a hyperlink. If you are using an existing page, simply select the text or image you want to use as a link. Then use the **Link** field in the Properties Inspector to specify the file or URL to be linked to.

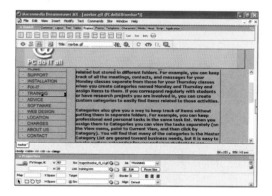

❸ Look at the Targets

Often, you will want the page to which the hyperlink points to display in a different frame on your page. You can choose the frame in which you want the linked page to open from the **Target** drop-down menu in the Properties Inspector. Click the arrow next to the **Target** field to display the list of frames in the page.

Click

4 Choose the Target Frame

In this example, we want the page referenced by the selected link in the left frame to display in the main frame, so we select **mainFrame** from the **Target** drop-down menu.

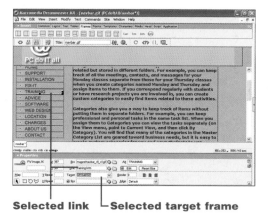

Selected link └**Selected target frame**

5 Open a Link Outside the Frameset

It is considered very bad manners to open other peoples' Web sites inside your own frameset. If the link you want to display is to an external site, you can specify that the contents open either in a new window (use the **blank** option) or into a complete page in the same browser window without frames (use the **top** option).

Click

6 Open a Link in the Same Frame

To open a linked page in the same frame as the link itself, choose **_self** from the **Target** menu. In this example, we want the link on the page in the **mainFrame** frame to open its referenced page in the **mainFrame**. To make this happen, select the link text and choose **mainFrame** or **_self** from the **Target** drop-down menu.

Click

How-to Hint

What Does _parent Do?

If you create a nested frameset, the outer frameset become the parent frame. When targeting your links, use the **_parent** option to point a link to the parent frameset and out of the nested frame.

How to Fix Links in a Frameset

When you use frames on your page, it's essential that you check the links between the frames. Your site will simply not work if you have full pages opening in navigation-sized frames and other peoples' sites trying to open into your layout. In this task, you learn how to check the links in your frameset—and how to fix any errors you find.

❶ Preview the Page in a Browser

When you are finished with your preliminary page design—including frames and links—open the frameset in the default browser for testing. To do this, choose **File**, **Preview in Browser**.

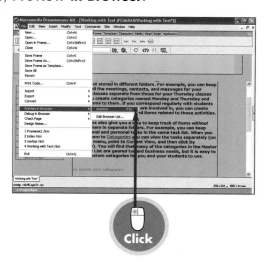

Click

❷ Check Internal Links

Click each of the internal links to be sure they open where they should. Make a note of any links that don't act as expected.

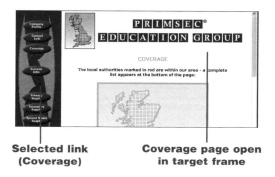

Selected link (Coverage)   **Coverage page open in target frame**

❸ Fix Any Problems

Switch back to Dreamweaver and open the Site window. Choose the frameset you want to work with (opening the frameset file opens all the associated HTML pages as well). Use the **Link** and **Target** fields in the Properties Inspector to retarget any links that went wrong during testing.

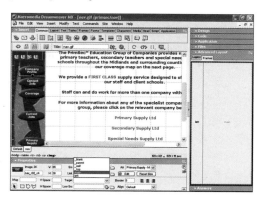

108   Part 6: Frames and Framesets

Check Links from Other Pages

It makes sense to manually work through all the links in a logical fashion because Dreamweaver has no feature that checks the target of links for you. Work through the links on each page in succession, and then move to the next page. This logical approach is the only way to guarantee success with targeted links. In this example, you can see what happens when a page that should open in the main frame is targeted incorrectly.

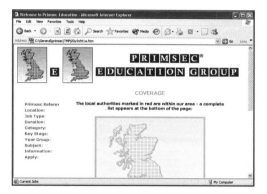

Set a Base Target Command

If you know that all the links on your HTML page have to open in a particular frame or window, you can edit the HTML code to set a base target that will operate for all the links on the page. Open the HTML source for the page by clicking **View**, **Code** and add the following line into the <Head> tag: **<base target="_self">**. Setting the base target to **_self** tells all links to open into the same frame as the link appears; setting the base frame to **_blank** opens all links in a new browser window.

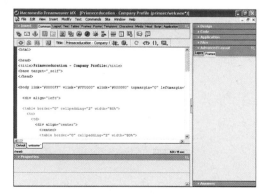

Use the Base Target Carefully

Using the HTML base target code shown in Step 5 can save you a lot of time and effort (using it can eliminate the need to keep targeting individual links on pages). However, you must still set targets for any links that you want to open in a new window or a whole page.

Test and Test Again

Dreamweaver's **Link Check** command checks to make sure that your internal links point to valid pages within your site. However, this command cannot check that targets for links are logically correct; only you can do this through manual testing.

How-to Hint

Task

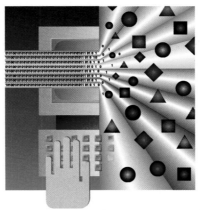

Introduction to Fireworks

By the end of this part of the book, hopefully you will feel confident to play with images, maybe even create your own, and most importantly, be able to use Fireworks with self assurance.

Let's start by getting back to basics and understanding what Fireworks actually is. Back in the last millennium, there was no such thing as a graphics program designed just for Web graphics—that is, until Fireworks came along. Unlike everything before, it was designed simply to create graphics to be seen on the Internet—not to be printed. That has changed slightly in that Fireworks graphics are often used in Flash and Director files in CD-based applications, but the original idea is still there.

Most graphics programs let you create either vector graphics or bitmap images, but not both. Fireworks gives you that flexibility and has built-in tools for both modes. This introduction to Fireworks takes you through the differences between the two modes, not only to help you understand the differences, but also to enable you to put that understanding into practice.

How to Find Your Way Around the Interface

When you open Fireworks for the first time it can appear very daunting—and possibly like something from another world. Luckily, Macromedia has spent the time and energy to standardize its applications where possible, so because you've been using Dreamweaver, the Fireworks interface should have a familiar feel, even if the buttons and toolboxes are different. In this first task we simply look around, identify the workspace elements, and explain why everything is there.

① Open Fireworks and Look Around

Launch Fireworks via your **Start** menu or desktop shortcut. The application opens with everything looking a little dull.

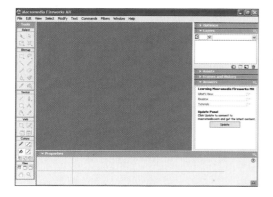

② Create a New Document

All the tools and panels are grayed out until you create a new document. From the **File** menu, choose **New** to open the New Document dialog box.

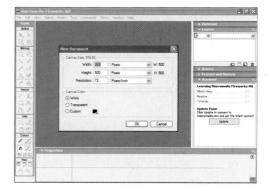

③ Complete the Dialog Box

Set the dimensions for this document. The **Width** and **Height** are in pixels. For this look-around task I'm creating a blank image that is 250×250 pixels. Simply type in the dimensions you require. Web graphics are normally sized in pixels, although you can use centimeters or inches instead.

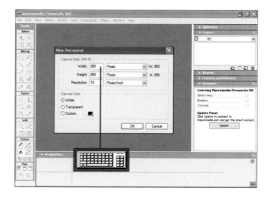

4 Choose a Canvas Color

Fireworks enables you to set the canvas to be any color you choose or even to have it set as transparent. To choose a color, use the color picker.

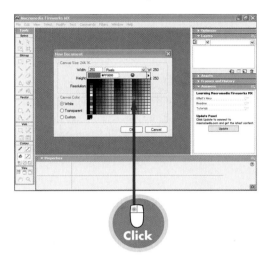

5 View the Canvas

Click **OK** to continue. Your canvas is ready and the toolbars and panels become active ready for use.

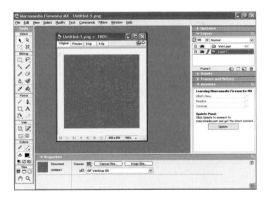

6 Maximize the Document

Fireworks creates a new file called untitled1.png. The document window is created per your dimensions. Maximize the document window by clicking the **Maximize** button at the top of the document window.

How to Navigate the Fireworks Workplace

Like Dreamweaver, Fireworks uses a combination of menus and panels to give you control over how the application works. The overall look of the workspace is similar to Dreamweaver. In this task, we look at and identify the actual components that make up the Fireworks workspace. Specifically, we'll look at the differences between Dreamweaver and Fireworks. Okay, you've created a new document and chosen the size of the canvas—surely they are the same? Well, not at all.

1 Understand the Terminology

Look at the workspace with the document maximized. The document is in the middle of the workspace—the canvas is the actual work area located in the center of the document.

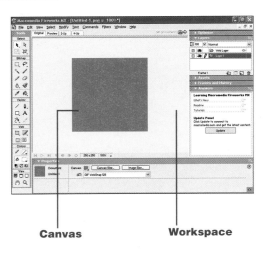

Canvas   Workspace

2 Look Left

On the left of the screen is the Tools panel. If this is not visible, choose **Window**, **Tools** to show it. The Tools panel is filled with graphics tools, text tools, and Web-related tools. This panel is perhaps the most important single part of Fireworks.

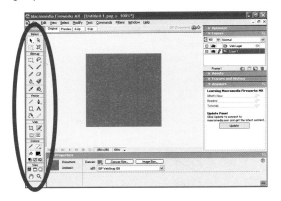

3 Look Right

On the right of the screen are the panels that enable you to work with layers, frames, behaviors, and assets—just like in Dreamweaver. Just as with Dreamweaver, they are opened and closed from the **Window** menu. We will work through these as we progress through the book.

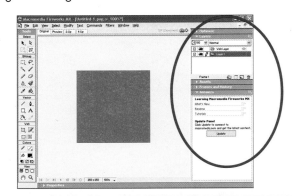

4 Look Up

At the top of the workspace are the title and menu bars. The title bar works in the same way as any other application, showing the name of the current document, while the menu bar gives you access to all the Fireworks options.

Title bar

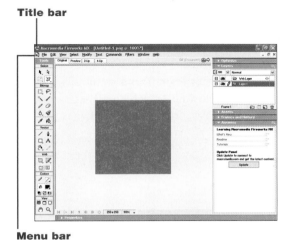

Menu bar

5 Look Down

At the bottom of the workspace is the Property Inspector. If you've used Fireworks before, you'll recognize this as a new feature bringing Fireworks in line with Dreamweaver. The Property Inspector displays the properties for selected items on the canvas. With a blank canvas such as ours the Inspector shows the canvas details.

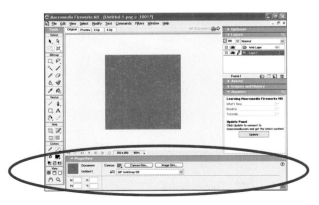

6 Change the Size of the Property Inspector

The Property Inspector displays at either full (seen in Step 5) or half size. To shrink or expand the Property Inspector, click the arrow at the bottom of the Inspector. To change size back, simply click again.

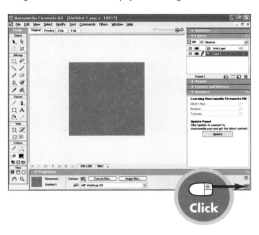

How to Change Fireworks Panels

As I've mentioned, Fireworks is jam-packed with handy features to give you great control over your new designs and edits to existing images. This task shows you all the features with a short explanation of what each does. When you've finished this task, you should be confident enough to use these features regularly and correctly. The panels in Fireworks are all movable and can be shown, hidden, and positioned to suit you. Each panel has a specific function within the application, and a title bar with an attached menu to give you control over the visibility.

1 Show a Panel

Fireworks opens with some panels already visible. The rest are available simply by using either the **Window** menu or by clicking the appropriate panel menu to show, hide, maximize, or minimize it. Click the sideways arrow in the Optimize panel title bar to open it to full size.

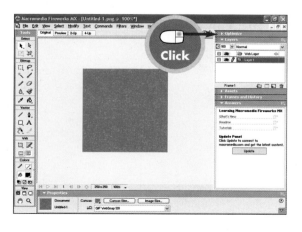

2 See the Difference

The arrow in the title bar changes and now points downward to indicate that the panel is expanded. Note that when maximized, the panel causes others to shrink.

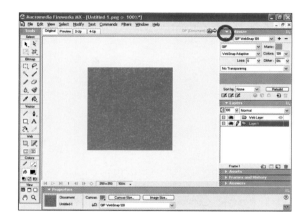

3 Grab a Panel

Each panel can be moved (undocked) from the main panel area. Click and hold in the title bar on the grabber. The cursor changes to a cross head, as shown here.

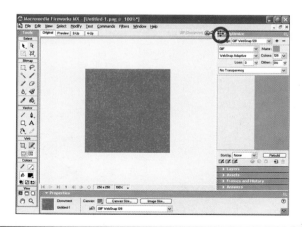

4 Move a Panel

With the cross head cursor you can drag a panel to any location within the Fireworks workspace. Simply drag to the location you want and let go. I suggest a more sensible location than in the middle of the canvas as shown here!

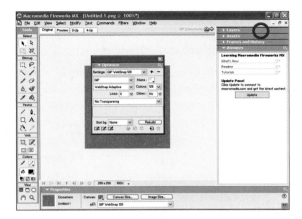

5 Redock a Panel

To put the panel back, simply grab and drag the panel again. When you see the thick line at the top of the panel area (the line is cyan on a Windows machine and gray on a Mac) you can safely let go and the panel will be redocked.

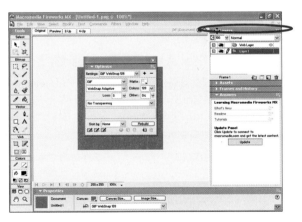

6 Show the Menu

Right-click (Ctrl-click for the Mac) in the panel title bar to show the context menu. This is the same for all panels, and enables you to close the panel or panel group completely, or simply to maximize or collapse it. Click the option you want.

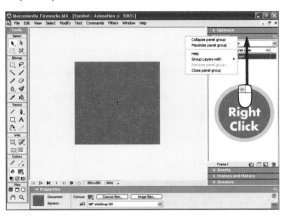

How-to Hint

Closed a Panel by Mistake?

The **Close** option mentioned in Step 6 removes the panel group from the right side of the screen completely. To reshow it at any time, simply use the **Window** menu and select the panel you want. When the panel reopens, it isn't docked in the panel area—it opens as a standalone panel, which you can then dock into the Panel area if you want, or simply use it, and then close again.

Rename a Panel Group

Fireworks MX enables you to rename some of the panel groups. Right-click a panel title bar and, if the **Rename Panel Group** option is available, simply select it and type a name that you prefer. If the option is grayed out, the feature is not available (Optimize, Layers, and Answers panels cannot be renamed). I suggest leaving them as they are until you're confident about using the application.

How to Use Panel Groups

As mentioned earlier, each panel or panel group has a specific function within Fireworks, so before we get going in the creation and editing of graphics, we'll look at what each panel is designed to do. This task covers all the panels and panel groups that are visible when the application launches. These are the most commonly used. Panel groups not covered here will be addressed as we use them throughout the book. Each panel and panel group has a title bar, is expandable, can be closed, and has an options menu located at the top right of the panel. Each options menu contains items specific to the open panel.

1 Examine the Optimize Panel

The Optimize panel is designed so that you can get the best from your image files, selecting the correct file format, size, and, where necessary, compression. All these are controlled by the Optimize panel, which helps you prepare your files for display on the Internet. Don't worry if the explanations here are a little bit brief. I'll expand on each panel as we use it later in the book.

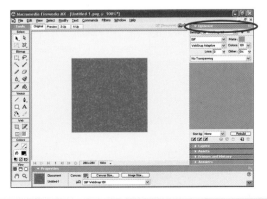

2 Understand the Layers Panel

Layers are used in Fireworks to enable you to place different image elements on different levels (or planes). Each layer can contain many objects that can be shown, hidden, or stacked however you want. This gives you control over the layout of your image files. The Layers panel is used to create and edit layers and their content.

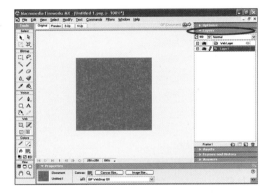

3 Use the Assets Panel Group

The Assets panel group has three panels within it: Styles, URL, and Library. Each is accessible by clicking the appropriate tab in the panel group title bar. Here we see the Library panel selected.

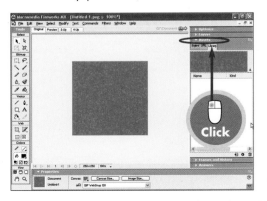

④ About the Library Panel

The Library panel contains symbols that can be reused over and over again in multiple documents. You can change a library item once and have it update wherever it's used. The panel shows the name of the item and the type of symbol, such as graphic, button, or animation. Here we see some existing symbols.

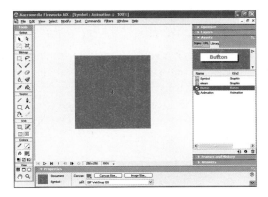

⑤ About the URL Panel

The URL panel enables you to add frequently used URLs as library items that can then be used over and over. This feature is particularly handy when you're creating buttons and imagemaps. Simply type in the URL or link info, then click the **+** button to store the information.

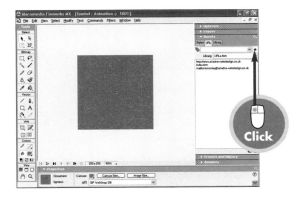

⑥ About the Styles Panel

The Styles panel lets you either save your own styles for future use or apply one of the 30 preset styles that ship with Fireworks.

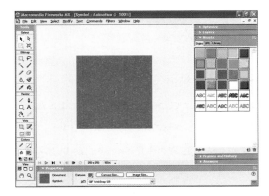

⑦ The Frames and History Panel Group

Use the tabs in this panel group to select either **Frames** or **History**. The panel options menu shows different options depending on whether you have the Frames or History panel selected.

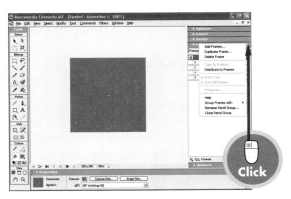

Continued **2**

⑧ The Frames Panel

The Frames panel is used for creating or editing animations. In an animation, each change to the object is recorded in and played back as a different frame, as shown here. The panel enables you to create, delete, and manipulate frames in your files.

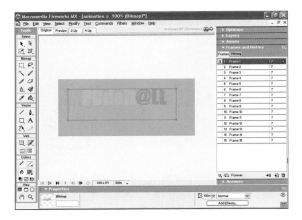

⑩ The Answers Panel

The Answers panel is a great new feature in Fireworks MX that enables you to jump straight to certain key help files and also connect directly to the Macromedia Web site to get updates, access forums, and so forth.

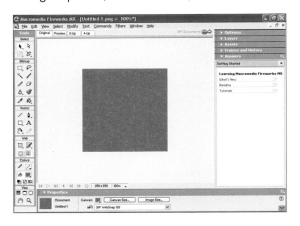

⑨ The History Panel

Every time you perform an action in Fireworks, it's remembered. You can use the History panel to undo actions, replay them, and even save actions as commands that can be used over and over. The slider enables you to move through the actions.

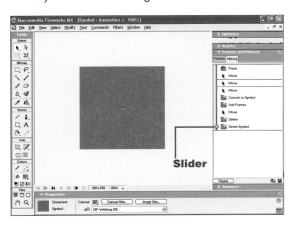

Slider

⑪ Using the Answers Panel

Make a selection from the Answers panel's drop-down menu to choose which area you want to use to find your answer. Here I am selecting technotes.

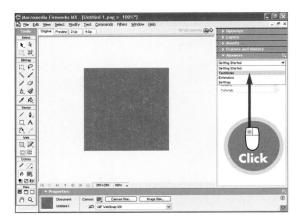

Click

12 Make a Selection

The panel updates to show you recent information from your selected area. These are links. Click on any link to jump to the Macromedia Web site to learn more, or you can type a search term into the the box at the bottom of the panel.

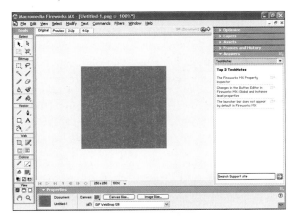

13 Other Panels

We have looked at the most common panels and groups here; however, there are others you can access through the **Window** menu—simply click a menu item to show the panel. We will look at these other panels as we work through the book.

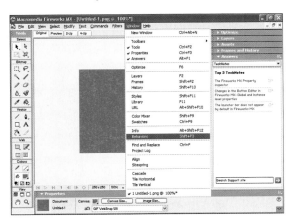

14 Showing Toolbars

Most application have toolbars visible. Fireworks has two toolbars available, but you have to choose to show them. From the **Window** menu choose **Toolbars** and make your selection.

15 About Toolbars

The Main toolbar displays at the top of the screen and has buttons for **Open**, **Save**, **Print**, and so forth. The Modify toolbar is located at the bottom and allows you to group, rotate, and generally modify your document objects.

Main toolbar

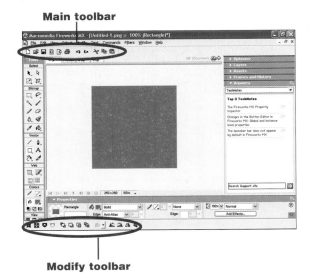

Modify toolbar

How to Set Preferences

Dreamweaver has many built-in preferences. In many cases, the defaults are fine and don't need changing. However, this task shows you how and where to change things if you need or want to. The preferences cover everything from the number of steps stored in the History to setting locations for plug-ins. This task will cover the General Preferences and Folder options for those of you with additional files compatible with Fireworks.

❶ Open the Preferences Dialog Box

From the **Edit** menu, choose **Preferences** to open the Preferences dialog box. (On a Mac running OS X, the **Preferences** option is located in the Fireworks **Application** menu.)

❷ Set General Preferences

The **General** tab lets you set the number of steps for the History panel (the default is 20). **Color Defaults** allow you to set default colors for fill and brush stroke, as well as update the color for highlighting paths—all of which we address as we work through the book.

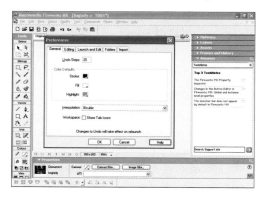

❸ Set Interpolation Option

By default, Fireworks uses Bicubic interpolation, which gives the best overall image results. It can be changed to one of the other Interpolation options. You should not need to change this. (The Hint at the end of this task provides more details.)

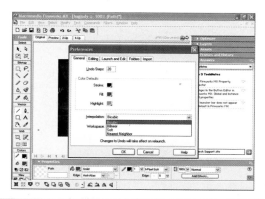

122   Part 7: Introduction to Fireworks

④ Show Tab Icons

If you used a previous version of Fireworks, you'll be used to the icons at the bottom of the document window. Checking the **Show Tab Icons** option restores them as shown here.

⑤ Select the Folders Tab

The **Folders** tab in the Preferences dialog box lets you specify the location for Photoshop plug-ins, textures, and materials that you have stored in other locations on your hard drive. Click the **Browse** button by the option you want to add, and then browse to the folder on your hard drive or CD-ROM that holds the information

What Is Interpolation?

Interpolation is the term used when a graphics application attempts to add extra pixels to retain resolution when an image is resized. It's never perfect, and each option in Fireworks does something different. The default option, **Bicubic**, gives the best results and really doesn't need to be changed. However, here are some definitions of the other options:

Bilinear—Better than **Soft**, but not as good as **Bicubic**. If you want to play with the settings this is probably the second-best option to try.

Soft—This effect was the original one used by Fireworks in earlier versions. It eliminates hard edges and usually gives a soft blurred effect.

Nearest Neighbor—Personally, I dislike this option because the effect is often rough and messy. The best description of the effect is that of using a zoom tool.

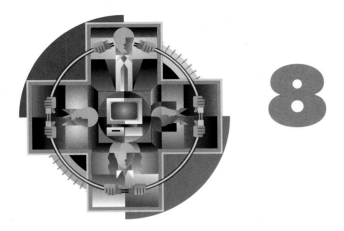

Images

It's funny to think that a decade ago not only were there hardly any Web sites, but most of those that did exist were text only. The idea of streaming media, sounds, and even images were just a distant dream. Now, however, images are an integral part of almost every Web site. Images are now a necessary part of the Internet, and every site, however basic, is likely to have them.

Knowing what type of images to use, how many, and what sizes is vital to the successful use of images on Web pages. An image that is too big will never be seen, one that is too small will be missed, and so on. Fireworks and Dreamweaver work so well together, letting you create, edit, change, and size images for the perfect balance. In this part, we look at some different image types and where they are best used. We'll create a simple graphic from scratch, place it into Dreamweaver, and use Dreamweaver to place an image that does not yet exist.

How to Choose an Image Type

If you are new to graphics, the different types of image files available will mean nothing to you. Let's look at the options and highlight which file types are used where and why. When that's out of the way, we'll get started with you creating your own basic images for your Web site. The first two types discussed are the ones that will actually end up on your Web pages; the rest all have their place and might be file types that you already have.

① About JPEG Images

The JPEG (JPG) image file, developed by the Joint Photographic Expert Group (hence the name), is the perfect file format for photographs to be used on the Internet. It supports millions of colors and should be used for any image needing more than 256 colors, such as the digital photograph shown here.

② About GIF Images

GIF (Graphics Interchange Format) files make up the bulk of Internet graphics, support up to 256 colors, and have the option for transparency; they are perfect for animations, bullets, and buttons, as shown here.

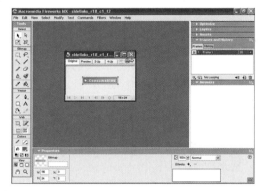

③ About PNG Image Files

PNG (Portable Network Graphic) image files are the Fireworks default image type. This format can support up to 32-bit color, allows transparency, and is very handy—unfortunately, not all browsers display PNG files, so for now they are best used within Fireworks.

④ About TIFF Images

TIFF is the most common file type for printed media. TIFF images are cross-platform and therefore are very popular for people using both Windows and Mac systems. TIFF images, which display as bitmaps when opened in Fireworks, are not supported on the Internet; they must be converted to either JPG or GIF.

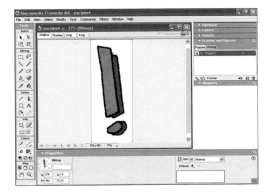

⑤ About BMP and PICT Images

BMP and PICT are operating system-specific: BMP on Windows and PICT on a Mac. They can both be pretty much universally read by applications on the corresponding systems. BMP files are commonly used as wallpaper on Windows systems, as shown here.

⑥ The Little-Known WBMP Image

WBMP is the newest of the image types and is used solely for imaging on mobile phones and personal data assistants (PDAs). The images are small, 1 bit, and therefore black and white. Fireworks can read these images, but they are not suitable for normal Web development.

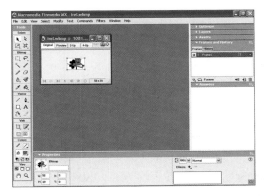

How-to Hint

Keeping the PNG

Even though it's best to stick to `.gif` and `.jpg` images for your Web site, always remember to keep a copy of the underlying Fireworks file. That way, you can come back and edit it whenever you need or want to.

Other File Types

We have looked at the main types of image file that Fireworks can create and export; however, such is the power of the application that you can also open Photoshop, Flash (`.swf`), and Illustrator files.

Editability

When you open an image file, such as a `.jpg` or `.gif`, in Fireworks, the word **Bitmap** often shows in brackets after the filename. You can make changes to the size of the image, add a text overlay, or slice the image, but you cannot edit any layers or textures that were previously added. However, you have full editability over all features when you open a `.png` file.

How to Create a New Image File

We've already had a look around the Fireworks workspace in Part 7 of the book, and now we'll actually use the application to create a graphic from scratch, giving you a better feel for how things work and where they are. By now, you have a good understanding of panels from earlier in the book, so the terminology should be familiar, even if the techniques to be used are new. Let's start simply, by opening the application and having a quick reminder of how it looks.

❶ Open Fireworks and Create a New Image Document

Choose **File**, **New** to open the New Document dialog box. In the **Width** and **Height** boxes, type values for the size of the canvas you want to create (you can always adjust the size later). The units of measurement can be pixels, centimeters, or inches. The **Resolution** field defaults to 72 pixels per inch, the most suitable for Web images.

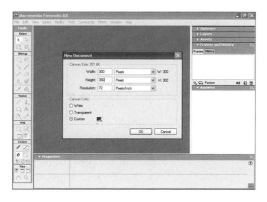

❷ Set the Canvas Color

The **Canvas Color** area of the dialog box controls the background for your image. You can select the **White** or **Transparent** option, or use the **Custom** drop-down button to choose a color using the color picker. Click **OK** to close the dialog box, and observe the canvas on the screen.

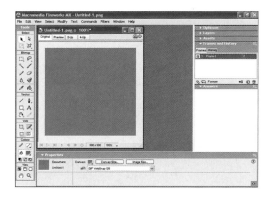

❸ Save the File

When you save a file in Fireworks, the default format is PNG. To save the current document, choose **File**, **Save As**. In the dialog box, navigate to the folder in which you want to save this file, and then type a meaningful filename. (On a Windows system, the **Save As Type** option lists **PNG** as the file format.) Click **Save**.

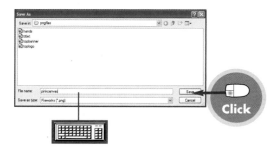

Click

④ Save a Copy

You can save versions of the same file at different stages of development—a great idea if you know you'll want to return and revise an earlier version. Choose **File**, **Save a Copy**. In the dialog box, navigate to the folder in which you want to save the file, type a new filename, and click **Save**.

⑤ Reopen Files

Just like Dreamweaver, Fireworks retains a record of the 10 files you've most recently worked on. Open the **File** menu and choose **Open Recent** to see the last 10 files you have opened. To reopen a file, simply click the filename in the list.

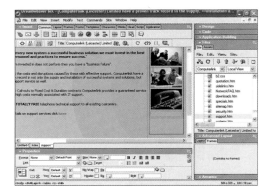

How to Insert an Image in Dreamweaver

When you create, scan, or otherwise receive images, you still have to place them into your Web pages. Dreamweaver makes this an easy process. Before you start, be sure the images you want to use are located in the folder you're using for your Web site. If they aren't, you will get constant reminders from Dreamweaver to copy them there.

① Open Dreamweaver

Start by opening Dreamweaver to either a blank page or one where you would like to place an existing image.

② Decide Where To Put the Image

Place the insertion point in your Dreamweaver page where you want the image to appear.

③ Show the Common Panel

Make sure the Common panel is showing on the Insert bar by clicking its tab.

Click

4 Open the Select Image Source Dialog Box

Click the **Image** icon on the Common panel to open the Select Image Source dialog box.

Click

5 Browse to the Image You Want to Insert

Use the dialog box to locate the image you want to place on the page. The image can be within the Web site folder, on your hard drive, a floppy disk, or on a CD. Click **OK** to continue. If working on a new page you will be prompted to click **OK** a second time.

Click

6 View the Property Inspector

The image is placed on the page at the insertion point. Click the image once, and then view the Property Inspector to see the information about the image you inserted.

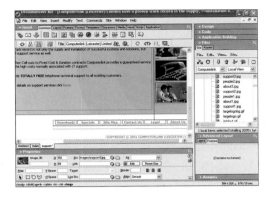

How-to Hint

Copy Images into Web Site Directory

If the image file you are inserting is not already in your Web site folder, Dreamweaver prompts you to copy it there. You should always say **Yes** to the question. Without being in the correct location, the file will not display correctly when uploaded to your final Web site.

How to Use the Property Inspector with Images

Task 4

The Property Inspector shows the details of the image you inserted. Initially, it tells you the width (**W**) and height (**H**) of the image and shows you a thumbnail and the source (**Src**) of the image. The Property Inspector can also be used to change and add image information, such as alternative text (**Alt**). Images should always have alternative text, which displays in the browser when the mouse is moved over an image, can be read by a screen reader for the visually impaired, or displays as a caption if the image fails to load or in a browser with no image support.

1 Add Alternative Text

Alt text can be read by accessibility aids and can be seen in browsers that don't support images. Type your descriptive text into the **Alt** text box on the Property Inspector. The description should be enough to give those using accessibility aids an idea of what the image is.

2 Edit the Display Size

You can change the width and height display settings for the image directly in the Property Inspector by typing in new dimensions. Note that this does not edit the image—merely the size it will display at. Here I have made a silly change to make the effect obvious.

3 Reset the Size

As you can tell, you must be careful making these edits! Luckily, Dreamweaver lets you put it right with a single click. Click the **Reset Size** button to put the image back to its original dimensions.

④ Add an Image Border

Type a number in the **Border** box to add a border to your image. The border is automatically the same color as the link color for your page, so you should avoid having an image border unless you are using the image as a hyperlink. It can be confusing to visitors.

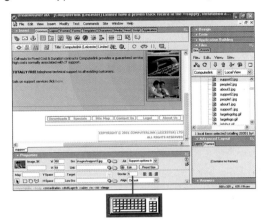

⑤ Give the Image a Name

Type a name for the image in the box next to the thumbnail. This name will be used for any scripts or behaviors that you associate with the image. (See Part 12 for more information.)

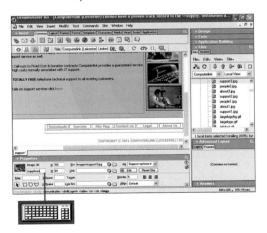

⑥ Align the Image

Use the **Align** buttons to align the image in a table data cell or layer. Use the **Align** drop-down menu to set how text aligns with the image.

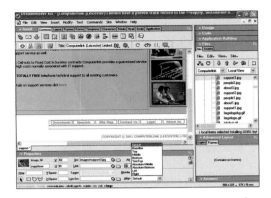

How-to Hint

Links and Images

I have not mentioned hyperlinks here because they're well and truly examined in Part 5, "Links, Navigation, and Structure," and Part 15, "Slices and HTML in Fireworks," looks at imagemaps. If you want to check there, you should find everything you need to know about hyperlinks in Dreamweaver—and possibly a whole lot more besides!

How to Use Image Placeholders

Task 5

One of the great new features in Dreamweaver MX and Fireworks MX is the capability to use placeholders. In simple terms, you now have the facility to tell Dreamweaver where you want to put an image and how big it will be, and then go off to Fireworks, create it, and watch Dreamweaver automatically update the display. That's the theory at least, so let's take a look at how to do it. For this task we'll start with a blank page. Open Dreamweaver and use the **File** menu to create a blank HTML page.

❶ Select the Image Placeholder Icon

From the Common panel of the Insert panel group, click the **Image Placeholder** button. The Image Placeholder dialog box opens.

❷ Complete the Dialog Box

Type a **Name** for the image—this is a friendly name, not a filename (which you'll create later). Add dimensions for the image in the **Width** and **Height** boxes— I am using 300×300 pixels. Use the color picker to set a **Color** for the placeholder; this does not affect the image, only the placeholder. You can add **Alternate Text** at this point as well.

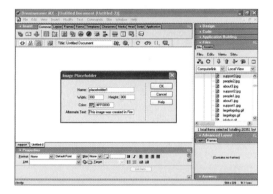

❸ View the Placeholder

Click **OK** to continue, and the placeholder is immediately visible in your document. You can now plan your page around the image, knowing that the placeholder is there, or you can go ahead and create the image.

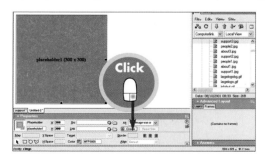

④ Launch Fireworks

From the Property Inspector, click the **Create** button. You are prompted to save your page before creating the image. Click **Yes**; name the file, and click **Save** to continue.

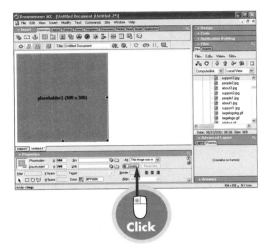

⑤ Look at Fireworks

Fireworks opens. Note that it already has a canvas set to the size you specified and an icon on the document window that shows you are editing from Dreamweaver. The title bar uses the same name that you used in the previous steps.

⑥ Set the Canvas Color

The default canvas color is white, so change it to be whatever color you prefer. Use the **Modify**, **Canvas**, **Canvas Color** option to choose the color you want.

How-to Hint

Finishing the Process

We'll continue this process through the next two tasks and take the opportunity to learn a little more about Fireworks as we go.

How to Create Your First Image

Now that you have a new file in Fireworks and have a blank canvas to work with, let's put some of the Tools panel and Property Inspector options to use. First, let's use some of the most common tools, starting with the Ellipse tool. Drawing shapes of any description is easy in Fireworks. The Tools panel makes it simple by letting you choose the shape you want.

1   Choose the Tool You Want

The Fireworks Tools panel has many tools (almost 40, in fact). To choose a tool, click it. Some tools have other tools hidden in a menu; these "parent" tools have a tiny arrow in the bottom-right corner. To access the hidden tools, click the visible tool and hold the mouse button down; a menu of related tools pops out. Drag across the additional tools to select the one you want. When you release the mouse button, the tool you selected displays on the button in the Tools panel.

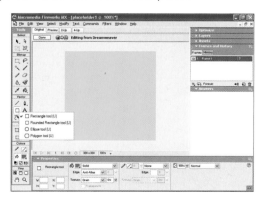

2   Draw an Ellipse

Select the Ellipse tool from the **Shape Tool** pop-out menu in the Tools panel. Move the mouse pointer over the open canvas and click and drag to draw an elliptical shape.

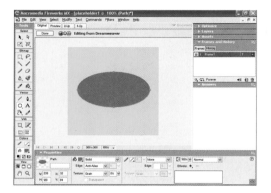

3   Select the Ellipse

You must select your shape before you can perform any other action on it. Click the Selection tool in the Tools panel (the dark arrow in the top-left corner of the Tools panel) and then, for this example, click the ellipse to select it. Fireworks adds a blue outline to the shape to show that it is selected.

Selection tool

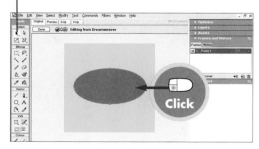

Click

4 Open the Color Picker

By default, the shape you draw is filled with the last color you used (or is white if you have not used Fireworks previously). With the ellipse selected, click the color picker next to the paint bucket icon in the Property Inspector.

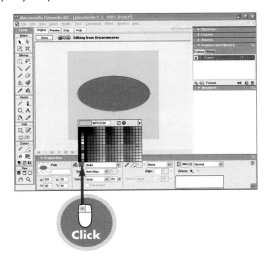

5 Select the Color You Want

Use the color picker to select the Fill color for your ellipse. As soon as you select a color, the document window updates and the new color fills your ellipse.

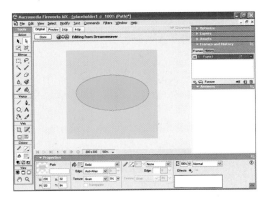

6 Add a Visible Outline

With the shape still selected, display the **Stroke Color** color picker located next to the pencil-like icon on the Property Inspector. Choose the color you want to use as a visible outline around the selected shape.

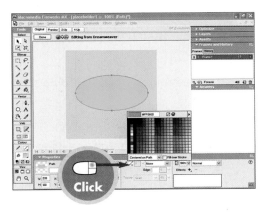

7 Set the Width of the Outline

Use the pop-up slider next to the stroke color picker to set the width of your outline. The higher the slider, the wider the outline. I want a thin outline, so I'm setting the slider to 4.

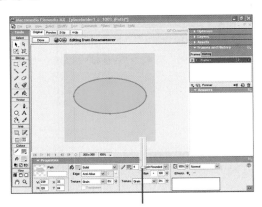

Border width slider

How to Send the Image Back to Dreamweaver

Now you have an image—it might be simple on this occasion, but the process of using a placeholder is the same no matter how complicated the image you create. Your imaging techniques will improve as you work through the parts of this book, and you'll no doubt be creating much more complex images to send straight back to Dreamweaver, but this part focuses on teaching the processes and terminology rather than the imaging techniques.

① Finished in Fireworks?

When you are happy with your creation, click the **Done** button at the top of the document window.

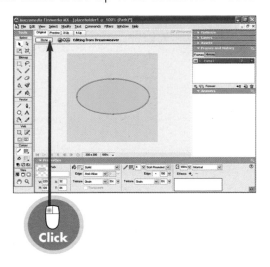

② Save the File

The Save As dialog box opens for you to save the PNG file. The filename defaults to your original name in Dreamweaver, but should be changed to a more meaningful name. Browse to the correct location to save the file and click **Save** to continue.

③ Export the Image

When you save the PNG file, Fireworks prompts you to save the file to be used in Dreamweaver. This will usually be a GIF image. Because the file type is different than PNG, Give this file the same meaningful name as the one in the previous step. Click **Save** to continue.

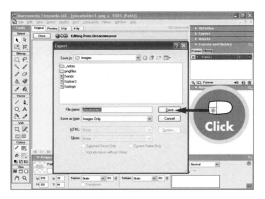

④ Return to Dreamweaver

Fireworks closes automatically when the image is exported. Return to your page in Dreamweaver, and the image you created is now in place in the document.

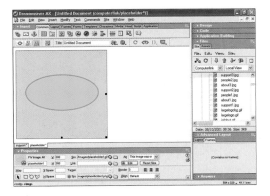

⑤ Look at the Property Inspector

The Property Inspector fills in the filename for the exported file, and also completes the **fw** (Fireworks) **Src** box at the bottom of the Inspector. This information tells Dreamweaver the name and location of the underlying PNG file. You will see how handy that is in the next step.

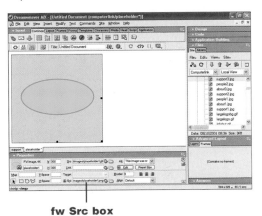

fw Src box

⑥ Edit the File

When we first looked at the Property Inspector to create our image, we found the **Create** button. Now that we have an image, the button is called **Edit**. Click this button to relaunch Fireworks and make changes to your file. Dreamweaver opens the underlying PNG file for you. Repeat the previous steps.

Task

Working with Images in Fireworks

We've looked a fair amount at Dreamweaver now, and have created a nice basic image via Dreamweaver, saved it, and reopened it for editing. Because images are such an important part of any Web site, we'll take a thorough look at Fireworks before going back to Dreamweaver and adding images to our Web pages. This part of the book is designed to show you enough of the basic techniques to make sure you can make images look the way you want them to, rather than just dumping an image into a Web page.

Like any graphics application, Fireworks can take a long, long time to master; however, the tasks in this part will give you the confidence to work with images in Fireworks.

Images you create in Fireworks can be seamlessly integrated into your Dreamweaver pages. Even after an image is exported in a Web-acceptable format (primarily the GIF or JPEG format), Dreamweaver will remember the originating Fireworks file format, making image editing easy.

Regardless of where your image files originated—in Fireworks or in some other graphics editor—the tasks in this part show you how to manipulate and fine-tune those images in Fireworks with the ultimate goal of exporting them for use in a Dreamweaver Web page.

When working with graphics, it's a good idea to save your work often—and in some cases, with many different filenames. You never know when something might need tweaking or changing. The more versions of a file you have saved during the development of an image, the easier it is to go back. When you export a PNG file from Fireworks to another format, you should keep the original PNG file—just in case.

How to Understand Modes

We've looked at some of the basics of Fireworks in the preceding parts, so let's move on a little and understand more of the terminology that will become common to you as you use the application more. Most graphics applications allow you to work in either *Vector mode*—when you work with the lines that comprise an image—or *Bitmap mode*—modifying pixels within a new image or editing an existing image, such as a photograph or scanned file. Fireworks enables you to work in both modes, and even swap between them, depending on what you're doing at any given time and the type of file you are working on.

1 What Is the Default?

When you first open Fireworks to create a new image, you are in Vector mode, the usual mode for drawing shapes and (as you'll learn later) adding effects to images you create. Everything you draw is a vector graphic, and you can edit and amend the lines, curves, and so forth. Select the **Rectangle tool** from the Tools panel and draw a rectangle.

Rectangle tool

2 Notice the Points

When you create a new shape in Fireworks, it has editable points. The rectangle you have just drawn has such a point at each corner. The points can be edited in a vector graphic. Select the **Sub Selection tool** from the Tools panel (also called the toolbox).

Sub Selection tool

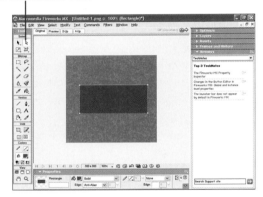

3 Ungroup the Rectangle

Click and drag any of the four points on the rectangle, and you are prompted to ungroup the rectangle and turn it into a vector. Click **OK** in the Fireworks alert box to continue.

④ Edit the Points

When the rectangle is ungrouped, you can manipulate it into a new shape. Handles appear, allowing you to push or pull the points in any direction to create whatever shape you want.

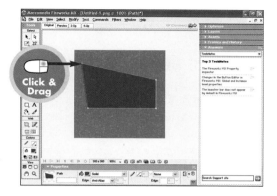

⑤ Open in Bitmap Mode

When you open a non-Fireworks image, such as a photograph, into the application, it automatically opens into Bitmap mode. This is identified by the word **(Bitmap)** in the document title bar.

⑥ Different Controls

In Bitmap mode, you can cut, crop, and resize images (all of which we cover in the next part), but even when you select the Sub Selection tool you cannot alter the shape of the underlying image as you could with a vector image. Here, you can see that using the Sub Selection tool only resizes the image.

How to Open Foreign Images in Fireworks

Fireworks supports images created in other applications or those obtained directly from a digital camera or scanner. These "foreign" files can be opened in Fireworks with some of the original editability intact. These steps explain how to open most graphics files in Fireworks; you also learn how to work with an animated GIF file.

1 Open a GIF or JPG File

GIF and JPEG files are the two most common file types used in Web pages; they are the file formats you are most likely to have. Simply choose **File**, **Open** and navigate to the desired file to open GIF and JPEG files in Fireworks. The selected file opens in the workspace. Fireworks adjusts the magnification to fit the workspace.

2 Get an Image from a Scanner

Assuming that you have a scanner or a digital camera, you can use the TWAIN options to move your images into Fireworks. Choose **File**, **Scan**, **Twain Acquire**, and select the software you usually use to scan or import an image from the external device. The resulting image opens in Fireworks as a new document.

3 Open Files from Other Applications

As noted in Part 8, Fireworks can open many image formats. If Fireworks cannot open a particular file (that is, if it doesn't recognize the file type), you see an error message, and you'll have to use a different application to work on the image. Fireworks supports all the file types suitable for Web pages, so you shouldn't have too many problems.

④ Open an Animated GIF File

Animated GIF files are fun to view and can add some visual excitement to your Web pages without adding megabytes of storage space to the site. Choose **File**, **Open** and navigate to the animated GIF file you want to open. The first frame of the image opens in a new document window. (There are many places on the Internet from which you can download small animations to use on your sites. A simple search in any search engine will produce results.)

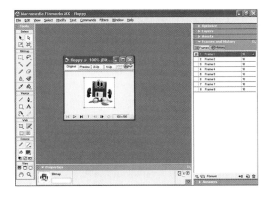

⑤ Open the Frames Panel

Initially, the animated GIF file appears as a single static image. The only evidence that it's an animation comes from the document window, which now has playback controls at the bottom. In fact, Fireworks has split the animation into frames. Expand the Frames panel to see the individual frames.

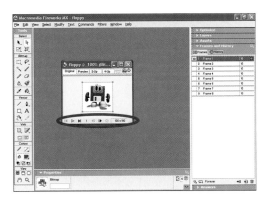

⑥ Look at the Frames

Scroll through the list of frames in the Frames panel to get an idea of how many individual images make up the animation. Click each frame in the list individually and watch the document window to see the image change slightly with each new frame displayed.

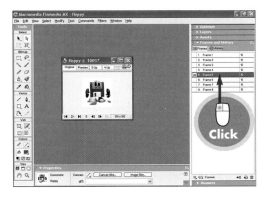

⑦ Watch the Animation in Fireworks

Use the playback controls at the bottom of the screen to see the animation play within Fireworks. You can view the animation frame by frame (in a kind of stop-action manner) or play it as a continuous file.

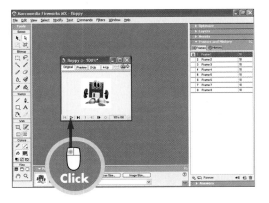

How to Resize Images

Frequently, image files are simply not the size you need or want them to be. In Fireworks, it's easy to change the dimensions of an image file, as you learn in this task. Resizing an image in Fireworks merely changes the dimensions; it does not affect the resolution.

① Open the Image to Resize

Open the image you want to resize. If the image file is foreign to Fireworks (that is, if it is not a PNG file), it opens in Bitmap mode. This means you can make certain changes to the image, but not to the components that were originally created. When you're working with a file created in Fireworks, the file opens into Vector mode and you can edit all components.

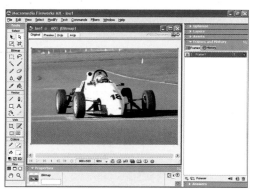

② Open the Image Size Dialog Box

You can control the size of the image down to the pixel level. Choose **Modify, Canvas, Image Size** to open the Image Size dialog box.

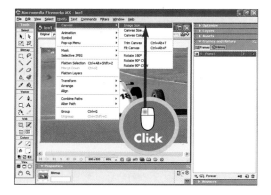

③ Fill Out the Dialog Box

Select the **Constrain Proportions** check box (bottom left) so that you do not inadvertently distort the image. In the **Pixel Dimensions** area at the top of the dialog box, type the new horizontal or vertical value you want the image to assume. (As you change the horizontal or vertical value, the other updates automatically.) Click **OK** to close the dialog box and resize the image.

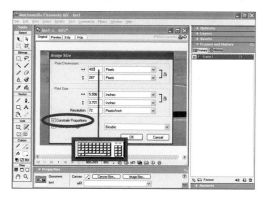

④ Transform the Image Size with Percentages

Rather than specifying exact measurements in the Image Size dialog box, you can resize an image to a percentage of its original size. Right-click the image and choose **Transform**, **Numeric Transform** from the context menu.

⑤ Adjust the Percentages

The Numeric Transform dialog box opens. Select the **Constrain Proportions** check box to ensure that the width/height ratio of the image is maintained. Specify the percentage by which you want to scale the image. Click **OK** to close the dialog box and resize the image.

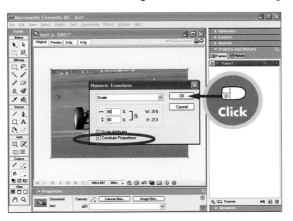

⑥ Modify the Canvas Size

When you resize an image, the canvas size stays the same and you might have excess space around the image. To change the size of the canvas so that there is less extra space around the image, choose **Modify**, **Canvas**, **Canvas Size**; the Canvas Size dialog box opens.

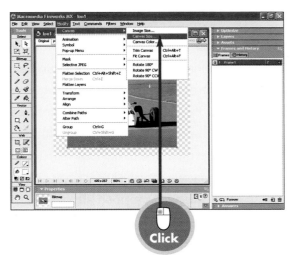

⑦ Enter Values

In the horizontal and vertical size fields, type new values for the canvas size and click **OK**. The canvas shrinks or enlarges around the image to your specifications. Be sure you don't make the canvas too small, or you'll lose part of the image itself. The Properties Inspector shows the current dimensions for the image.

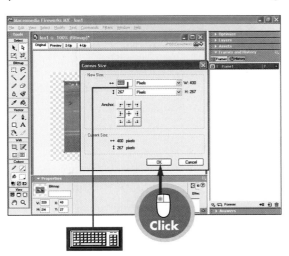

How to Crop Images

Frequently, you will have an image that could benefit from having some of its background eliminated. *Cropping* is the process of cutting away that portion of the image you don't want to see (with the side benefit of shrinking the file size). Fireworks offers a simple Crop tool that squares up the image to your specifications. You can also produce some specially cropped shapes with the tricks you learn in this task.

➊ Open the File to Be Cropped

In the workspace, open the file you want to crop. In the Tools panel, click the **Crop** tool.

➋ Draw the Area to Keep

Move the mouse pointer over the image and drag a rectangle around it. The portion of the image inside the rectangle will remain; everything else will be removed. If you make a mistake drawing the rectangle, press **Esc** and drag again, or use the handles that appear around the selection when you let go of the mouse to resize the selection.

➌ Crop the Image

Double-click inside the area to be cropped to perform the cropping action. Note that everything outside the rectangle that you drew disappears.

4 Crop Creatively

Consider the original image before you cropped it. Suppose you want to crop the image so that just the boy at the front remains and appears in an oval shape. As you know, the Crop tool cuts away the background in a rectangular shape. If you want to crop more creatively, click the **Marquee tool** in the toolbox and choose the **Oval Marquee tool**.

5 Draw the Area You Want to Keep

Click and drag the mouse to draw a nice oval around the area of the image you want to keep. A dashed line appears around the area you draw.

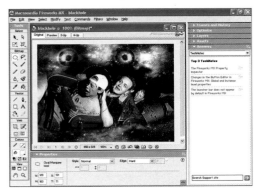

6 Copy the Selection

Choose **Edit**, **Copy** to copy the area inside the marquee onto the Clipboard. Copying the image in this fashion saves only the area inside the marquee, not the entire image.

7 Paste into a New Document

With the cropped area you want safely on the Clipboard, open a new file. Choose **Edit**, **Paste**. Fireworks automatically suggests a canvas size that matches the copied area of the original image. Make the canvas color transparent, and the image will blend nicely into your Web page.

How to Flip, Rotate, and Distort Images

As with many things, images don't always look how you want them to when you first open them in Dreamweaver. This is especially true when you're working with files created by others or with scanned images that have come from somewhere else. Being able to make changes to the overall look of the image, even in small ways, will make your image files look more professional.

❶ Open and Select an Image

Open the image you want to work with in the workspace. Click the **Selection tool** in the Tools panel, and click the image to select it.

❷ Rotate an Image

From the **Modify** menu, choose **Transform**; from the submenu, select one of the rotation options: **Rotate 180°**, **Rotate 90° CW** (clockwise), or **Rotate 90° CCW** (counterclockwise). When working with a single image that makes up the whole file, you can also use **Modify**, **Canvas**, **Rotate** followed by the direction you want.

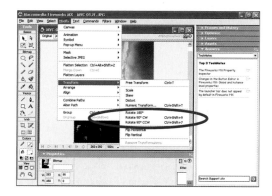

❸ Skew an Image

Skewing an image slants it either vertically or horizontally (or both if you like). Select the image and choose **Modify**, **Transform**, **Skew**. Handles appear on the selected image.

④ Drag to the Shape You Want

Drag any of the handles to slant the image in any direction.

⑥ Flip an Image

You can flip an image vertically or horizontally within the canvas. When you flip an image, the text appears mirrored, right hands appear to be left hands, and so on. Select the image and choose **Modify**, **Transform**, **Flip Horizontal** or **Flip Vertical**. In this example, I used the image of the boy at the theme park—notice he is now facing the other way.

⑤ Distort an Image

Distorting an image changes its dimension with no regard for ratio or appearance. Select the image and choose **Modify**, **Transform**, **Distort** to make handles appear around it. Drag any of the handles to change the shape of the image.

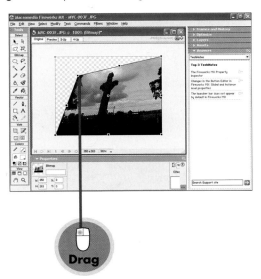

How to Add Text to an Image

Now that you know how to do some basic image manipulation in Fireworks, let's look at adding text to an existing image. (In Part 13, "Text and Simple Image Effects in Fireworks," you'll learn much more about using text in and as image files.) For example, a company logo in a non–Web-safe font is best converted to a graphic for use on the Internet. In this task, you learn a quick and easy way to add text to an image in Fireworks and save the text as part of the Fireworks file.

① Open the Image

Open the image on which you want text to appear. Click the **Text tool** in the Tools panel and then click the image to see the text insertion point.

② Type the Text

Type the text you want to show on the image. Select the text box, and then use the Property Inspector to set the font, size, and other attributes of the text.

③ Move the Text

The text might not appear where you expected and might not even be totally visible. Click the **Selection tool** in the toolbox and drag the text to the location on the image where you want it to appear.

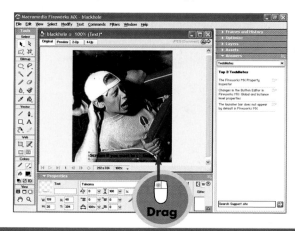

④ Edit the Text

With the text selected, right-click (Mac users Ctrl+click) and choose **Editor** at any time to open the Text Editor. Edit the text itself by retyping or changing the font, size, or color of the type. Click **Apply** to keep the dialog box open so you can view the changes on the image; click **OK** to close the dialog box and return to the image.

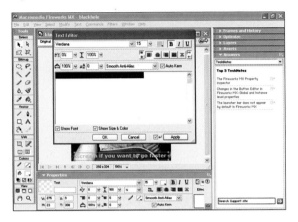

⑤ Split Text Over Lines

You can split the text over multiple lines. (By default, Fireworks places all the text horizontally across the image, regardless of whether it actually fits on the image.) Open the Text Editor and position the cursor after the word where you want the split. Press **Shift+Enter**.

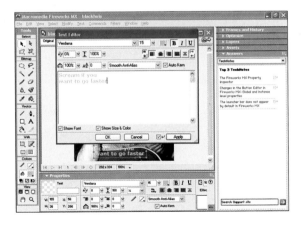

⑥ Save the Image and Text

When you save an image file in Fireworks, any text you've added to the image is saved as part of the file on its own layer, with no special treatment afforded to the text. To save your Fireworks image as a PNG file, choose **File**, **Save**. To save as a GIF or JPG, use the **Export** options.

Click

How-to Hint

Making Text Go Vertical

In Part 12, we'll look further at using text in Fireworks, but it's worth mentioning here that you can have vertical text as well as horizontal text. In the Text Editor, click the **Vertical Text** button to make the text change direction. Note that the text appears vertical only in the document window and not in the Text Editor.

Task

Navigation in Fireworks

Having nice buttons and a Web site that's easy to navigate can make your site more successful. We looked at navigation options using only Dreamweaver in Part 5. Now we'll look at how Fireworks can work alone to create navigation systems, or how it can work with Dreamweaver.

Creating buttons and navigation systems in Fireworks is a really easy process. The design of your buttons can be as simple or complex as you like, and Fireworks still writes all the code for you. You can create buttons that change in appearance as the mouse moves over them or clicks them. These appearance changes are known as *rollovers*: The image "rolls over" into a new one as the mouse moves over or clicks the button.

These effects are achieved using JavaScript; hand-coding the rollover effect is not only time-consuming, but also very easy to get wrong. Letting Fireworks do all the script writing for you not only saves time but also guarantees that the code is correct.

Buttons in Fireworks have *states*; this is a reference to the different ways a button can look in the browser. The Up state is how a button looks when it is simply sitting on the page with no interaction; the Over state is how the button looks when the mouse pointer is over it. The Down state is a "depressed" image that's displayed after the button is clicked. The Over while Down state, as the name implies, is displayed when the mouse is over an already depressed button. It really is very simple to create even the most complex buttons in a small amount of time. After you have mastered the creation of a single button, you'll be ready to move on to a navigation bar.

A *navigation bar* is a collection of buttons, each of which links to a different page in your site. Navigation bars give a consistent feel to your site and create a way of grouping your buttons together in a single image file. And just as it does for button rollovers, Fireworks writes all the navigation bar code for you.

One of the best tools in Fireworks, in my opinion, is the pop-up menu feature. The results can be great with the minimum of effort—what could be better?

How to Create a Simple Button

Fireworks has a built-in button editor, designed specifically to make your life easier. Not only can you use it to create the button designs you want, but Fireworks will write the script that controls the button's behavior. Start by creating a new, blank document.

❶ Create a New Button

In Fireworks, create a new file with a canvas about 300×300 pixels. From the **Edit** menu, choose **Insert**, **New Button**. The button editor opens, ready to create a new button.

❷ Choose a State

Treat the button editor as a canvas onto which you create the graphic you want to use as the button. You can draw shapes, import bitmaps, or drag objects from your main document into the button editor. The first four tabs across the top of the editor enable you to select in which state you'll design your button. I've selected the **Up** tab.

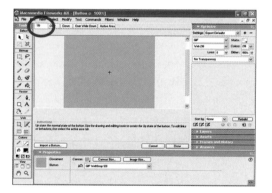

❸ Create the Button

For this task, just draw a rectangle in the center of the canvas using the drawing tools. Add some text to it by using the text tool. I simply typed **Button**.

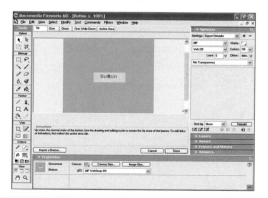

④ Move to the Over State

For a button to look different in each state, you must create a button for each state. Click the **Over** tab at the top of the button editor to show the blank canvas ready to create the next state of the button.

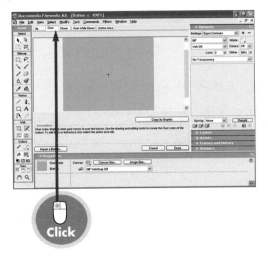

⑤ Copy the Up Button

If you want the Over state of the button to be similar to that of the Up state (for example, you might want the images to be the same in everything but color), click the **Copy Up Graphic** button. Edit the copied graphic using the drawing and fill tools on the Tools panel. I've changed the rectangle's fill color and the text color.

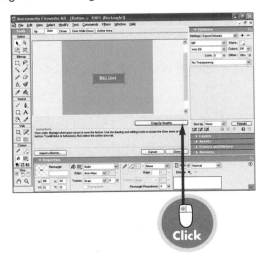

⑥ Set the Active Area

Now that you have images for a couple of the button states, click the **Active Area** tab to establish the area of the button that will respond to the mouse. The active area is represented by a "slice" that probably appears on your screen as a semi-opaque rectangle. The slice automatically covers the whole area of the button.

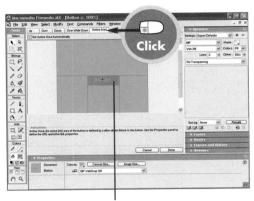

Active area (slice)

⑦ Create a Link

With the button's active area selected, use the Property Inspector to add a link (Link text box). Type some alternative text (**Alt** text box) that users will see if the button does not display—for example, "Click here for Irish information." Save your file; we'll continue with this button in Task 2.

How to Edit and Add Button States

In the previous task, we created a simple button that changes colors when the mouse moves over it. So far, that button doesn't change when it's clicked. After you've created a button, you can go back and add states or edit the images you've already created for the states. The single button you created in Task 1 can be used as the basis for a navigation bar, which you'll learn how to create in the next task.

① Add a Down State

Open the file you saved at the end of Task 1. The image opens as a graphic file with the active area highlighted. To open the button editor so that you can further edit the image, double-click the graphic. For this task, we'll add a Down state to the existing button: Click the **Down** tab to open the button editor for the Down state.

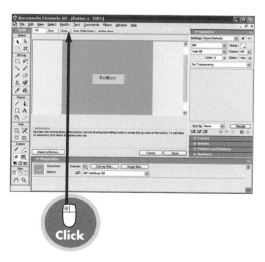

② Copy the Over State

Click the **Copy Over Graphic** button to copy the image from the **Over** tab to the **Down** tab so that you can edit the image to create the Down state of the button.

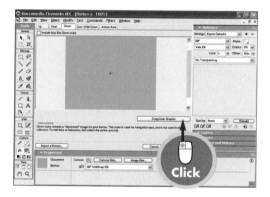

③ Edit the Image

Edit the Over graphic to create the Down button. Be sure the changes you make to the image are enough to make the Down graphic distinct from both the Up and the Over graphics. In this example, I'm changing the colors only.

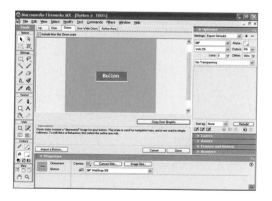

④ Add an Over While Down State

Click the **Over While Down** tab and repeat Steps 2 and 3 to create the Over While Down state for the button. This button now has images for all four button states. Close the button editor and resave the file. Because the graphic is a PNG file, saving the file automatically saves all the button states with it.

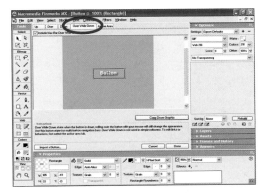

⑤ Edit Button Text

You can edit the text just as you can any aspect of the graphic. Open the button editor and click the appropriate state tab; right-click the text on the button to open the Text Editor. Change the text and click **OK**. When prompted to update the text on the other buttons, click **Yes** if you want the text change to appear on all the other button graphics.

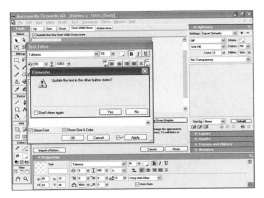

⑥ Edit Button Graphics

You can edit the button graphics at any time by opening the button in the button editor (double-clicking) and selecting the tab for the button state you want to change. Edit the graphic as you would any other object in Fireworks. Close the button editor and resave the file to retain your updates.

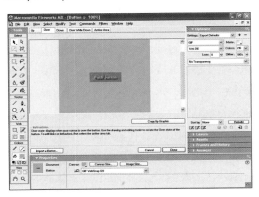

How to Create a Navigation Bar

A *navigation bar* is a collection of buttons used together to create a navigation system for your Web site. Starting with a single button symbol, you can make the navigation bar as simple or as complex as you want it to be. Once we have a collection of buttons, we'll make it look more professional and then export it into Dreamweaver.

1 Create the Graphic and Text

Begin by creating the graphic and text that you want to use for the first button.

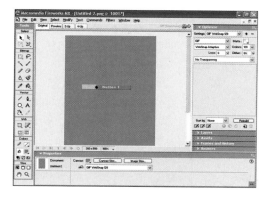

2 Convert to a Symbol

Select the graphic and text on screen, From the **Modify** menu choose **Symbol**, **Convert to Symbol**.

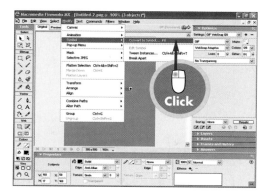

3 Complete the Dialog Box

In the Symbol Properties dialog box, check the **Button** type for the symbol and give the symbol a name, such as **NavButton**. Click **OK** to continue.

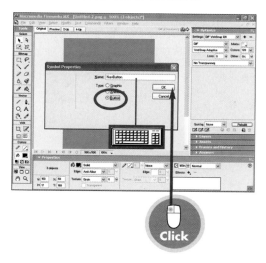

4 Check the Screen

The graphic you created is now a button. It appears in the Library, and the version onscreen is an instance of the button—this is indicated by the arrow at the bottom left of the graphic.

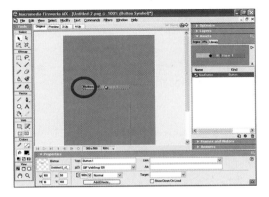

5 Add Button States

Now you have the simple button, complete the steps from tasks 1 and 2 to add the other button states that you want. You can have two, three, or four button states. Here you see the Over state for the button with color changes in place.

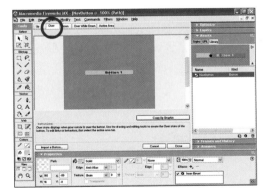

6 Add More Buttons

A single button is hardly a navigation bar, so create some more buttons. Select the current button on screen and choose **Clone** from the **Edit** menu.

Click

7 Position the New Button

The cloned button appears immediately on top of the original. To position the clone, use the arrow keys on your keyboard. I'm creating a vertical navigation bar, so I've moved the clone down, but you can move the button horizontally if you prefer.

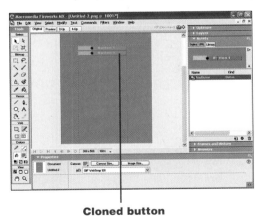

Cloned button

(8) Edit the Clone

Change the text on the cloned button—you would not want two buttons with the same text! Select the button, and use the Property Inspector to edit the text. All states for the button will be updated. Don't use the button editor to change the text because that affects the original symbol.

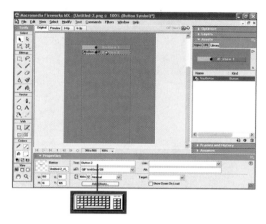

(9) Complete the Bar

Repeat steps 6, 7, and 8 until you have all the buttons you require, with appropriate names. Use the Property Inspector to add a link for each button.

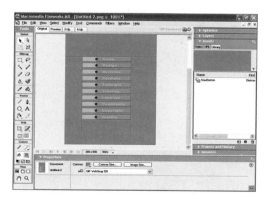

(10) Use a Separator

Instead of just lumping the buttons together, you could organize them into sections, separated by a plain graphic. Here I use a simple rectangle graphic with text on it. I've added a blank rectangle at the bottom for neatness.

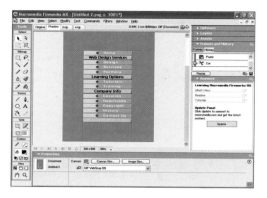

(11) Add a Company Logo

Take the opportunity to publicize your company or group. Add your company logo to the top of the navigation bar by selecting **File**, **Import** and locating an image to insert.

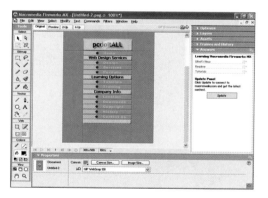

12 Trim the Canvas

Use the **Modify**, **Canvas**, **Trim Canvas** option to fit the canvas to the size of the navigation bar. This clears any excess space around the navigation bar before exporting it to Dreamweaver. The result is that only the actual area containing buttons will be exported.

14 Export the Navigation Bar

Now that you have your navigation bar, it's time to export it to Dreamweaver. Click the **Quick Export** button at the top of the document window and choose **Dreamweaver**, **Export HTML**.

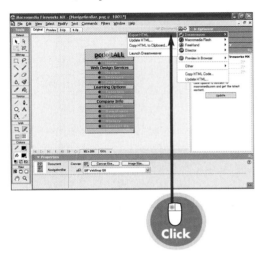

13 Save the PNG File

Save the navigation bar as a PNG file, so that you can come back later, edit the file, and re-export it.

15 Complete the Export Dialog Box

In the Export dialog box, choose the location for the HTML file that Fireworks will create. Assuming you have an images folder in your site, check the **Put Images in Subfolder** option and browse to your images folder. Click **Save** to continue.

How to Insert the Navigation Bar in Dreamweaver

In the previous tasks, you created and saved a navigation bar. Now let's look at how to insert it into your Web page(s) in Dreamweaver. The export process at the end of the previous task created all the code and images required to add the navigation bar as well as an HTML page holding it all together.

❶ Open Dreamweaver

Open Dreamweaver and the file to which you want to add the navigation bar. Click where you want the bar to appear. This can be in a blank page, a frame of a frameset, or within a table cell or layer, as shown here.

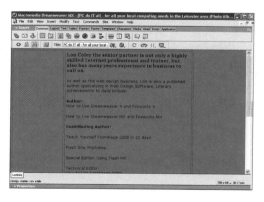

❷ Insert the Fireworks HTML

From the **Common** tab of the Insert bar, click the **Fireworks** icon.

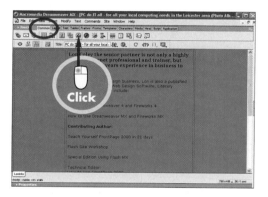

❸ Locate the File

From the Insert Fireworks HTML dialog box, choose the file that you exported from Fireworks. Click **Open** and then **OK** to continue.

4 Adjust As Required

If the navigation bar is not where you want it, amend as needed. Here I need to change the cell alignment and size for the cell the navigation bar is in. Select the cell, and then use the Property Inspector to make changes.

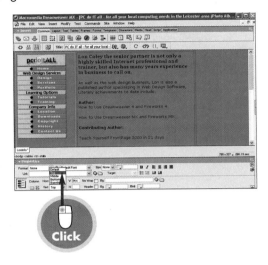

6 Preview the File

Preview the file in a browser and check that all the links work. Your Alt text should be visible whenever you move your mouse over a button—unlike the figure here! Check out the hint after this task for more on Alt text.

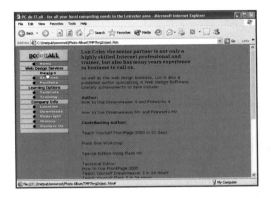

5 Save the File

Save the page in Dreamweaver. Saving the file saves all the information required for the navigation bar into the Dreamweaver document. If you used an existing page, simply choose **Save**; otherwise, choose **Save As** and name the file.

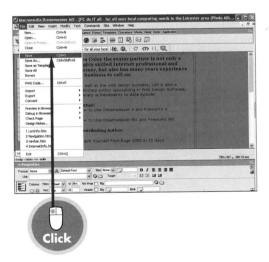

How-to Hint

Testing and Previewing

As with all things in Web design, you should test your files in at least one browser. In this case, you should check that not only are the links correct, but that the Alt text displays. This is a great opportunity for you to visually check the spelling on your Alt text—after all, it isn't displayed in your page and is not normally picked up on a spell check. It would be a real shame to ruin a really good layout and design by some silly typos in your Alt text. Just remember, it could be a prospective customer who spots it!

How to Troubleshoot Links

So, you've created your navigation bar and inserted it in your Web page. What do you do if there's a problem? Maybe a link goes to the wrong page. There are a couple of options available, so let's work through them now. Start with the page in Dreamweaver to which you added the navigation bar.

1 **Select the Navigation Bar**

In Dreamweaver, select the navigation bar in the document window. Notice that the Property Inspector shows that it is a Fireworks Table. Because we saved the PNG file and exported directly to Dreamweaver, the Property Inspector shows the original source file.

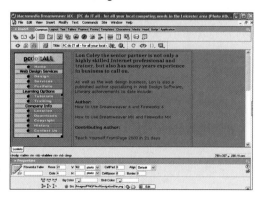

2 **Edit the Source File**

Click the **Edit** button in the Property Inspector to launch Fireworks, ready to make any edits. Note that Fireworks tells you that you are editing from Dreamweaver.

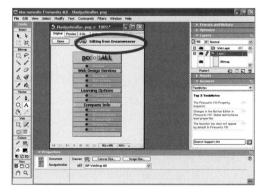

3 **Make the Changes**

Select a button that has an incorrect link, and then use the Property Inspector to correct the error. When you are finished, click the **Done** button in the Fireworks workspace.

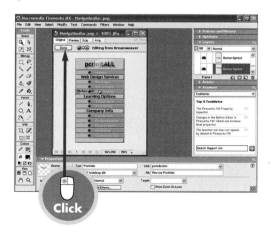

Click

4 Edit Inside Dreamweaver

You can also edit links directly from within Dreamweaver. To do so, select the button for which you want to change the link or Alt text. The current information displays in the Property Inspector.

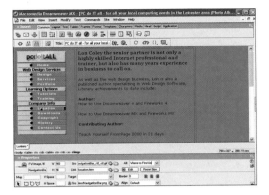

5 Save and Preview in Dreamweaver

When you have made the changes or corrections, save the file again in Dreamweaver, and retest the links.

Click

6 Deleting the File

If you decide you don't want the navigation bar, you can delete the HTML file and all the sliced images from within Dreamweaver. You must delete *all* the individual files. Deleting the HTML file alone does not remove all the sliced images. Select the files in the Site panel and use the panel's **Options** menu to delete them.

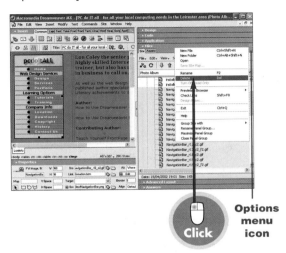

Click

Options
menu
icon

How to Create a Pop-Up Menu

Pop-up menus enable the user to navigate your site by means of a menu that responds to either a mouseover or mouse click. Unlike a navigation bar, pop-up menus can have submenus within them. To test your menu, you must preview it in a browser window, because Fireworks can't display it correctly in the document window. When you export your menu, Fireworks creates all the required HTML and a JavaScript file that has all the necessary code for the pop-up menu.

① Create the Trigger

Pop-up menus must be located on either a slice or a hotspot (a *hotspot* is an area of a graphic with a link attached). These act as the triggers for the menu items. Start by opening or creating a graphic. I'm using a graphic that looks similar to the buttons in the previous tasks.

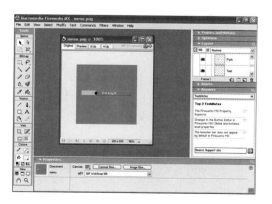

② Add a Hotspot or Slice

On the graphic you want to use, draw a hotspot or slice that covers the complete image. This is the area that will cause the menu to display. The **Slice** and **Hotspot** tools are located in the Web section of the Tools panel.

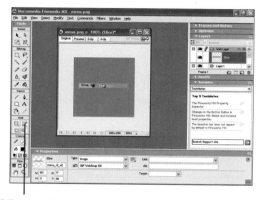

Slice tool

③ Open the Menu Dialog Box

With the slice or hotspot selected, choose **Modify**, **Pop-up Menu**, **Add Pop-up Menu**.

Click

④ Complete the Dialog Box

The Pop-up Menu Editor opens to the Content page. Click the **+** (plus) symbol at the top of the Editor to add the first menu item.

⑤ Enter the Details

Add the text to display on screen; the link; and, if necessary, a target for where the link will open. Press **Enter**, and a blank line is added for you to put in the next line.

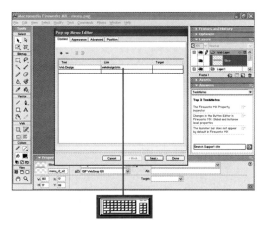

⑥ Repeat the Process

Repeat Step 5 until you have listed all items that you require for your menu. We'll continue working on the menu in Task 7.

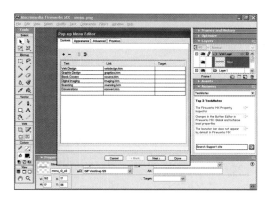

How to Set the Menu's Appearance

You're off to a good start on your new pop-up menu, having listed all the items you want on it. Now move on to how you want your menu to look on your page.

1 Choose the Appearance

After you've added all your menu items (Step 6 in the preceding task), click the **Next** button at the bottom of the Pop-up Menu Editor to move to the **Appearance** tab. The Editor now shows you a preview of your menu, which gets updated as you add your settings.

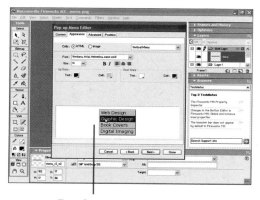

Preview pane

2 Set the Orientation

On the **Appearance** tab, select either **Vertical Menu** or **Horizontal Menu** in the text box at the top right (use the drop-down menu to choose). This controls the direction the menu pops up.

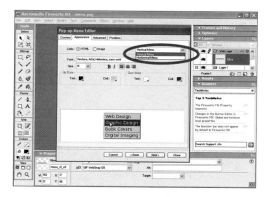

3 Choose the Font

From the **Font** drop-down menu, choose the font group for your text on the menu.

Click

4 Choose the Font Size and Alignment

Using the **Size** drop-down menu, set a font size for the text. You can use the alignment buttons to set how your text will align on the menu buttons, and you also can make that text bold or italic by clicking the appropriate buttons.

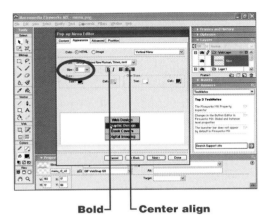

Bold— └—Center align

5 Choose Font Colors

You need to choose a font color for both the Up and Over states of the menu text. Although this can be the same color, I suggest that you choose two colors so that the user sees a change. Use the color picker by the Text fields to set the color.

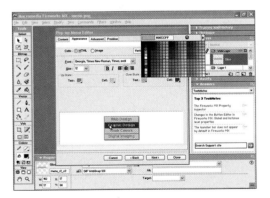

6 Choose the Cell Colors

Use the **Cell** color pickers to choose the two colors that the menu items will have. The cell color can change in the same way as the text.

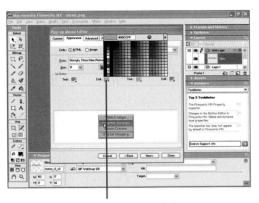

Up State Cell color picker

How to Set Advanced Options

When you've finished your menu's Appearance settings (previous task), click the **Next** button to show the Advanced tab. You can use the **Cell Width** and **Cell Height** fields at the top to set a precise size for menu items. Unless you particularly need them a set size, however, it's better to leave these set to **Automatic** and let Fireworks decide. Let's look at the other advanced settings now.

① Set Spacing and Padding

You can add cell padding (space between the text and the edges of the cell) and cell spacing (the amount of space between menu cells) to put space between the cells created by the menu. Here I've left the default padding set at 3 and set spacing to 10 to give you the idea.

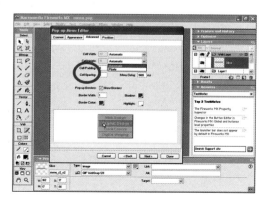

② Indent the Text

You can indent the text to keep it further away from the edge of the cell by typing a number in the **Text Indent** box. (This indent is in from the left of the cell and is in addition to the padding.)

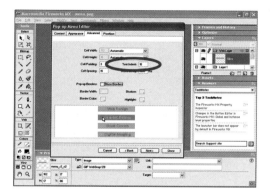

③ Show or Hide a Border

Use the **Show Borders** check box to add or remove a border around the menu cells. Check it and uncheck it while looking at the Preview pane to see how your menu looks with and without the border. With a border, you can choose the border color and border width, and add shadow and highlight.

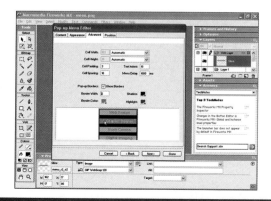

④ Set the Position

Click **Next** to progress to the **Position** tab of the Pop-up Menu Editor. You can choose where your menu will pop up by clicking one of the **Menu position** buttons. This automatically fills in the coordinates (**X** and **Y**) for the menu location. You also can type in coordinates manually.

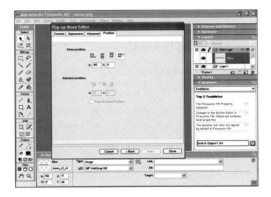

⑤ Return to Fireworks

When you're finished, click **Done** to close the Pop-up Menu Editor and return to the Fireworks document window. Note that your menu is displayed as a highlight on screen. From the **File** menu choose **Save** to save the PNG file. It's a good idea to save the file within your Web site folder.

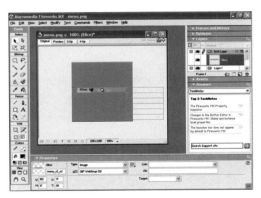

⑥ Export the File to Dreamweaver

Use the **Quick Links** menu (explained in Task 4) in Fireworks to export the menu to Dreamweaver.

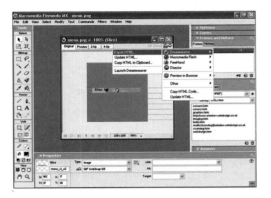

How-to Hint

Uploading

One important fact about using a Fireworks pop-up menu comes when you upload your files to the Internet. You *must* upload the mm_menu.js file to the same location as the page that contains the menu. If you don't, the menu won't work and causes all kinds of errors.

Using Submenus

We haven't had time to talk about submenus; however, they are easy to use. If you want any item in your menu to appear as a subitem, simply select the item in the Pop Up Menu Editor dialog box and click the **Indent** button. Fireworks adds an arrow image to the selected menu item so that users are aware it is a submenu.

How to Edit a Pop-Up Menu

If the pop-up menu does not look how you expect, you can make changes quickly and easily within Fireworks. Let's look at editing pop-up menus.

1 Open the File That Contains the Menu

Open Fireworks and open the PNG file that you created. Select the slice or hotspot to which you added the menu.

2 Open the Menu

Double-click the menu outline to open the Pop-up Menu Editor.

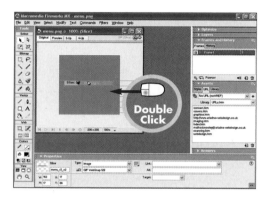

3 Make Adjustments

In the Editor, make any changes or additions that you want. You can make some items into submenus, using the **Indent** menu button, or add or delete items as required.

Change the Order

You can reorganize your menu items inside the Pop-up Menu Editor. Select the item that you want to move and simply drag it to the new location.

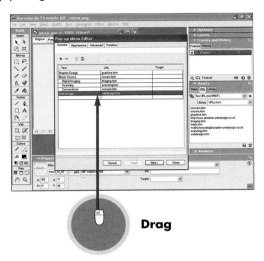

Drag

Change Submenu Items

To turn a menu item into a submenu item, select the item and click the **Indent** button. Clicking the **Outdent** button moves an item back to being a normal menu item.

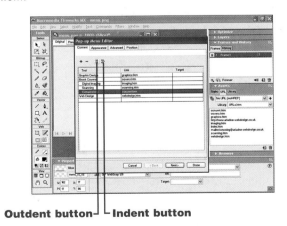

Outdent button ⌐ ⌐ **Indent button**

Multiple Menus

In the last two tasks, we looked at attaching a menu to a single button-style object. However, by using a series of buttons, each with its own menu, you can create handy flowing menus across your whole site. There is no limit to the number of pop-up menus you can create in Fireworks.

Editing from Dreamweaver

In the final task we edited the pop-up menu directly in Fireworks. You also can use the method we looked at for a navigation bar, and open the file after it has been added to your Dreamweaver page. Click **Edit** in the Property Inspector, make the changes, and click **Done** to return to Dreamweaver.

How-to Hint

Task

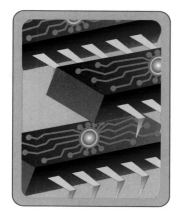

Working with Layers

Layers are best described as containers or holders for your page content. Layers can hold any page element, have their own properties and settings, and also have the advantage of being positioned or repositioned exactly on the page (this is where the Dynamic HTML comes in). In Web design terms, layers are still an innovation, implemented quite recently into the vocabulary of Web designers and developers. The idea behind layers is to give Web designers complete control over the appearance of their content at all times.

So, if layers are so wonderful, why do we still talk about laying out pages using tables? It's simple really: Layers are still quite new, and if you use them, anyone with a browser before version 4 simply sees a garbled mess (or nothing at all) instead of your page. Even some of the newer browsers are a little buggy in their support of layers. Unless you are designing your site for only those people who have new browsers, you should remember that your site visitors might have display problems with layers.

The good thing is that Dreamweaver has a built-in command that lets you convert your layers to tables. This command gives you the flexibility to design with layers, but ensures a greater audience by also posting the page converted to tables.

You can create animations in Dreamweaver by positioning layers on your page at different points in a timeline. The moving layers create the effect of an animation. At the same time as they move around the screen, layers can also be made to change size, visibility, position, and depth (in relation to other layers).

The layers that you animate can contain text, images, or other objects (such as a Flash movie). Because the timeline only controls layers, you can animate only objects that are in layers.

Because Dreamweaver uses JavaScript and DHTML to animate the layers, remember that your animated pages will be viewable only in browsers of version 4.0 or later. This restriction might limit your potential audience

How to Create Layers

Dreamweaver gives you options on how to create layers—all are easy to use and straightforward. Layers don't have to be created on blank pages; you can use an existing page and move content into the layers. However, for this task, we'll start from scratch. You can have as many layers as you need to hold your page content. Layers can be as large or as small as you want, and each layer can contain text, images, plug-ins, or any combination of these elements. You can place layers inside other layers to create nested layers or stack them on top of other layers, and you can use the Layers panel to control and manage your layers.

❶ Use the Insert Bar

Open a blank document in Dreamweaver, click the **Common** tab of the Insert bar, and click the **Draw Layer** button. The mouse pointer changes to crosshairs.

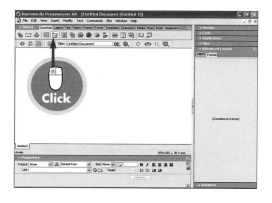

❷ Draw the Layer

Draw the layer on the page where you want it by dragging the crosshairs to define a rectangle of the size you want, and then letting go of the mouse. Normally, you know what content you are planning to place in the layer, so draw the layer to an appropriate size. Remember that you can draw a layer anywhere in the document window.

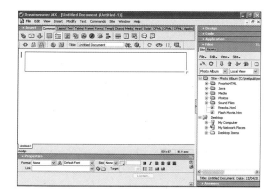

❸ Draw Multiple Layers

Click the **Draw Layer** button again and hold down the Ctrl key as you draw another rectangular layer. Each layer is created when you let go of the mouse. You can draw as many layers as you want for the layout of the page as long as you hold the Ctrl key. As you draw each layer, a marker (visible only in Dreamweaver) appears at the top of the screen. (If you don't see these markers, check the How-To Hints box at the end of this task.)

4 Insert Layers Using the Menu

Instead of dragging a rectangular layer on the page, you can let Dreamweaver insert layers for you. Choose **Insert**, **Layer**. A rectangular layer appears automatically at the top of your screen.

6 Drag from the Insert Bar

You can also drag the **Draw Layer** icon from the Insert bar onto the page to insert a layer. The cursor appears as a little page icon with a + on it. On a blank page, this layer appears at the top of the screen and can be resized or repositioned as described in Step 5.

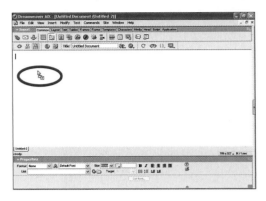

5 Move the Layer

You can move and resize the default layer that Dreamweaver inserts at the top of the screen. Click the square handle at the top left of the layer to select it. Now drag the layer to reposition it, or resize it by dragging the handles. (The square appears atop any layer when the mouse is clicked inside it.)

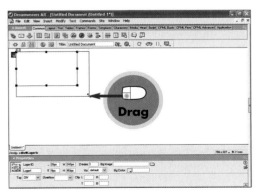

How-to Hint

Can't See the Layer Icon?

For each layer you insert on the page, a layer icon appears in the top-left corner of the page. If you can't see the layer icon, open **View**, **Visual Aids** and enable **Invisible Elements**. When you insert layers into a blank page, the layer icons appear at the top of the document window. The icons appear farther down the page after you add content or insert paragraph breaks in the page. These layer icons are a quick and easy way to select layers and view their properties in the Layers panel (described in Task 2).

How to Work with Layers

Layers give you control and flexibility over the exact layout of your pages. You can insert content into your layers in the same way you can in tables, except that layers are more flexible and easier to manipulate than tables. When you work with layers, you'll make extensive use of the Layers panel.

1 Understand the Layers Panel

Choose **Window**, **Others**, **Layers** to display the Layers panel, which shows all the layers you have created for the page. Click any layer in the panel to select it. When selected, the layer has handles around it, and its marker at the top of the design view is highlighted.

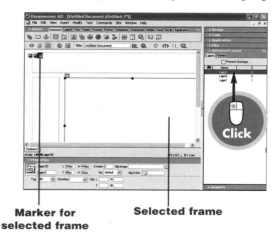

Marker for selected frame

Selected frame

2 Look at the Layer's Properties

When a layer is selected, its properties are visible in the Property Inspector, which shows you the name of the layer (under Layer ID), the width and height of the layer in pixels, and the layer's location on the screen. (The T entry means the distance from the top of the page, and the L entry refers to the distance from the left edge of the page.)

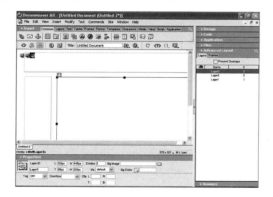

3 Create a Nested Layer

A nested layer is a layer inside another layer. By default, the nested layer has the same properties as its parent. To create a nested layer, click inside an existing layer and choose **Insert**, **Layer**. You can resize this layer to fit neatly inside the existing layer. The nested layer's marker appears inside the parent, not at the top of the screen.

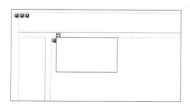

④ Ensure That It Is Nested

Choose **Edit**, **Preferences**, **Layers** to open the Preferences dialog box. Select **Layers** from the **Category** list and enable the **Nesting** option (**Nest When Created Within a Layer**) to ensure that the new layer appears as a nested layer. This option ensures that any layers you draw inside existing layers in the future are automatically nested.

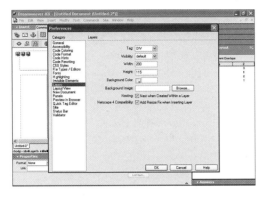

⑤ Activate a Layer

Before you can insert content into a layer, you must first activate the layer by clicking anywhere inside the layer box. The active layer has a border around the edge. Activating a layer is not the same as selecting a layer. Activating a layer simply means that the insertion point is within the layer, ready for you to insert content.

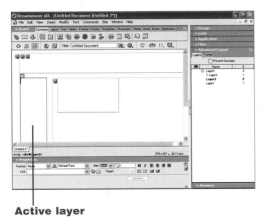

Active layer

⑥ Select a Layer

To select a layer, click the layer icon for the layer you want. The icon is highlighted, handles appear around the selected layer on the page, and the layer's properties display in the Property Inspector. Selecting a layer lets you move, resize, and (if you want) delete it.

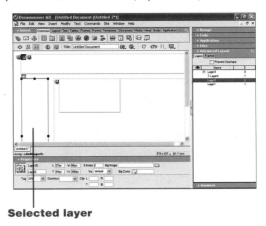

Selected layer

⑦ Select More Than One Layer

You can select multiple layers on the page by holding **Shift** as you click the border of the layers you want to select. Each selected layer has handles around it. With multiple layers selected, you can move them all at once—to the left, right, up, or down.

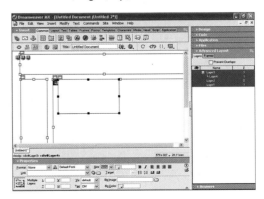

How to Set Layer Properties

Each layer you create has individual properties you can view and edit through the Property Inspector. Most of the properties are set automatically when you draw or insert a layer, but you can change them in the Property Inspector at any time. You can rename the layers from the Layer1, Layer2 defaults Dreamweaver generates, and control the background image or color. You also can control the visibility (whether the layer is seen onscreen at all times) and whether visitors can scroll through the layer if the content outsizes the layer's dimensions.

1 View the Properties

Select a single layer in Dreamweaver and view the Property Inspector. If necessary, use the arrow at the bottom of the Properties Inspector to expand it.

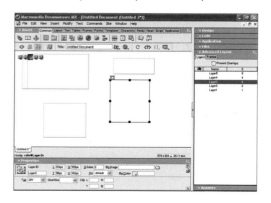

2 Name the Layer

By default, Dreamweaver assigns the layers you create sequential numbers: Layer1, Layer2, and so on. In the **Layer ID** box in the Properties Inspector, type a unique name for the layer (you can use only letters or numbers for the name—no spaces or punctuation). Use an appropriate name; in this example, the layer will contain navigation links at the top of the page, so I've named it **NavTop**.

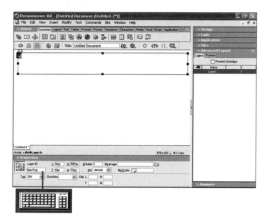

3 Set the Position

The T and L boxes in the Property Inspector show the position of the layer's top-left corner on the page, in pixels from the top and left corners of the screen. If the layer is not exactly where you want it, change these values. These fields are especially handy when you want layers to line up with one another exactly.

④ Set the Size

The W and H boxes determine the width and height of the layer in pixels. You can specify a different unit of measurement by typing it in the field. For example, type **80mm** if you want to use millimeters or **7in** if you want to use inches. You can even specify that a nested layer is a percentage of its parent by typing **60%**.

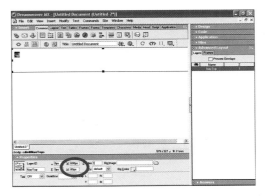

⑤ Set a Background

To select a background color for the layer, type the hex value of the color in the **BgColor** field, or use the color picker. To select a background image, click the folder icon next to the **BgImage** field and browse to the image file you want to use. The background image and color you set for the current layer affect any layers nested within it.

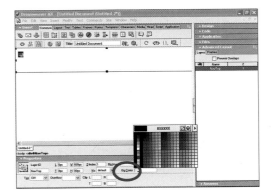

⑥ Understand the Z-Index

The z-index sets the stacking order for your layers. When displayed in a browser, the layer with the highest z-index appears at the top of the stack. You can see in this example how the yellow layer (z-index 4) sits atop the other layers.

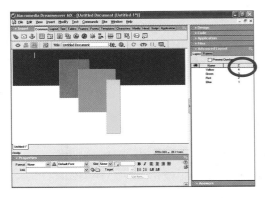

How-to Hint

Background Image Files

Background images are used all over the Internet and come in many different guises. The best file type to use for backgrounds tends to be a GIF file because these files are small and quick to download. With any background—for a page, a table, or a layer—you must use a file that appears very quickly. If you don't, your text might be invisible to the visitor until the background loads (imagine a nice black background image with white text; no background equals no text). Although you can use JPEG files for backgrounds, this is less common because they tend to be larger files and take longer to download.

Continued **3**

7 Set the Visibility

Layers are normally visible unless you tell them not to be. Nested layers inherit properties from their parent unless you change the visibility for the child. Having invisible layers might seem odd, but when you're creating timelines and animations, they're a great way to control what is seen and when. When a layer is hidden, the layer icon remains visible onscreen in Dreamweaver.

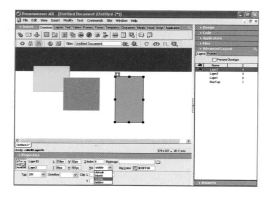

8 Choose the Tag

Dreamweaver supports the use of CSS layers, which use the SPAN and DIV tags, within Dreamweaver. Within Dreamweaver there is little or no difference in these, so stick with the default, leaving the **DIV** setting in the **Tag** field. These HTML tags are created whenever a layer is created in Dreamweaver. CSS layers give you the greatest audience for your layered site.

9 Set Overflow Settings

The **Overflow** option determines what will happen if you insert content that's too big for the layer to hold. Overflow values include **Visible** (the layer expands to hold the content); **Hidden** (cuts the content to fit the layer); **Scroll** (adds scrollbars to the layer whether they're needed or not, as you can see in this example); and **Auto** (adds scrollbars only when they're needed).

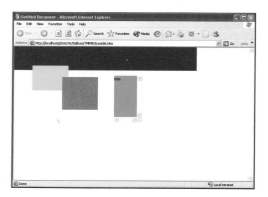

10 Specify Clip Settings

You can use the Clip options to set a visible area within the layer, which can be useful if you're placing an image in the layer and want to crop part of it without editing it. The values you enter in the left, right, top, and bottom (**L**, **R**, **T**, and **B**) fields are in pixels and relate to the current layer, not to the page.

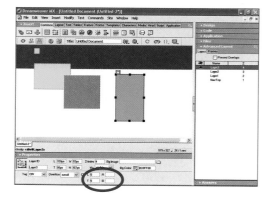

⓫ Set Properties for Multiple Layers

After you use Shift+click to select multiple layers, you can set properties for all the selected layers simultaneously in the Property Inspector. You can add a background color or image to all selected layers, set text attributes across the layers, and even set the visibility for multiple layers at the same time. The Properties Inspector shows only those options that can be changed across layers.

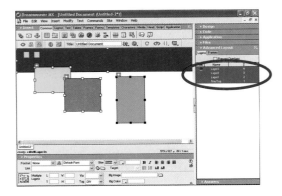

⓬ Snap Layers to the Grid

Dreamweaver has a design grid that you can display to help you position and resize layers and other elements on the page. Choose **View**, **Grid**, **Show Grid** to turn on the grid, and then choose **View**, **Grid**, **Snap To Grid** so that the layers will snap to the lines of the grid.

⓭ Snap a Layer

With the grid displayed and the Snap To Grid feature enabled, drag a layer to reposition it on the page. Note that the layer snaps to the nearest grid line as you drag. Choose **View**, **Grid**, **Grid Settings** to change the spacing of the grid lines and to specify how close an object must be to a grid line before it snaps to the line.

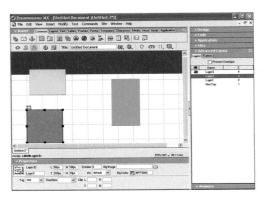

How-to Hint

Layer Tags

I mentioned previously that there are two tag options (DIV and SPAN) and recommended the use of the DIV tag. In older browsers that do not support layers, an extra line break is often added before and after a DIV tag, and this can cause serious display issues. However, this should not be a problem with modern browsers.

How to Convert Layers to Tables

Because some older browsers don't support layers, Dreamweaver lets you easily convert layers to tables. However, you can't convert layers that overlap because table cells can't overlap, and any attempt to create a table from overlapping layers fails. You should first check the **Prevent Overlaps** checkbox in the Layers panel, and then, if your page design contains overlapping layers, you'll have to redesign the page before you can convert the layout to tables. Note that "overlapping" includes nested layers, so you must move or delete any nested layers before converting the file.

❶ Convert Layers to a Table

To convert all the layers on your page to a table, choose **Modify**, **Convert**, **Layers to Table**. The Convert Layers to Table dialog box opens.

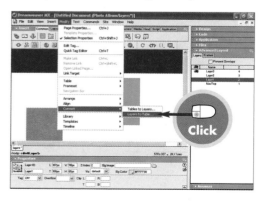

❷ Select Conversion Options

I recommend that you select the **Most Accurate** and **Use Transparent GIFs** options to achieve the most accurate conversion possible. The **Most Accurate** option creates a table cell for each layer (plus additional cells for the areas in between); the **Use Transparent GIFs** option creates a table that views the same in all browsers. Click **OK** when you are done.

❸ View the Result

Look at the result of the page conversion in your default browser. Be sure the page still looks the way you want it to look. If the conversion went awry, go back to the Dreamweaver document window and choose **Edit**, **Undo Convert to Table** to return the page to the layer layout.

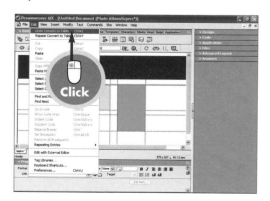

④ Convert for Version 3 Browsers

Choose **File**, **Convert**, **3.0 Browser Compatible** to create a version of your page that's compatible with older browsers. The Convert to 3.0 Browser Compatible dialog box opens. Choose whether you want to convert **Layers to Table**, **CSS Styles to HTML Markup**, or **Both**. (I suggest **Both**.) Click **OK** to close the dialog box and begin the conversion.

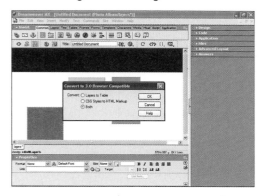

⑤ View the Results

Dreamweaver creates a new, unsaved, untitled version of your document, leaving the original intact. You can then make any edits you require and save the page into your Web site folder. When you're happy with the results, it's safe to delete the original file.

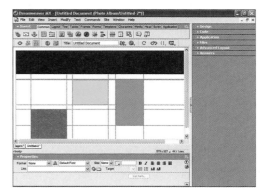

How-to Hint

Save Some Time

If you convert your page to a page that version 3.0 browsers can view, be sure you have completed development of the page before you convert it. Because Dreamweaver creates a new page when it does the conversion, you will have to keep converting the original to a version 3.0–compatible page whenever you change the original. It makes more sense to complete the page and convert it once.

⑤ How to Create a Simple Animation

Creating a timeline animation is easy. The hard part comes later when you have to test, edit, and amend it to look how you really want. This task gets things moving onscreen; after we have an animation in place, we can look at making changes to it. For this example, I use a simple page that contains a single layer with an image of a flower. You can put animations on pages with as much content as you want, but I'm keeping this simple to ensure that you can see what's happening.

① Open a Page and Create a Layer

Either open an existing page with content, or create a new page. Add a layer to the page, and insert an image into the layer. In this example, the page contains a single layer that sports the image of a flower.

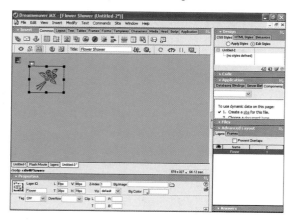

② Show the Timeline Panel

Choose **Window**, **Others**, **Timelines** to display the Timelines panel.

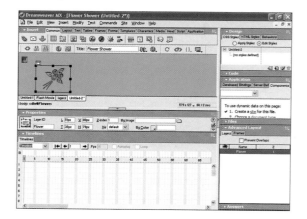

③ Record a Path for the Animation

Select the layer you want to animate and choose **Modify**, **Timeline**, **Record Path of Layer**. This command lets you define a path along which the image (the flower in this example) will travel. Recording the path puts it into Dreamweaver's memory.

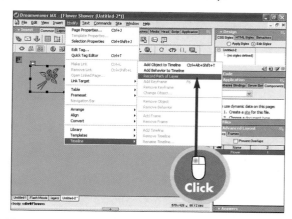

Click

④ Draw the Path

Select the layer and drag the layer handle around the screen to create the path of movement that you want to use. Let's start with a simple, short path. As you move the layer, a dotted line appears on the screen.

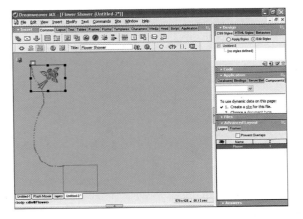

⑥ See the Animation in Action

Click the **Play** button on the Timelines panel to see the animation move through each frame in turn. Hold down the **Play** button to see a smoother movement.

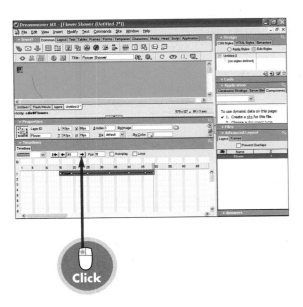

⑤ Let Go of the Layer

When you release the mouse button to let go of the layer, a dialog box appears, telling you that Dreamweaver can animate the layer. Click **OK** to continue. The dotted line created by dragging the layer now becomes solid.

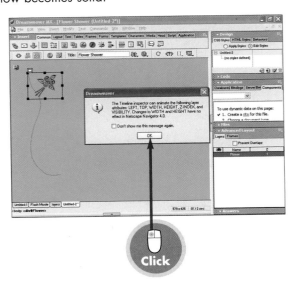

How-to Hint

Animating Images

Although Dreamweaver gives you a reasonably easy way to animate objects on your page, if you want to create real animated images, you should turn your attention to Fireworks. Part 14, "Layers and Frames in Fireworks MX," introduces you to creating animations in Fireworks.

The Timelines Panel

Think of the Timelines panel as a clock with a timer switch. Objects are activated and deactivated at specific times. This is the basis of all timeline animations. The important word is time, not necessarily animation.

7 Set a Trigger

As the name implies, a *trigger* tells the animation when to start. Let's make this animation start when the page loads. On the Timelines panel, enable the **Autoplay** checkbox. An alert box appears, telling you that the timeline is being added to the onLoad event. Click **OK** to continue.

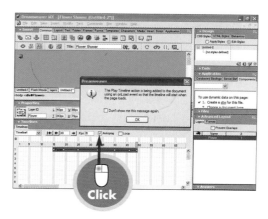

8 Set the Animation to Loop

Setting the animation to **Loop** causes it to restart when it reaches the end of the timeline. To make the animation play continuously, enable the **Loop** checkbox in the Timelines panel. Dreamweaver displays an alert box telling you how to edit this effect.

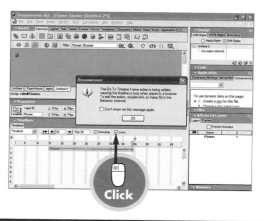

9 Save the Page

If this a new page, save it into your Web site folder now, by choosing **File**, **Save**. In the Save As dialog box, give the file a name, navigate to the appropriate folder, and click **Save**.

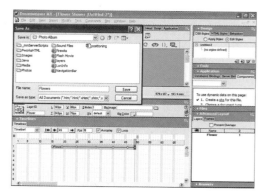

10 Preview the Page

Because you have added a trigger to the animation (the onLoad event), the animation should start as soon as the page loads. Choose **File**, **Preview in Browser** to see how the animation looks in a browser window. Notice that the flower keeps falling down the screen.

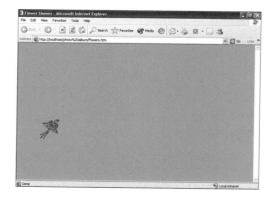

11 Remove the Loop

If you don't like the way the animation loops, disable the **Loop** check box in the Timelines panel. Save the file and preview the page again. Notice that the animation stops when it reaches the end of the timeline, and the object remains in its end position.

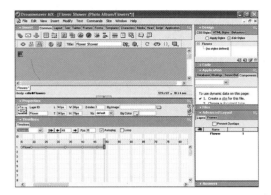

12 Name the Timeline

Name the timeline in case you want to use it again. On the Timelines panel, select the name **Timeline1** and type a new name in the text box. For this example, I named the timeline **Flower**. Although this simple example doesn't require a name other than the default, you should get into the habit of naming your timelines so that you can later create more complicated animations that use many timelines.

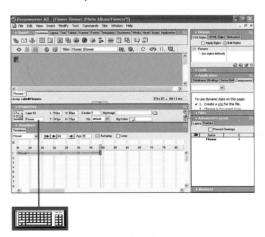

How-to Hint

Language Issues

Creating timeline animations can be confusing, so let's try to dispel some of that confusion now. Dynamic HTML (DHTML) is the terminology used to position layers on a screen. DHTML is a combination of HTML with a scripting language (JavaScript). When you create timeline animations, DHTML gives you the control over where and when the layers appear using JavaScript. When you create a timeline animation, Dreamweaver creates the required JavaScript for you and places it all inside a `<script>` tag located in the `<head>` of your document so that the browser knows how to interpret it.

Task

Behaviors and Scripts in Dreamweaver

The Behaviors panel in Dreamweaver is used to attach JavaScript behaviors, such as status bar messages and alerts that show when the page loads, to your pages and page elements. Dreamweaver behaviors add interaction to your pages in a way that is far more straightforward than any other Web design application. The Behaviors panel enables you to avoid hand coding and the errors associated with it.

Behaviors are Dreamweaver-specific scripts. You can use them in many different ways, such as to show and hide elements such as layers, to create messages in the status bar, and to create navigation bars. Scripts are perhaps the single most powerful element of the software.

To add this type of JavaScript interaction with almost any other piece of software, you would need to learn how to code in HTML and JavaScript. The great thing about Dreamweaver behaviors is that the JavaScript is inserted for you, so all you have to do is attach an action (behavior) to an event such as a site visitor's click on a particular area or when a page loads into the browser.

The only drawback to using behaviors is that some older browsers offer little or no support for JavaScript. For this reason, Dreamweaver lets you choose the type of browser you anticipate that most of your visitors will have. The newer the browser version you choose, the more behaviors you have access to. Even better is that the behaviors that ship with Dreamweaver are written to work with both Internet Explorer and Netscape.

How to Attach a Behavior to a Page Element

Attaching a behavior involves defining an action that takes place when the visitor to the page causes an event to occur. The easiest way of remembering this is that an event plus an action equals a behavior. It's a simple process in Dreamweaver as long as you are careful. In this task, you attach a behavior that shows text in the status bar when the user moves the mouse pointer over a hyperlink.

1 Open the Behaviors Panel

All behaviors are inserted and controlled from the Behaviors panel. To open the Behaviors panel, expand the Design panel group and click the **Behaviors** tab.

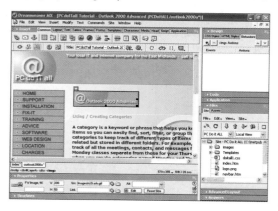

2 Select the Element to Be Affected

Select a hyperlink or image you have inserted on any page, or create a new page element for this exercise. Behaviors should not be attached to plain text, only to hyperlinks, images, forms, or complete pages.

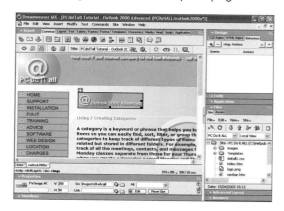

3 Choose the Action

In the Behaviors panel, show the Action list by clicking the **+** button. The list of actions available for the currently selected page element is displayed. Choose **Set Text**, **Set Text of Status Bar**.

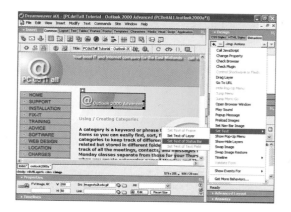

4 Set the Text to Appear

In the Set Text of Status Bar dialog box, type the text you want to appear in the status bar when the user moves the mouse pointer over the selected page element. Click **OK** when you're finished.

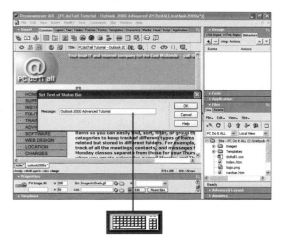

5 Look at the Event

Dreamweaver has filled in the event for you. The Behaviors panel shows that when the user passes the mouse over the selected page element (this event is called onMouseOver), the specified text will appear in the status bar. We'll look at how to edit behaviors later in this task.

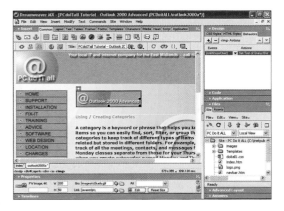

6 Test the Behavior

Save the page and preview it in your browser. Move the mouse pointer over the selected element, and the specified text appears in the status bar, as expected. However, when you move the mouse away from the element, notice that the text remains in the status bar—which is not what you'd expect.

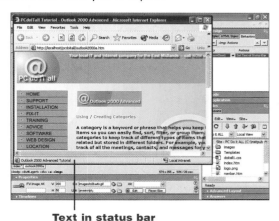

Text in status bar

7 Solve the Behavior Problem

An event has been triggered, but it has not been stopped. We must add another action (displaying a blank status bar) that is triggered when the mouse moves away from the selected page element. Select the same element you selected in Step 2, and choose **Set Text**, **Set Text of Status Bar** from the Actions list in the Behaviors panel.

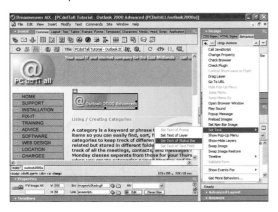

10 Preview the Page Again

Open the page in the browser and move the mouse pointer over the link. The text appears in the status bar as expected. Now move the mouse pointer away from the link; the text disappears from the status bar. Problem solved!

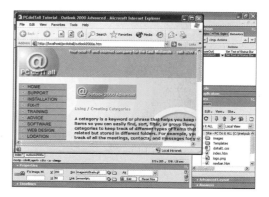

8 Set the New Message

In the Set Text of Status Bar dialog box, type the text you want to appear in the status bar when the user moves the mouse pointer away from the selected page element. In this case, leave the Message field blank because you don't want any text to appear in the status bar when the user moves the mouse away from the page element. Click **OK**.

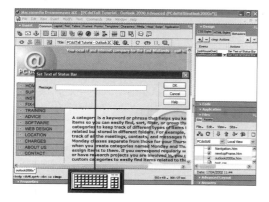

11 Open the Code View

Now is a good time to see what is happening behind the scenes and to view the code that Dreamweaver has generated. If you don't know any JavaScript, this is a great way to start understanding it. Select the element to which you attached the behavior and choose **Code and Design** from the **View** menu.

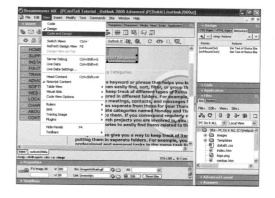

9 Change the Event

By default, Dreamweaver has assigned the onMouseOver event to the action you just defined. To change the event for the second action, click the down arrow next to the event to display a list of other possible events. Choose onMouseOut, meaning that the mouse pointer has moved away from the selected page element.

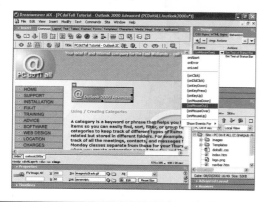

⑫ View the JavaScript

The code for your Web page opens to the section for the selected element. You can clearly see the code showing the status bar message being turned on and off in the browser. (It's also worth viewing the code in the <head> section of the page at the start of the document where the script language command is inserted. Scroll to move up the code.)

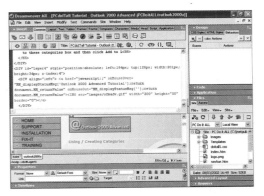

Different Events

How-to Hint

When you selected the onMouseOut event, you noticed that many other events were in the list. The names of the events give big clues about what each event does. For example, the onClick event is triggered when a user clicks a page element; the onDblClick event occurs when a user double-clicks, and so on. Other events have less obvious names. For example, onKeyDown is activated when a user presses any key on the keyboard, regardless of whether the key is released; onKeyPress is activated only when a key is pressed and released.

For a complete list of names and descriptions of events available for different browsers, go to http://www.macromedia.com/support/dreamweaver.

Specifying a Browser

As you know, different browsers support different JavaScript functions. The older the browser, the fewer options you have available. If you are designing a site and expect it to be viewed mainly by people using older browsers, you should set events that are compatible with those older browsers. To show events for a particular browser version, select an event in the Events column of the Behaviors panel, click the down arrow next to the event, and choose **Show Events For**. As soon as you select a browser from the list, the list of available events changes to reflect your selection.

How to Add a Behavior to a Page

You can attach a behavior to a whole page if, for example, you want to cause an action to happen as the page is loading into the visitor's browser. For example, you might want to send the visitor to a different URL if you have recently moved your Web site to a new server, or if the visitor is accessing an out-of-date page. This option is also commonly used (as it is in this task) to redirect visitors to a new page if they are using older browsers that might not display your content correctly.

1 Select the <body> Tag

Open the page to which you want to attach the behavior and click the **<body>** tag at the bottom-left corner of the screen.

2 Show the Behaviors Panel

If the Behaviors panel is not visible, choose **Window**, **Behaviors** to show it. Notice that the panel's title bar shows that you have already selected the <body> tag.

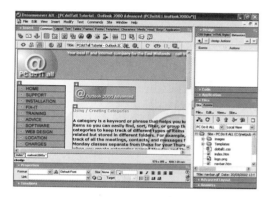

3 Choose the Behavior

Click the **+** button at the top of the panel to access the **Actions** drop-down menu, and choose **Check Browser**. The Check Browser dialog box opens. This option creates some JavaScript code that will check the version of the browser the visitor is using before the page loads.

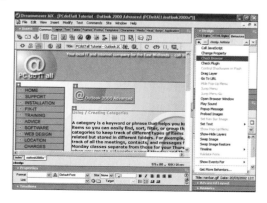

④ Complete the Dialog Box

Use this dialog box to specify which page will be displayed to visitors using **Netscape Navigator 4.0 or later**, **Internet Explorer 4.0 or later**, and **Other Browsers**. You can specify different URLs for browser versions earlier than 4.0 as well, by selecting an option in the appropriate **otherwise** box. For this example, select options so that version 4.0 or later browsers stay on the current page; the next step explains how to send visitors to a different URL.

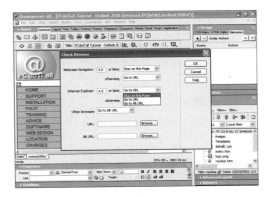

⑤ Set the URLs

If you selected the **Go to URL** option for any of the browsers in the top part of the dialog box, specify the URL of the page you want to display in those instances in the **URL** box. If you selected the **Go to Alt URL** option for any of the browsers, specify the URL of the page you want to display in those instances in the **Alt URL** box. If you are redirecting visitors to a remote URL (one that is not part of the current site), you must include the full `http://www` part of the address. Click **OK** to continue.

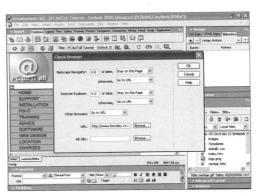

⑥ Learn from Dreamweaver

Even if you never intend to write your own code, understanding what it is doing can help if things ever go wrong. The Behaviors panel now shows that you have an onLoad event in the <body> tag that checks which browser is being used; the page holds all the code to accomplish this check. Click the **Show Code View** button on the toolbar to see just what Dreamweaver has written for you.

Click

How-to Hint

Very Old Browsers

Some people still use browsers that are so old they won't even respond to the script you just set up to check browser versions and redirect browsers to other URLs. Therefore, it's always a good idea to add a straightforward hyperlink on the main page that people can click to get to a simpler page that will display in their older browsers.

How to Create a Navigation Bar

In Part 10, we created a navigation bar in Fireworks and placed it into Dreamweaver. You also can use your own images to create a navigation bar (with fewer design options) in Dreamweaver. Use images you already have or check out the Fireworks section of this book for instructions on making your own images. Start with an open page in Dreamweaver. Click to place the insertion point where you want the navigation bar to appear—in a layer, frame, or table cell. In this example, the navigation bar is on a separate layer.

① Name the First Element

Choose **Insert**, **Interactive Images**, **Navigation Bar** to open the Insert Navigation Bar dialog box. Each element on the navigation bar must be named. For example, you might have a series of images that link to a family page; you could call that element Family. In the **Element Name** box, type a name for the first element you want to add to the navigation bar.

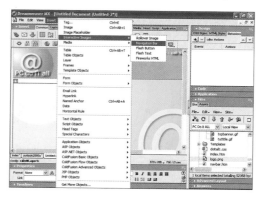

② Select the Images to Use

Each element needs at least an **Up Image**—the image visible when the mouse isn't over or clicking the image. Also use an **Over Image** (displayed when the mouse moves over the element); otherwise, you could just add static images and links. Although not required, the **Down Image** (displayed after a mouse click) and the **Over While Down Image** (displayed after the element is clicked and the mouse is still over it) make the navigation bar more professional. Specify the folder and filename of each image you want to use.

③ Insert the Link Information

In the **When Clicked, Go to URL** box, type the URL of the HTML page to link to or use the **Browse** button to navigate to the page. If your site uses frames, use the **In** drop-down list to the right of the **Browse** button in the Insert Navigation Bar dialog box to specify the frame in which you want the page to appear.

4 View and Modify

Choose the orientation for your navigation bar using the **Insert** drop-down menu. If you want to use tables, check that option. Click **OK** to close the Insert Navigation Bar dialog box and view the navigation bar on the page. (At this point it has only the one button.) You can edit the navigation bar at any time by selecting **Modify**, **Navigation Bar** to reopen the dialog box.

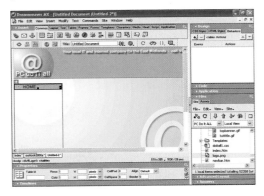

5 Add More Elements

Click the **+** button in the Modify Navigation Bar dialog box to add more elements to the navigation bar. Remember that you must name each button element you add to the navigation bar, and you must specify an image file in at least the **Up Image** field before the element can appear on the page. When you finish adding buttons, click **OK**.

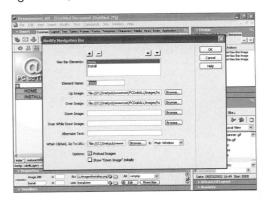

6 Preview in Browser

Open the page into the browser. Move the mouse over the elements to see the rollover effect (the image changes). Click an element to observe the change in the image. If you used only one image per element, there will be no change! Check your links to be sure the page you expect to appear when you click the navigation button is actually the page that does appear.

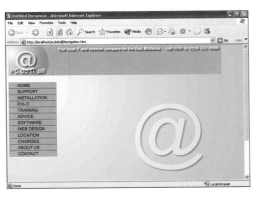

How-to Hint

Navigation Bar Options

The Insert Navigation Bar and Modify Navigation Bar dialog boxes offer several other options you can choose from.

As stated before, in the Insert Navigation Bar dialog box, you can use the **Insert** drop-down list to insert the navigation bar either vertically or horizontally. If you want the navigation bar to be created as a table, with the elements in individual cells, enable the **Use Tables** check box. These two options must be set when you create the bar; they aren't available in the Modify Navigation Bar dialog box.

Enable the **Preload Images** check box to ensure that all required files for the current element are downloaded when the page first opens. This option ensures that there is no delay in image rollover when passing the mouse over the element or when clicking the element.

Because the navigation bar includes buttons for every page in the site, you can enable the **Show 'Down Image' Initially** check box for each button element. When that page opens, the Down Image state of the element linked to that page appears.

How to Change or Remove Behaviors

After you have attached a behavior to an element on the page, you can change or remove that behavior at any time without affecting the page element in any other way. For example, if you have a hyperlink to which you have attached a behavior that displays a message in the status bar, removing the behavior does not affect the link itself; clicking the link still takes you to the page you expect to see.

1 Select the Page Element

Click to select the element on the page to which you have attached a behavior that you want to modify. If necessary, choose **Window**, **Behaviors** to display the Behaviors panel.

2 Change the Behavior

In the Behaviors panel, double-click the action you want to modify. A dialog box appropriate to the specific action opens. In this example, the action being modified is **Open Browser Window**; when this action is double-clicked, a dialog box opens to allow you to change the URL and the frame in which that page opens. Note that every action has a different dialog box. Make your adjustments to the action and click **OK**.

3 Change the Event

You can also change the event that triggers the action. In this example, the onClick event triggers the Open Browser Window action. You can change this event to onDblClick (the action occurs when the user double-clicks the page element) simply by clicking the arrow next to the event and choosing a different event.

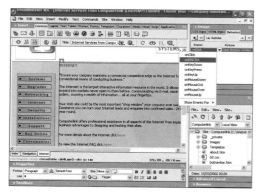

④ Delete a Behavior

You can easily delete a behavior from your page, too. Select the page element and, in the Behaviors panel, click to select the behavior you want to delete. Then click the **–** button to remove the event and its associated action.

⑤ Open a New Browser Window

Behaviors can be used to open a link in a new browser window. Select an element on the page that you want to use as the trigger for the event. I am using a null link. Using the # as a link allows you to attach a behavior to an element. Choose **Open Browser Window** as the event. The Open Browser Window dialog box opens.

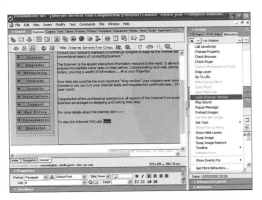

⑥ Complete the Dialog Box

In the **URL to Display** field, type the URL to the file you want to open. In this example, I use another HTML file that contains more information. You also can set the exact width and height of the new window to match an image size (or page content). Don't forget to name the window you want to open. (This name is then referenced in the code.)

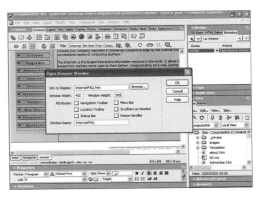

⑦ Specify Additional Options

The Open Browser Window dialog box has additional options, called attributes, with which you can set or remove menus and toolbars on the new window. Enabling any of the check boxes adds that attribute (toolbar, scrollbars, and so forth) to the page. These options affect only the new window. Click **OK** to continue and add the behavior to the page.

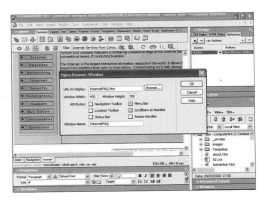

How to Get More Behaviors

We've looked at some of the default behaviors that come with Dreamweaver; for those of you new to Dreamweaver, these behaviors are probably enough to last for a while. After you really get into using behaviors, however, you might want to try new things. People who have been using Dreamweaver for a while have created some interesting behaviors for elements on their Web pages and are kind enough to share these JavaScripts with the general public. You can download these behaviors and then install them for use in your own pages.

❶ Choose the Option

Be sure you are connected to the Internet, and then open the Behaviors panel. From the **Actions** menu (click the **+** button), choose **Get More Behaviors**. Dreamweaver uses your default browser to open the Macromedia Exchange Web site.

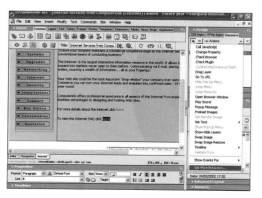

❷ Use the Web Site

If you have already registered with Macromedia, the Web site will recognize who you are. If you haven't registered, click the **Get a Macromedia ID** link on the page. If you want the Macromedia site to remember you, you must allow cookies to be enabled in your browser.

❸ Browse the Extensions

Open the **browse extensions** drop-down list at the top of the page and look through the list of options. Because behaviors are categorized as scripts, select the **Scripting** option to see which files are available in that category.

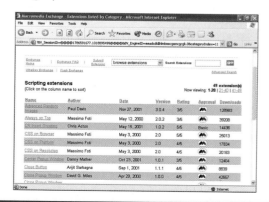

④ Choose a File

Each of the files listed has information associated with it. The title of the file is a good indicator of what the script actually does. Click the title of the script to open the script's details page, which contains all the information for the file, including its features and possibly comments from users. In this example, you see the details for a script entitled CSS on Platform Extension.

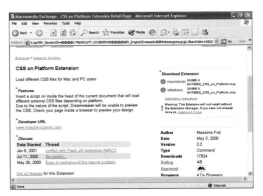

⑥ Install and Use the Script

After you have downloaded the file, double-click it to install it into the Package Manager. After it is installed, you can access full instructions about where and how to use the script by choosing **Commands**, **Manage Extensions** to open the Macromedia Extension Manager.

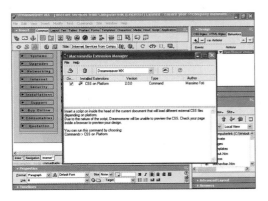

⑤ Download the Script File

To download a script file you have decided to try for yourself, click the download button for your operating system (generally either Windows or Macintosh) in the Download Extension section on the detail page. The file is downloaded to the location you specify.

How-to Hint

Don't Get Carried Away

The Macromedia site provides many files you can download for use with Dreamweaver. Before you start downloading everything in sight, spend a little time getting used to the behaviors that Dreamweaver has already. A word of caution: Some of the files you can download might have bugs or problems. Become familiar with the scripts that Dreamweaver comes with, and then move on. By the time we look at Part 24, "Applications and Beyond," with the purpose of extending Dreamweaver, you should be more than ready to download selectively.

Task

Text and Simple Image Effects in Fireworks

Working with text—entering and editing characters—is a simple process in Fireworks. It's very much a case of what you type is what you get. You can add text to an existing image (for example, if you want to add a fancy heading), or you can create a new file that uses the text as its basic element (such as a button graphic). Remember that when you use text in a graphic, you are not limited to the narrow range of Web-safe fonts required of most regular text.

Fireworks makes it easy to apply and edit effects such as shadows, bevels, and glows. You can use effects to make objects appear highlighted onscreen. The careful placement of a drop shadow, for example, can make an object appear to jump out of the page at the visitor.

You can use Fireworks's standard effects, create and then save your own custom effects for use later on other documents, or just edit Fireworks's default settings for an image each time you use an effect.

After you apply an effect to an object in Fireworks and then export that document, the effect is exported along with the image. The result is that your effects appear as you intended them to look when the image is inserted into your Dreamweaver pages.

How to Work with Text

Using text within graphics, either to create a text-based heading or to enhance an existing graphic file, is common throughout the Internet. Fireworks makes the process of working with text easy; it offers a text tool to type with and access to all Fireworks tools, enabling you to change sizes, colors, fonts, fills, and almost anything else you can think of. You can also add effects, such as shadows, glows, and bevels, to your text after you have typed it.

① Open a New Fireworks Document

Choose **File**, **New** to open a blank document. The New Document dialog box opens. Type the dimensions you want for the new document. Because this document will contain text only, let's keep it reasonably small— in this example, the document is 150 pixels by 150 pixels. Click **OK** when you are done.

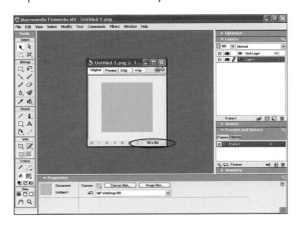

② Select the Text Tool

In the Tools panel, click the **Text** tool to select it.

③ Activate the Text Tool

Click once inside the document window to open the Text Area. The Property Inspector updates to show you text properties.

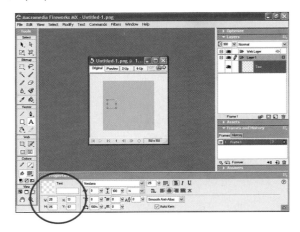

4 Select the Font and Size

Use the **Font** drop-down menu in the Property Inspector to select the font you want to use, and select the size for your text using the Size slider.

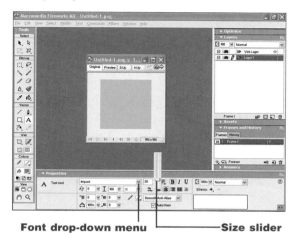

Font drop-down menu ⎯⎯⎯⎯⎯⎯⎯⎯⎯⎯⎯⎯Size slider

5 Start Typing

Type several words onto the canvas. As you type, the text appears onscreen in the font and size you selected.

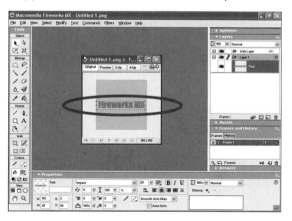

How-to Hint

Format the Text You Added

After you create the text, it remains a separate object that you can change simply by selecting it and using the Property Inspector to make changes. You can change the text characters, reformat the text, and even change the color of the text. Reformat the text by selecting new fonts, sizes, and attributes such as bold, italics, and underlining (click the **B**, **I**, or **U** button).

To move text you have created, click to select it in the document window, and then drag the text box wherever you want.

Traditional Alternative

An alternative way to make changes in your text is to select the text, right-click it, and choose **Editor** from the context menu. This opens a traditional Text Editor dialog box, with which some people find it easier to work.

How to Set Text Properties

In Fireworks, setting the size, font, and color of your text as you learned to do in Task 1 is merely the start of your options. You can set other text properties, such as kerning, leading, and the baseline shift by using the Properties Inspector or Text Editor dialog box (right-click and select **Editor**). The more you use text in an imaging environment, the more you will probably want to. Fireworks gives you control over the flow of the text—even vertical and right-to-left text is possible.

1 Set the Baseline Shift

The Baseline Shift field in the Property Inspector lets you move selected letters to positions above or below the baseline (the line on which the letters rest) to create subscript and superscript characters within your text. Select the character or characters you want to shift, and use the Baseline Shift slider to reposition the characters.

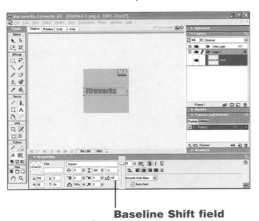

Baseline Shift field

2 Specify the Leading

The leading value controls the amount of space between the lines of text (in other words, leading is the line spacing). Use the **Leading** slider to change the amount of space between the lines of text onscreen. You can see the bottom version here with a large gap between the lines.

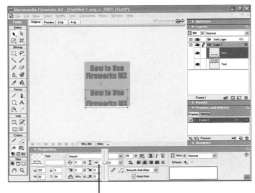

Leading field

3 Set the Kerning for the Text

Changing the kerning value changes the amount of space between two or more letters. Leave the **Auto Kern** check box enabled, and Fireworks improves the kerning of your characters automatically. You can manually change kerning by positioning the flashing cursor between two letters and using the **Kerning** slider to bring the letters closer together or spread them out.

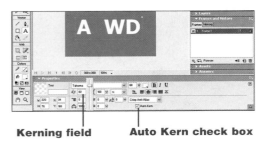

Kerning field   **Auto Kern check box**

④ Align the Text

You can change the alignment of the text in a paragraph. In addition to making the text centered, left or right aligned, or fully justified, you can make the text appear vertically. Select your text and open the **Text Direction** pop-up menu by clicking the button in the Property Inspector to change text layout.

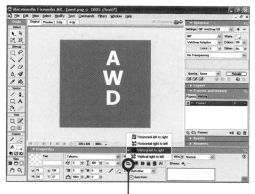

Click very small arrow to open menu

⑤ Change the Text Color

When you create text, it automatically appears onscreen in whatever color is currently selected. To change the color, select the text and use the color picker in the Property Inspector to select the color you want.

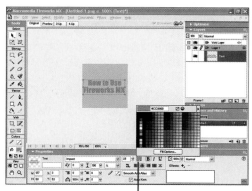

Click here to access Text color picker

⑥ Allow Anti-Aliased Text

Anti-aliased text has a nice, smooth edge that blends into the background: **Smooth Anti-Alias** is Fireworks's default setting. To change the anti-alias level, select your text and use the Anti-Alias drop-down menu in the Property Inspector. Experiment with the settings to see which you prefer.

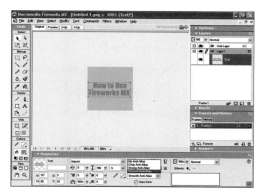

How-to Hint

Alignment Options

The alignment options in Fireworks let you lay out your text the way you want it to appear. Just remember that some of the alignment options will be displayed only in the document window and not in the Text Editor if you use that rather than the Property Inspector (for example, vertical text appears only in the document window).

Fireworks remembers the alignment settings you have enabled; the next time you use the Text Editor, it will use the alignment settings from the time before. Remember to check these settings before you start typing, or you might get some strange results that you'll then need to edit!

③

How to Create a 3D Effect in Fireworks

Fireworks has the capability to help you create incredibly powerful effects in a simple manner. We have had a fair look around the software now, so let's jump in and start playing with some of the effects. In this task, we'll create the illusion of 3D using gradients and fill effects. We'll keep this pretty simple, but the technique can be applied in many different situations.

❶ Create a Document and Draw a Circle

Create a new document in Fireworks, select the **Ellipse** tool, and draw a circle—hold down the Shift key while dragging to ensure it is a circle.

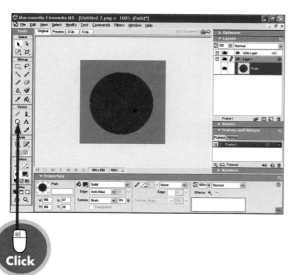

❷ Adding Gradient Fill to the Circle

By default, the circle fills with the last color you used. To change this to a linear fill, select the circle. Then, in the Property Inspector use the **Fill** drop-down menu to select **Linear**. The circle fills with the last used gradient.

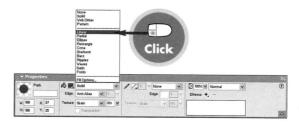

❸ Edit the Gradient Fill

Click the **Paint Bucket** to edit the gradient used in the fill. You must choose two shades of the same color for the effect to work. I have used a gray and silver combination. Using the color picker, choose one color at the left end of the gradient and a second color at the right end of the gradient to set the colors.

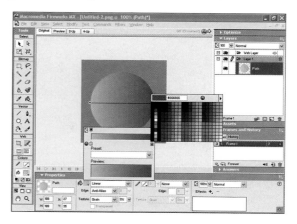

4 ⃝ Open the Effects Menu

With the circle selected, click the **Effects +** button in the Property Inspector to open the **Effects** submenu. Choose **Bevel and Emboss**, **Inner Bevel** to open the Settings panel. I've selected **Flat**, a distance of **10**, an angle of **165**, and **Raised**, leaving the default values for contrast and blur. Click inside the document window to close the Settings panel.

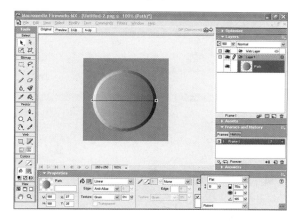

5 ⃝ Clone the Circle

With the circle selected, click **Edit**, **Clone**. You now have two circles, one on top of the other. You can see both circles listed in the Layers panel. Right-click the top circle and choose **Transform**, **Numeric Transform**. In the Numeric Transform dialog box, add a value of 75. Be sure **Scale Attributes** and **Constrain Proportions** are selected. Click **OK** to continue.

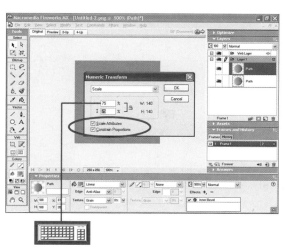

6 ⃝ Change the Inner Circle

Select the top circle, which is now smaller. Notice two handles joined by a line. These control the look of the gradient. Select the square handle and rotate it by 180 degrees. It will look strange for a minute, but don't worry.

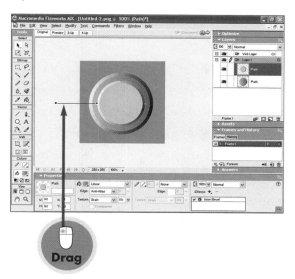

7 ⃝ Complete the Effect

Now drag the circle handle toward the right edge of the inner circle. Note how the gradient moves with you! When you like the look, click away from the circles and you should have a nice 3D effect. Save this file for the next task.

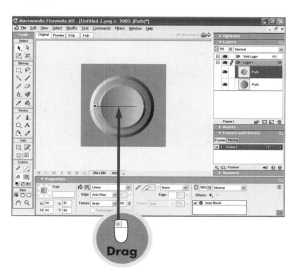

How to Edit or Remove an Effect

After you have modified your image with some special effects, you might decide to edit those effects—or remove them altogether. Being able to change or delete special effects is a vital skill, and this task explains how to make these changes. In this task, we will modify the 3D effect from Task 3.

1 Select the Object

In the main document window, open the file you saved at the end of Task 3. Select the object that has the effect you want to remove or modify. Any effect applied to the object is listed in the Property Inspector. I have selected the bottom (larger) circle from the previous task.

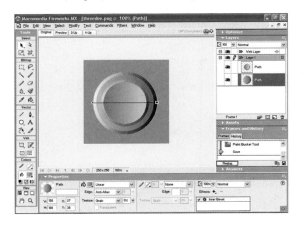

2 Select the Effect

In the Property Inspector, click to select the effect you want to remove or modify.

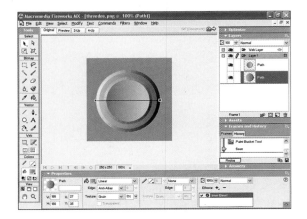

3 Change an Effect

To change any settings for an effect, double-click the selected effect in the Property Inspector to reopen the Settings panel.

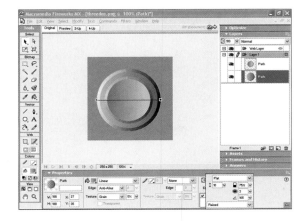

4 Adjust the Settings

Use the options on the Settings panel to adjust the special effect. I changed the bevel width on the bottom circle to 5, and then selected the top circle and reduced its bevel width to 3.

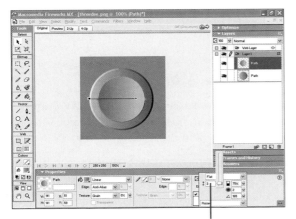

Bevel width setting

5 Change the Gradient

Even with the effects in place, you can change the gradient. Select both circles (Shift+Click), and then select the color picker next to the Paint Bucket in the Property Inspector. Change the colors in your gradient. I've selected red and black for this completed effect.

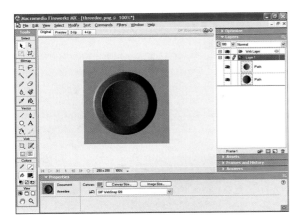

How to Create a Text Effect with Layers

We've looked at using basic text in Fireworks and have used effects a little to create our 3D look. Now let's look at using effects with text to create a split text effect that also uses layers.

1 Create a New Document

Open Fireworks and create a new blank document. For this example, I'm using a dark colored background for the canvas—you'll see why in a minute!

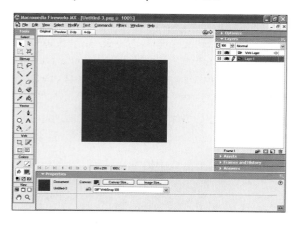

2 Draw a Rectangle

On the canvas, use the **Rectangle** tool to draw a rectangle. The size is not too important, but it must be large enough to hold some text.

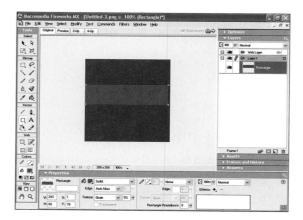

3 Fill the Rectangle

From the Tools panel, choose a color that contrasts with the canvas, and fill the rectangle. The rectangle should show up well against the darker canvas color.

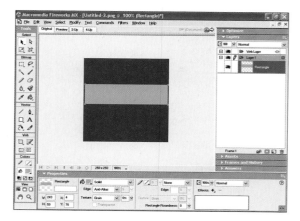

4 Add a Layer

Expand the Layers panel, then open the **Layers** options menu at the top of the panel. Select the **New Layer** option to add a new layer and name it **Text**. If the Layers panel is closed, select **Window**, **Layers** to show it.

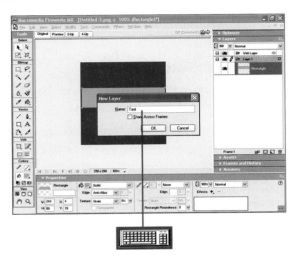

5 Type Some Text

Click the **Text** tool to select it, and then add some text to the new layer. Color the text to be the same as the rectangle.

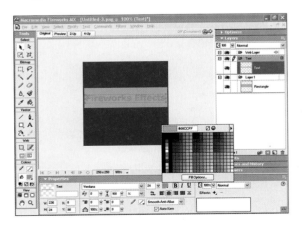

6 Position the Text

Drag the text so that it overlaps the edge of the rectangle onto the canvas.

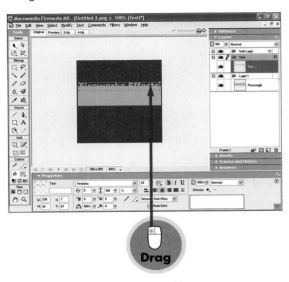

7 Blend the Layers

On the Layers panel, open the **Mode** drop-down menu and select **Difference**. You'll see the effect immediately. Simply crop any unwanted areas from around the text to have a complete graphic in next to no time!

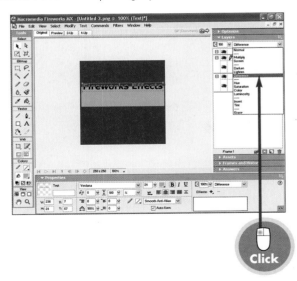

How to Create and Save Custom Effects

If you create a specific effect, such as a drop shadow with particular color and direction settings, you can save and name that effect and apply it to other objects. Applying the same effect to a group of objects makes your images more consistent and your Web pages more professional. For example, if you're creating text graphics to use as page headings on your site, applying the same effect to each ensures consistency, is a more professional approach, and saves time in the long run.

① Create the Effect

Apply the effect or effects to an object. Be sure that all the settings are exactly as you want them. In this example, I added a drop shadow to some text. I want to save the drop-shadow effect so that I can add the same effect to other text I will create.

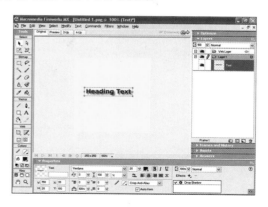

② Save the Effect

Open the **Effects** submenu and choose **Save as Style**. The New Style dialog box opens.

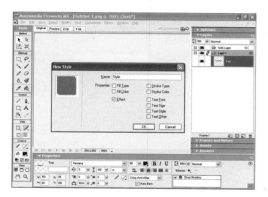

③ Name the Effect

In the dialog box, type an appropriate name for the effect and choose the settings you want to save. I'm saving the **Effect**, **Text Font**, and **Text Size** to ensure that they're applied correctly in the future. You can choose other options as well. Click **OK** when you have made your selections.

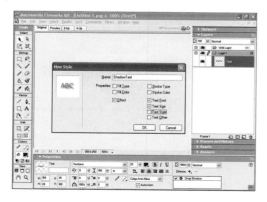

④ Apply the Style to Another Object

After you have saved an effect, you can reuse it with any other object. Open or select another object. Show the Styles panel by choosing **Window**, **Styles**. The effect you saved appears at the end of the list. Create a new object to apply the style to, select it, then click the style to apply it.

⑥ Delete a Saved Style

You can delete any custom style you have. Simply select it in the Styles panel, then from the **Styles** options menu, choose **Delete Styles**. That style is no longer available for you to apply to other objects, but any objects that have had the style applied are unaffected.

Click

⑤ Edit a Saved Style

You can edit a saved style at any time. Select it in the Styles panel, then from the **Styles** options menu, choose **Edit Style**. The Edit Style dialog box opens for you to make any changes or additions that you want. Click **OK** to save your changes.

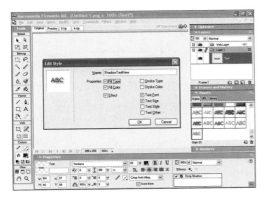

How-to Hint

Using Photoshop Plug-Ins as Effects

If you're a Photoshop user, you can install a Photoshop plug-in so that you can use Photoshop special effects in Fireworks as well. Unlike the effects you create in Fireworks, Photoshop plug-ins cannot be edited or removed after you have applied them.

To install the plug-ins, select **Options**, **Locate Plugins** from the **Effects** submenu, locate the plug-ins, and click **OK**. The plug-ins become visible only after you close and relaunch Fireworks.

How to Attach Text to a Path

Fireworks lets you manipulate text in many ways. To create curvy, swirly text that flows along the document, you must attach the text to a path. Start with a new blank canvas—mine is 250×250 pixels, with a peachy canvas color, but yours can be any size and color you want. We'll draw a line and then curve that line; because the line we draw is a vector graphic with editable points, it's called a *path*. At the end of this task, save the file because the last task in this part takes this text and adds some other bits and effects to create a complete graphic.

❶ Select the Pen Tool

Select the **Pen** tool from the Tools panel. The Pen tool draws a line (path) between two points. Click once at the left edge of the canvas and then again at the opposite point on the right. The line (path) will be drawn between the points. Hold the Shift key to force a straight line.

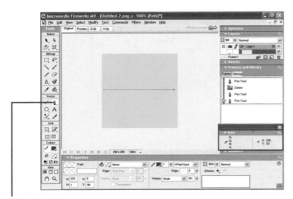

Pen tool

❷ Curve the Line

Click and drag the handle at the right edge to curve the line (path) you drew in step 1. When the handles are visible and the line has started to curve, it should look something like this image.

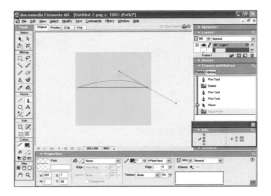

❸ Smooth the Curve

From the **Select** group in the Tools panel, choose the **Subselection** tool (white arrow), and click the right edge of the line. The handles should appear. Use them to create a nice smooth curve (path) as shown here.

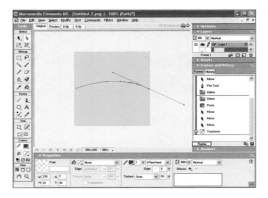

④ Add Some Text

Select the **Text** tool from the Tools panel and add some text—only one or two words. Use the Property Inspector to format the size, color, and font of the text.

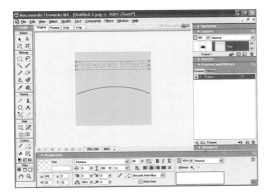

⑤ Attach the Text to the Path

Hold down the Shift key and click both the text and the path to select them. From the **Text** menu, select **Attach to Path**. The text now curves round the line!

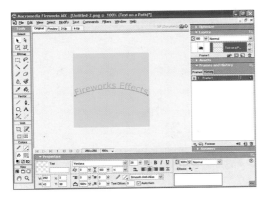

⑥ Skew the Text

To add perspective to the text, select it, right-click, and choose **Skew** from the **Transform** context menu. Click the upper-left handle and drag the text to create the look of perspective. Save the file—we'll use it the next task.

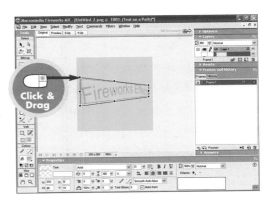

How to Combine Different Effects

In this task, we'll combine many of the effects from this part of the book and create a complete graphic with text, shadows, fill effects, and more. Start with the skewed text from the previous task. If you have not yet done that task, do so now because you will need the text on the path for this one. On your canvas, move the text to the top so it's out of the way for the moment.

① Draw a Circle

On the canvas, draw a circle using the Ellipse tool and holding down the Shift key.

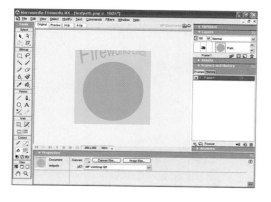

② Add a Fill

Select the circle and use the **Fill** options from the Property Inspector to select a **Radial** fill. I used white at one end and the same color as my text for the other. Move the gradient slider inside the circle until it looks similar to this image.

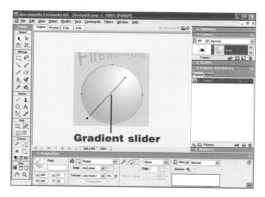

Gradient slider

③ Add a Stroke Color

We want the circle to have a nice, gentle, silver-gray outline. Use the **Stroke** color picker to select an outline color. Use the slider to set the tip size to **1** and leave the Stroke category set to **1-Pixel Soft**.

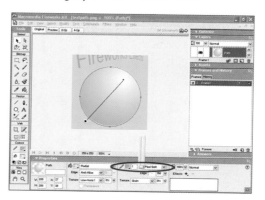

④ Draw an Ellipse

We want the circle to have a shadow set away from it. Rather than use effects, we'll create this ourselves. Draw a small ellipse and give it a solid dark gray fill and no edge.

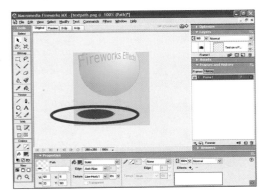

⑤ Add a Blur Effect

With the ellipse selected, click the **Effects** submenu and choose **Blur**, **Gaussian Blur**. The default setting is a radius of **4.1**, which is fine. Click **OK** to apply the effect.

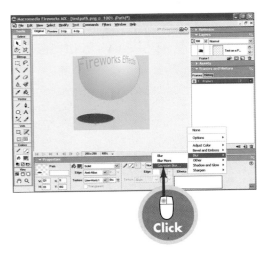

⑥ Change the Opacity

With the blurred ellipse still selected, use the **Opacity** slider located above the Effects box on the Property Inspector to reduce the opacity. Somewhere around 50% should be fine—after all, shadows are never as deeply colored as objects.

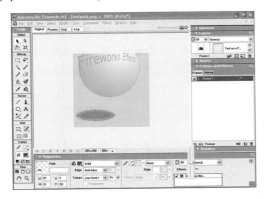

⑦ Put the Circle and Shadow Together

Place the shadow and circle in the correct positions on the canvas. Don't worry about the order they appear in—we'll sort that next. Be sure the gray ellipse is placed to look like a shadow.

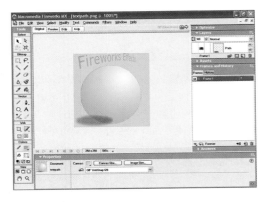

8 Change the Order

Click the circle. From the **Modify** menu, choose **Arrange**, **Bring to Front**. This brings the circle to the front of the canvas, covering enough of the ellipse to make a shadow.

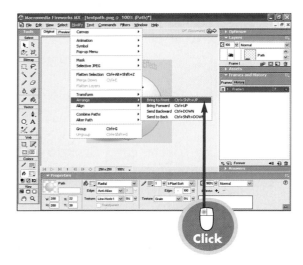

9 Edit the Text

Select the text from the top of the canvas and increase the font size so that the text flows wider than the circle. Move the text over the circle and bring it to the front. If necessary, increase the width of the canvas.

10 Duplicate the Text

Select the text, and from the **Edit** menu choose **Duplicate**. This creates an identical copy of the text directly on top of the original. Select the duplicate.

11 Edit the Duplicate

Change the Opacity of the duplicate text to around 30%, and add a drop shadow by selecting the **Effects** submenu and choosing **Shadow and Glow**, **Drop Shadow**.

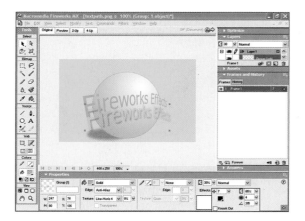

12 Move the Shadowed Text

Place the text with the effects so that it's behind the original (**Modify**, **Arrange**, **Send Backward**). This adds a pale shadow to the original and gives the appearance of depth. Save the file for future playing, or optimize it for exporting to Dreamweaver.

How-to Hint

Playing with Fills

You can add a normal fill to the text as well. This can give some interesting effects to the top layer of text. Try adding an outline color or bevel to give the illusion of height and depth.

As I said before, you can play with the settings to get the effects that best suit your Web site, so take the skills you've learned here and try different things. Just remember to save the file often with different file-names, so that you can go back to a previous version if you want to.

Layers and Frames in Fireworks MX

Layers are used in Fireworks to give you more flexibility when working with image files; you can simply place each object in your file onto a different layer. Layers are similar to having many pieces of clear acetate, each with a part of the image on it. When the layers are stacked on top of each other, the image becomes visible as a whole. However, for editing purposes, each component or layer is totally independent of the others.

The Layers panel in Fireworks displays the layers in your current file, including the names of the layers and whether they are visible or invisible, locked or unlocked. The stacking order of the layers in the panel reflects the way that the layers are stacked on the canvas. It's a good idea to give each layer a unique name so you can easily identify it.

When you change an object on your canvas, look at the Layers panel for the blue box that indicates which layer the object is on. When you add new objects to your image, they are placed on the layer that is selected in the Layers panel.

The new animation options in Fireworks MX make it easier than ever to create great-looking animations without bothering with the technical stuff behind them. All you have to do is create the objects you want to animate and let Fireworks do the rest. In the tasks in this part, you learn how to use layers and frames; the last task shows you how to create a more complicated animation using all the skills you learned in the preceding tasks in the part.

How to Add and Work with Layers

When you create a new document in Fireworks, two layers are created: Layer 1, which is where the initial content will go, and the Web layer. You cannot edit or delete the Web layer; it contains information needed when you use slices or hotspots. Layer 1 is created as a starting point for you to work with. If you are creating a document without adding any additional layers, everything you do appears on Layer 1.

❶ Create a New Document

Open Fireworks and create a new document, which we'll use to build on and add layers to. The size and canvas color can be whatever you want them to be. Expand the Layers panel using the arrow. Notice that, even though your new document contains no real content, the Layers panel shows that the document has two layers: the Web Layer and Layer 1.

Click to expand Layers panel

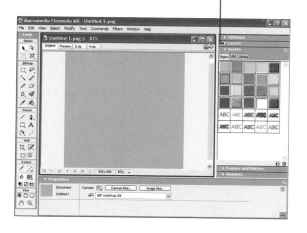

❷ Add a New Layer

To add a new layer to the document, open the **Layers** options menu at the top right of the panel title bar and choose **New Layer**. The New Layer dialog box opens.

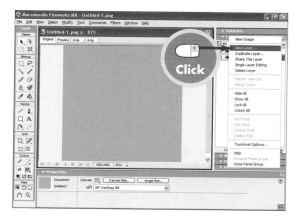

❸ Name the Layer

In the New Layer dialog box, either type a name for the layer you are adding or accept the default. In this case, the default layer name is **Layer 2**. Click **OK** to continue.

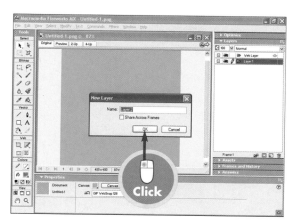

④ Activate a Layer

Any objects that you add to the canvas are automatically placed on whichever layer is selected. To select the layer to which you want to add an object or with which you want to work, click the layer in the Layers panel. The layer is highlighted in the panel. Click **Layer 1** and add a circle.

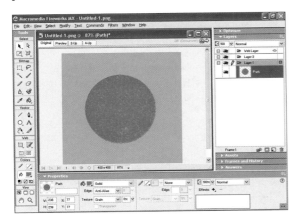

⑤ Add Further Content

Now click **Layer 2** and draw a square. Notice that the Layers panel shows you what is contained in each layer.

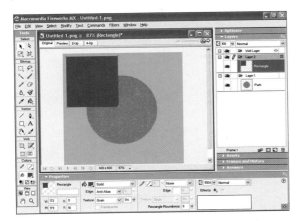

⑥ Rename a Layer

Layers can be renamed easily in Fireworks. In this example, I added a red circle to Layer 1 and want the layer name to identify what it contains. To rename a layer, double-click its name in the Layers panel and rename the layer to something more appropriate. Press the **Enter** key to continue.

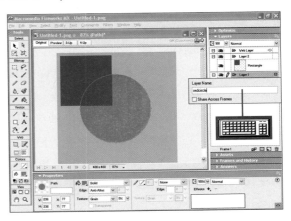

⑦ Delete a Layer

You can delete any layer (except for the Web Layer) just as easily as you can create a layer. To delete a layer, select it in the Layers panel and click the trash can icon. Fireworks deletes the layer without prompting you to confirm the action. All the content of the selected layer is deleted. If you delete a layer by mistake, use **Edit**, **Undo** to bring it back

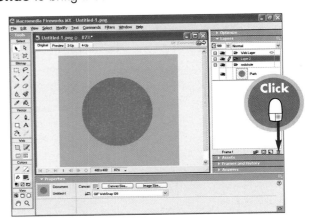

Click

How to Plan a Simple Animation

Animation adds movement and life to any Web site; however, too much animation can be bad visually and can detract from an otherwise well-presented site. Fireworks lets you create animated GIFs—a series of static images that display quickly in rotation, giving the appearance of movement. By changing the content of each frame in succession, you can create movement, resize images, change colors, create fades, and even present entire cartoons for your Web site. Fireworks can save you some work by *tweening*, a process that creates movement between frames. Let's use animation to make some text fade from view.

❶ Create a Document and Add Some Text

Create a new document that has the size and canvas color you want. Add some text and format it accordingly. Here I am simply using a company name and two colors for the text.

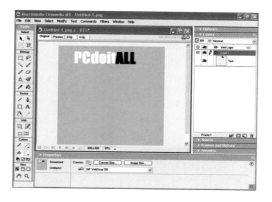

❷ Create the Animation

We're going to make the text fade totally from view. Select the text you have typed and from the **Modify** menu choose, **Modify**, **Animation**, **Animate Selection** to open the Animate dialog box.

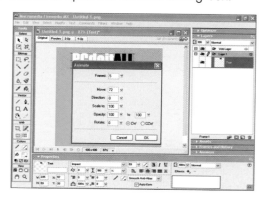

❸ Set the Animation

In the Animate dialog box, set the movement and direction for your animation. The movement is in pixels and the direction is in degrees. Here I am moving my text 100 pixels and 270 degrees. Use the slider knob to set the direction.

Direction slider knob

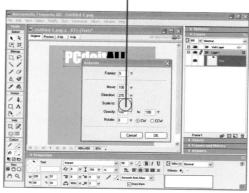

④ Add Some Frames

Change the number of frames for the animation. I'm using 15 frames to allow for a smooth movement. Change the number from the default 5 to 15 either by using the slider or by typing in the new number.

Frames slider bar

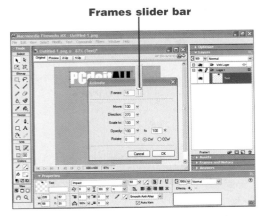

⑤ Let Fireworks Add More Frames

We want our text to move and fade out, so change the Opacity setting to read **100** to **0**. Click **OK** to continue. Fireworks displays a screen asking to add more frames. Click **OK** to continue. Fireworks generates the animation based on your settings.

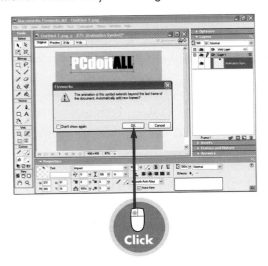

Click

⑥ View the Changes

If you look at the document you created, you will now see that there are some dots. The green dot is where your animation starts, and the red dot is where it ends. The blue dots show the animation frame by frame.

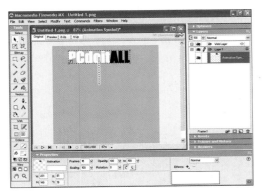

⑦ View the Animation

Click the **Play** button at the bottom of the document window to test the animation. When the animation is playing, the **Play** button becomes the **Stop** button, which you can click at any time to stop the playback.

Click

⑧ Show the Frames Panel

You can see where the movement is at any point in the animation by viewing the individual frames. Expand the Frames panel by clicking the arrow in the panel title bar, or by right-clicking in the panel's title bar and choosing **Expand**.

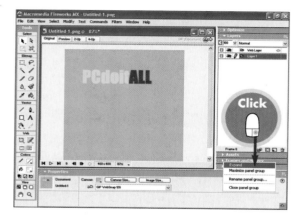

⑨ View a Single Frame

Click on any frame in the Frames panel to see the animation at that point.

⑩ Edit the Animation

You can make changes to the animation at any time before you export it to Dreamweaver. You can change the actual text simply by editing it in the normal way. Double-click the text in Frame 1 to open the text in the symbol window for editing.

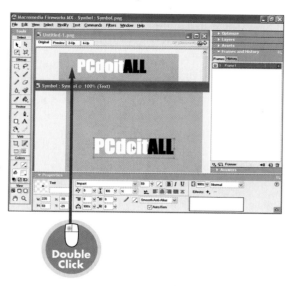

⑪ Text Is a Symbol

Notice that the text is now treated as a symbol in Fireworks. This is standard in an animation. We first came across symbols in Part 4, "Reusing Information"—Library items are treated as symbols. Once you have a symbol it can be used over and over from the Library.

12 Change the Animation Settings

You can change the actual animation (the movement, direction, fade, and so forth) by selecting the animation and choosing **Modify**, **Animation**, **Settings** to open the Animate dialog box.

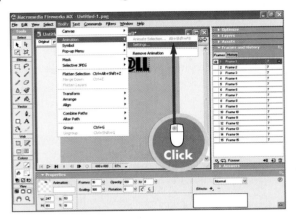

13 Make Some Changes

Use the Animate dialog box to change the animation. Try making the animation grow by changing the **Scale** to a number greater than 100 (or shrink by setting a lower number). You can also rotate the text by adding a setting using the slider. Click **OK** when you're done.

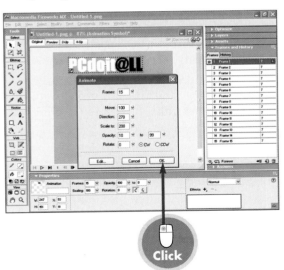

14 Test the Animation Again

Test your animation again to ensure it looks how you want before exporting it to Dreamweaver. You'll export the animation in the next task.

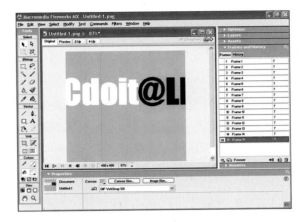

How-to Hint

Animation Hints

In this part of the book, you're making animated GIFs (you can't have animated JPEG files). The Optimize panel allows you to select the file format before you export the file to ensure that all the frames are correctly exported. If you forget to optimize the image, you will get only a single frame.

Looping

The **Looping** option in the Frames panel lets you set how many times your animation will run. Although animated GIFs often run forever, they don't have to. Remember that if you set your animation to play only once, it might not load quickly enough to display in slow browsers; a minimum of two plays is therefore advised.

How to Export an Animation to Dreamweaver

Like any other image file, animation files should be optimized when they are exported. Fireworks lets you export your animation as a single animated GIF, as multiple files that can be edited separately, or as a Macromedia SWF file. If you choose to export an animated file as a SWF file, you will be able to edit the file in Macromedia Flash (assuming that you have the software). For more information about Flash, see the Macromedia Web site at http://www.macromedia.com.

1 Start the Export Process

With your completed animation file open and saved in Fireworks, choose **File**, **Export Wizard** to launch the Export Wizard. Click **Continue** until you see this screen, where you will choose the type of export file you want to create. In this case, choose **Animated GIF** and click **Continue**.

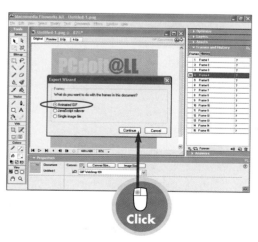

2 Optimize the File

In the Export Preview window, you will see the file ready to be exported. By default, unused colors are removed and the whole canvas area is exported. Click **Export** to continue.

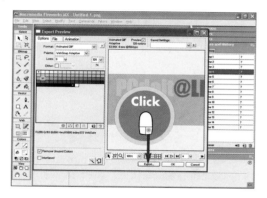

3 Select a Location for the File

In the Export dialog box, browse to the location in which you want to store your animation file (normally in the images folder of the site you are creating in Dreamweaver). Click **Save** to complete the export process. Remember to save a copy of the file as a PNG file so you can edit it later if you need or want to.

4 Insert the Animation into a Page

In Dreamweaver, open the page you want the image to appear in, click where you want the image to appear, and use the **Insert Image** button from the Insert bar to insert the animation file as you would any other GIF image. Here you see the image selected on the page.

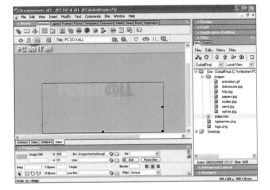

5 Preview the File in the Browser

Although you can see the first frame of the animation file in the document window, you cannot see the actual action in Dreamweaver. To do that, you must preview the page in a browser. Choose **File**, **Preview in Browser** and choose a browser from your list.

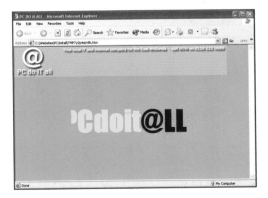

Exporting Options

In the tasks in this book, we are concentrating on creating animated GIF files; however, Fireworks allows you to export your animation in other formats as well. You can export your animation as a series of multiple files by choosing **File**, **Export Special**, **Layer/Frames to Files**. Select **Frames** from the pop-up menu, and each frame will be saved as an individual file.

Exporting to Flash

You can export your work to the Flash application for further editing by selecting **File**, **Export Special**, **Flash SWF**. Exporting an animation to Flash causes some Fireworks formatting to be lost. It's well worth your time to check the Fireworks help files for a full list of formatting options you might lose in this transfer.

How to Control Animations

The preceding tasks explained how to create a very simple animation in Fireworks and how to export it to Dreamweaver. Many factors control the way an animation looks and plays. This task looks at the panels and control options that affect those factors. Starting with a new document, let's create a series of shapes and letters that will change in the animation.

❶ Create a New Document

Create a new document and draw or insert all the objects you want to use in the animation. Don't worry too much at this stage about the layers on which the elements appear in the document—we'll sort them out later. Choose **File**, **Save As** and save it as a PNG file so that you can continue to work on it in Fireworks.

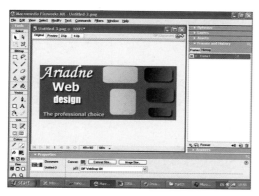

❷ Create a New Layer

Create a new layer that will contain all the shapes in the image. In the Layers panel, click the **New/Duplicate Layer** button at the bottom of the panel. The new layer, with the default name Layer 2, is added to the Layers panel and is automatically selected.

New/Duplicate Layer button

❸ Select the Shapes to Add to the Layer

Select all the shapes in the document (do not select the squares with text in them). To select all the shapes at the same time, hold down the **Shift** key as you click. Each shape is highlighted as you select it. Notice that the items are also selected in the Layers panel.

④ Move the Shapes

Notice the blue square next to Layer 1 in the Layers panel. This icon indicates that the selected items are currently on that layer. Drag the icon to Layer 2 to move the selected shapes to Layer 2. Now the shapes are on Layer 2, and the text remains on Layer 1.

⑤ Make the Text Visible in All Layers

We want the text to be visible at all times in the animation. To do this, we must share Layer 1 (the layer that contains the text) across all frames in the animation. Click **Layer 1** in the Layers panel to select it and then open the Layers panel options menu at the top right of the panel title bar.

⑥ Share the Layer

From the Layers panel menu, choose **Share This Layer**. Fireworks inserts a filmstrip icon to the right of the layer name to indicate that this layer is shared across all the frames.

⑦ Select and Move the Text

In the Layers panel, select **Layer 1** and move the text where you want it to appear in the animation.

⑧ Select and Move the Shapes

In the Layers panel, select **Layer 2**, which contains the shapes. Select each shape in turn and move it to cover part of the text. (The order doesn't matter; just cover the text with the shapes.) In your file, select the layer containing the objects you want to move and arrange them so that they appear in their initial locations.

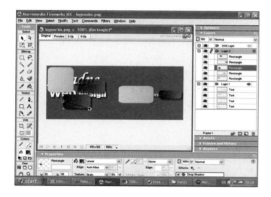

⑨ Select the Shapes and See the Frames

Select all the shapes by holding the Shift key as you click each shape in turn. Then show the Frames panel by clicking its tab. (If the Frames panel isn't showing onscreen, choose **Window**, **Frames** to display it.)

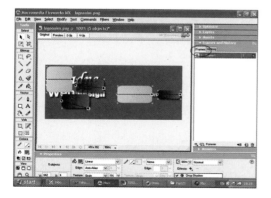

⑩ Distribute the Shapes to Separate Frames

Click the **Distribute to Frames** button at the bottom of the Frames panel. This action places each shape onto a different frame in the animation.

Distribute to Frames button

⑪ Preview the Animation

Use the animation playback controls at the bottom of the document window to see the animation in action. Notice that, as each frame appears, one of the shapes covers a different part of the text.

⑫ Optimize the Image

Open the Optimize panel. Choose **Animated GIF** from the options. (If you don't choose Animated GIF at this point, when you export the file for use in Dreamweaver, you will export only Frame 1.)

⑭ Save the File

Now save the file and export it for use in a Dreamweaver page. Refer to Task 3 for instructions on optimizing and exporting animation files.

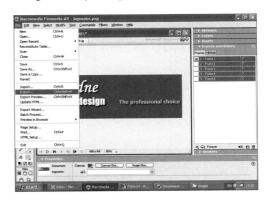

⑬ Set the Frame Delay

Press and hold the **Shift** key and click all the frames in the Frames panel. From the **Frames** panel menu, choose **Properties**. In the dialog box, set the **Frame Delay** (the amount of time each frame displays). The default is 20/100 of a second; 50/100 is half a second. To make the animation play faster, make the **Frame Delay** number smaller. Click away to close the dialog box.

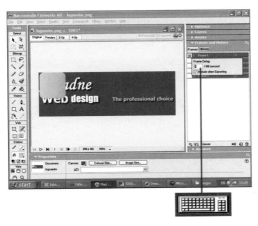

How to Work with Symbols and Animations

You can use many options to create and change animations in Fireworks. This task looks at some of those options and clarifies some terminology that you might have heard about. In the preceding tasks, you created the content for every frame in an animation. This task looks at how Fireworks can automatically generate the content for frames if you identify the starting and ending frames of the animation. This process is known as *tweening*.

1 Create a New Document and a Symbol

In a new document, draw a shape and convert it to a symbol by choosing **Modify, Symbol, Convert to Symbol**.

Click

2 Name the Symbol

The Symbol Properties dialog box opens. Choose **Animation** from the symbol options and give the symbol a meaningful name. Click **OK** in the Symbol Properties dialog box, then **OK** again to continue. The symbol now resides in the Library for this document.

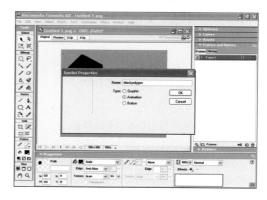

3 Insert the Symbol

Show the Library panel, and then drag two instances of the symbol you created in Step 1 into your document. Be sure there is some noticeable space between the two objects.

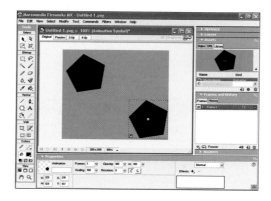

4 Tween the Symbols

Hold down the **Shift** key and click to select both instances of the symbol in the document window. Choose **Modify**, **Symbol**, **Tween Instances** to ask Fireworks to create frames to animate the selected symbols.

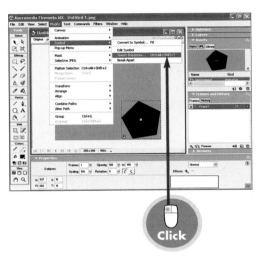

6 Test the Animation

Click the **Play** button at the bottom of the screen to see the effects of tweening. The first instance of the symbol moves across the screen and ends up where the second instance was. The Frames panel now shows all the frames for the animation. Notice that, as the animation plays, the panel highlights each frame in turn to show you the current frame.

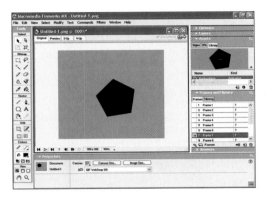

5 Distribute to Frames

Enable the **Distribute to Frames** check box. This option creates a new animation frame for each step that the polygon must take to move from the initial position of the first instance to the position of the other instance. Type the number of steps you want Fireworks to create to move the symbol from the first position to the second. Click **OK** to continue.

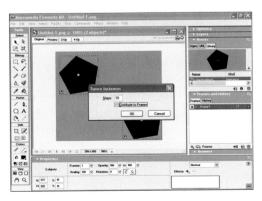

7 Choose an Instance to Transform

Now that the symbol moves across the screen, let's change some of the instances. In the Frames panel, click **Frame 5**. In the document window, you can see that the symbol moved slightly. Click to select this instance of the symbol and choose **Modify**, **Transform** to display a submenu of transformation options that you can apply to this instance.

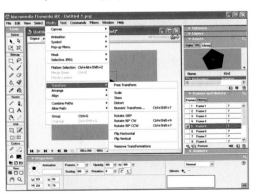

8 Apply Transformations

Choose any transformation option to apply it to this instance of the symbol. The effect affects only the instance in the selected frame, not all the instances in the other frames. Select other frames and adjust or transform them to create some variation in your animation. In this example, I transformed an instance to be 25% of its original size.

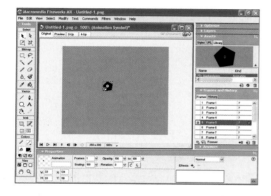

9 Set Looping Options

The **Looping** setting controls how many times the animation will play. Most animated GIF files play forever, but you can control this by clicking the **Looping** button at the bottom of the Frames panel.

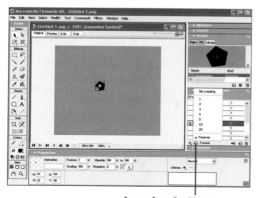

Looping button

10 Pick a Number

From the menu that opens, choose the number of times you want the animation to play. If you select 3, the animation will play once and then three more times before stopping. Choose **Forever** to cause the animation to play constantly as long as the Web page on which it's displayed is open.

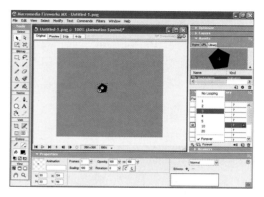

11 Fading

Select each frame in turn and adjust the **Opacity** settings in the Property Inspector to give the effect of fading in an out. Play with this setting to get an effect you like.

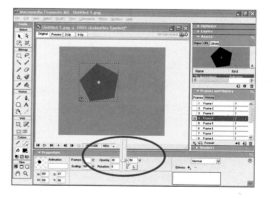

12 Rotate an Instance

Use the **Rotation** setting in the Property Inspector to rotate a symbol in a frame. Use the Rotation slider to select the angle of rotation; select the **Rotate Clockwise** or **Rotate Counterclockwise** button to specify the direction of the rotation.

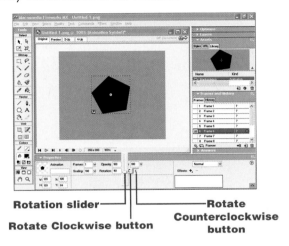

Rotation slider ——

Rotate Clockwise button

—Rotate Counterclockwise button

13 Scale an Instance

The **Scaling** slider changes the size of any instances of the symbol. Changing the properties of an instance has no effect on the underlying symbol. In the Frames panel, select the instance to change and use the **Scaling** slider to set the percentage. A setting of more than 100% makes this instance larger than the original, but does not show until you preview the animation.

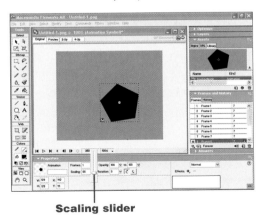

Scaling slider

14 Preview the Animation

Use the animation playback controls at the bottom of the document window to see the effects that you have added to your animation. Alternatively, preview the file in a browser.

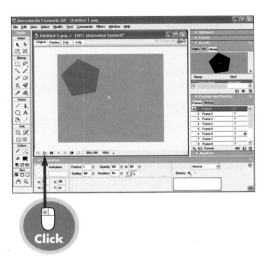

Click

15 Save the File

Choose **File**, **Save**; name the file and save it as a **PNG** file. Then, choose **Window**, **Optimize** to display the Optimize panel. Select **Animated GIF** from the drop-down menu and make any other optimization settings that you want. To export the optimized version of the file, choose **File**, **Export** and complete the dialog box. The file is now ready to be included in any Web page.

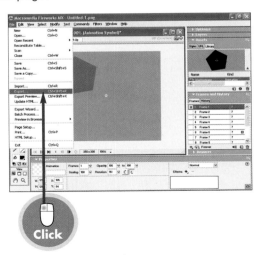

Click

How to Use Onion Skinning

Onion skinning is a common technique when working with animations. In simple terms, it allows you to see the contents of more than one frame at a time. Onion skinning can help you move an object a certain distance from one frame to the next; the "ghost images" of the objects in the frames before and after the current frame help you position the objects in the current frame.

1 Open the Onion Skinning Options

Open a file that contains more than one frame and be sure the Frames panel is displayed. Click the **Onion Skinning** button at the bottom of the panel to display a menu of options.

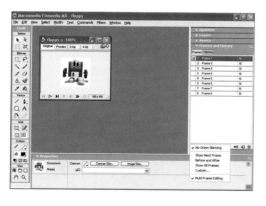

2 Turn On Onion Skinning

By default, the onion-skinning feature is turned off in Fireworks. To turn it on, click the option you want. In this example, I want to show the frames before and after the current frame, so I select **Before and After**.

3 Click Between Frames

In the Frames panel, click to select different frames. In the document window, you can see not only the contents of the selected frame, but also a dimmed version of the next and previous frames. Notice that the Frames panel shows you which frames are being displayed.

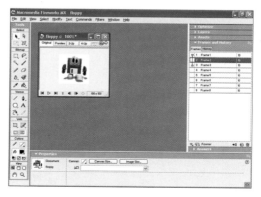

Use Multi-Frame Editing

By default, you can edit the visible contents of any frame in Fireworks, a feature called *multi-frame editing*. If you have turned on onion-skinning, you can manipulate all visible objects regardless of which frame they are on. Select objects from different frames and move them to see this feature in action.

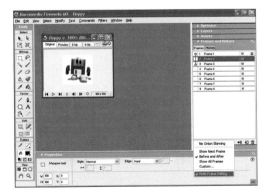

How-to Hint

Playing or Working?

Learning how to animate objects in Fireworks (or any other application) can be a time-consuming process. Even so, it should be fun! Start by playing with text, and see whether you can get your name to bounce across the screen, fading in and out. Then, you can use that knowledge to build the animations you want for your Web pages.

Getting Flash?

Remember that if you also have access to Macromedia Flash, you can save your animations as Flash files. Then you can open those files into Flash and edit them further, using some of the dedicated animation techniques in Flash to refine your animations even more. If you don't already have Flash, download a trial version from Macromedia at http://www.macromedia.com. Although the trial version will time out, you'll still have a chance to get to know the application.

How-to Hint

Frame Delay

The **Frame Delay** controls the playback speed of your animation. You have total control over the length of time each frame is displayed. The Frame Delay is specified in hundredths of a second. A value of 50 displays each frame for one-half second; a value of 300 displays each frame for three seconds. To change the frame rate, open the Frames panel option menu at the top right of the panel title bar and select **Properties**. Enter the desired value (in hundredths of a second).

Frames and File Size

You can make your animations as large and as complex as you want—there's no limit on the number of frames you can use. However, you must note that the greater the number of frames within your animation, the larger the file size will be and the longer the image will take to download into a browser.

No More Multi-Frame

If you decide you don't want multi-frame editing (maybe you don't feel confident about moving items around that are in different frames), simply reopen the **Onion Skinning** menu and deselect the **Multi-Frame Editing** option.

How to Create More Complex Animations

Fireworks MX makes it easier than ever to create complex animations. In this task, we'll create a banner for a Web site by employing layers, frames, and tweening to create a single animation that uses different objects from the Library and makes them all do different things at the same time. This more complex animation requires the techniques you learned from this chapter and from some previous ones. The standard size for Web banners is 470×60 pixels, so start with a canvas that size.

1 Add Static Content

Create the background for the banner, along with any other objects that will remain static throughout. All these objects must be placed on Layer 1 of the banner, which is the default layer.

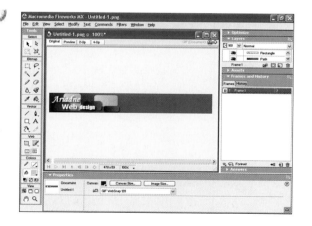

2 Edit Layer 1

In the Layers panel, double-click Layer 1 and rename it **Background.** Click in the **Share Across Frames** check box; we want this content visible at all times. Press **Enter** to continue.

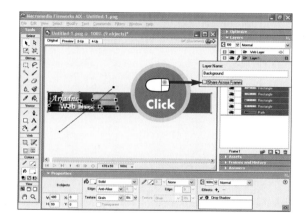

3 Add a New Layer

Open the Layers panel options menu at the top right of the panel title bar and choose **New Layer**. Name this layer **Animation**.

4 Create Symbol to Animate

With the Animation layer selected, type the text to be animated. Set the **Font**, **Size**, and **Color** as usual, and then from the **Modify** menu, choose **Symbol**, **Convert to Symbol**.

5 Name the Symbol

In the dialog box, type a name for the symbol (I've used **Text1**). Then be sure you select **Animation** from the **Type** options. Click **OK** to continue

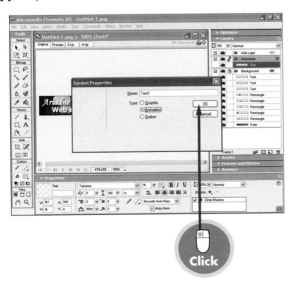

6 Complete the Animation Settings

We want this text to move, grow, and fade in, so complete the dialog box with the settings shown here. Note that we aren't using **Rotation** in this project. Click **OK** to continue and add the required frames.

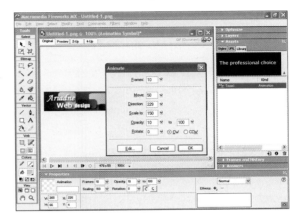

7 Set Frame Delay

Select **Frame 10** in the Frames panel and double-click the **Frame Delay** number (the default is 7/100 second). Change this number to **60**. Click away to close it. This gives the reader a chance to read the text when the animation loops. Be sure you check the **Include when Exporting** option.

⑧ Add a New Blank Frame

From the Frames panel, add a single blank frame. Set the frame rate back to 7 for this frame.

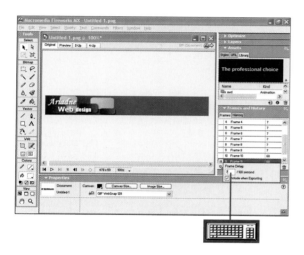

⑨ Add More Content

In this frame, I've added an instance of the text we used before, but this time it will be static; that is, with no animation. Add some different text to animate from this frame onward, then convert it to an animation symbol as before (**Modify**, **Symbol**, **Convert to Symbol**).

⑩ Animate This Content

In the Animation settings dialog box, choose the animation you want for this text. I have chosen to fade the text in by setting **Opacity** to **0** to **100**, **Scale** to **170%**, and **Move** to **0**. Click **OK** to continue and **OK** to add five new frames.

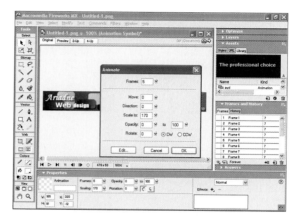

⑪ Move the Text

If the second symbol does not appear where you want it, simply select it in Frame 11 and move it. The animation settings will then adjust for that position.

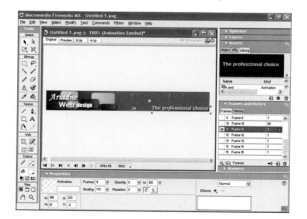

12 Change the Frame Delay

In the last frame, change the **Frame Delay** to **60**. This again gives the viewer the chance to read your text. Test your animation using the controls at the bottom of the document window.

13 Copy the Static Content

The static text needs to be copied into the remaining frames from 11 onward. Select the text in Frame 11, and paste it into each of the remaining frames in turn. If you do not do this, the static text will appear only in Frame 11.

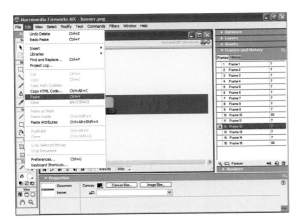

14 Save the File and Export It

Save the file as a PNG so that you can edit it if you need to, then optimize it, and export the file to Dreamweaver as an animated GIF.

Task

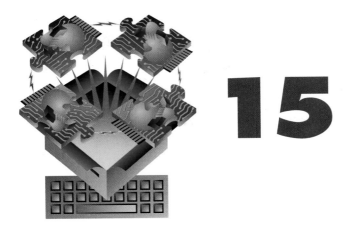

Slices and HTML in Fireworks MX

As its name suggests, a *slice* is a piece of an image. Large images can be sliced into smaller sections that are then rebuilt in the browser window into the complete original file. Slices are used in Fireworks when creating buttons and navigation bars, as you learned in Part 10, "Navigation in Fireworks." In this part, we'll look at using slices for other reasons.

Slices are the perfect way to use large images in your Web site without increasing download time. Slicing an image not only reduces download time, it also gives the site visitor something to see early in the browsing process—a must if you want to ensure that your visitors hang around long enough to see the rest of your site!

The slicing process actually cuts the image into smaller pieces, each an individual file. When the original file is exported, Fireworks generates a table that holds all the smaller images as well as the code required for a perfect rebuild in the browser.

You might choose to slice an image for any of several reasons: You can split a large image into pieces to enable a smooth and speedy download, you can use slices for text messages that have to be updated, and you can use slices to save different parts of an image in different formats, such as .gif and .jpg.

When you create a text slice, Fireworks creates a table cell that contains only your text. By using this approach to text slices, you can then edit this single cell in Dreamweaver without having to open the image file at all. This works well for a sales notice or for other information that changes regularly.

How to Split a Large Image

Fireworks enables you to split, or *slice*, an image into multiple pieces, each of which is stored in a separate file. When you slice an image in this way, Fireworks also creates an HTML document that instructs the browser how to reassemble the separate files back into the original image. You can slice the image into simple rectangles, or you can use the Polygon tool to create non-rectangular shaped slices. When you use polygons, remember that the code Fireworks creates is more complex and can make the end result take longer to download.

❶ Open an Image

Open a large image into the Fireworks window. Reduce the size of the image onscreen so you can see the entire image (select magnification from the **View** menu and select the percentage). Don't resize the image to do this; simply display it at a smaller percentage. I'm using a map that would take far too long to download as one image.

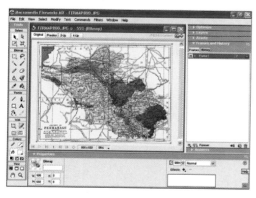

❷ Slice Rectangles

In the Tools panel, click the **Slice** tool to select it. Use the Slice tool to drag out rectangles over the image. Each rectangle represents an image slice. Draw as many rectangles as you need to split the image. In this example, there are no obvious breaks, so I am simply drawing rectangles of equal sizes.

Slice tool

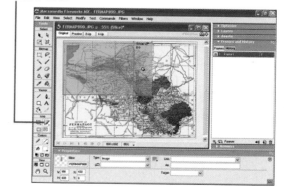

❸ Preview the Export

Choose **File**, **Export Wizard** and click **Continue;** choose **Dreamweaver**, and then click **Exit**. The Export Preview screen opens. Select either **GIF** or **JPEG**, depending on the type of file you are working with. Click the **Export** button to continue.

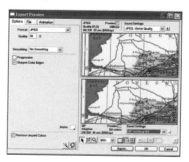

4 Select Export Options

In the Export dialog box, make certain that **Export Slices** is selected from the **Slices** drop-down options.

Click

5 Choose Save Options

Use the **Save in** field at the top of the dialog box to specify a location for the HTML file that Fireworks will create. In the **Save as type** box, select **HTML and Images** from the drop-down menu.

6 Save the Image Files

Having specified that the HTML file will be stored with your other pages, you must now tell Fireworks where to store the images that it creates. Assuming that your images are stored in a subfolder, enable the **Put Images in Subfolder** check box and browse to your images folder. Click **Save** to export the image as multiple image slices.

Click

How-to Hint

What Is Fireworks HTML?

Fireworks HTML is the code created when you use either slices or hotspots in an image. The HTML contains all the necessary information for the browser to rebuild your images, show links, and download correctly in the browser.

Fireworks creates a complete HTML page for you when you use hotspots and slices. As you work through the tasks in this part, you will see that you can use the page or just the code, or let Dreamweaver insert the HTML code into a page (and then delete the Fireworks page).

How to See a Rebuilt Image

If you followed the steps in Task 1, you have created several files from a single sliced image using Fireworks. You can rebuild the image by inserting the Fireworks-created HTML file into your Dreamweaver site and viewing the page with the **File**, **Preview in Browser** command. If you want, you can view the HTML code Fireworks generates for you: Click the **Code and Design View** button on the Dreamweaver toolbar.

1 Open Dreamweaver

If Dreamweaver isn't already open on your desktop, open it now by selecting **Start**, **All Programs** (or **Programs**), **Macromedia**, **Macromedia Dreamweaver MX**, or click a shortcut icon if you have one

2 Open a File

Choose **File**, **Open** to launch the **OPEN** dialog box. When you exported the sliced image from Fireworks, it created an HTML page that contains the information necessary to rebuild the image (see Step 6 of Task 1). Locate this file and open it. It looks exactly like it did before you sliced and exported it from Fireworks.

3 Preview the Page

The HTML file you loaded does not contain the image itself (the image files are stored in the images directory for the site); it contains references to those image files so that Dreamweaver can reassemble the slices into the original image. To see how the browser rebuilds the sliced image in stages, view the page in a browser. From the Dreamweaver **File** menu, choose **Preview in Browser** and select a browser.

④ Check the Download Time

The image rebuilds completely into the browser window. The time it takes to assemble the sliced image files into a whole takes less time than it would to display the original large image file, partly because it's easier to download smaller file sizes. (It's also part illusion, because the visitor is seeing something straight away and isn't just looking at a blank screen.)

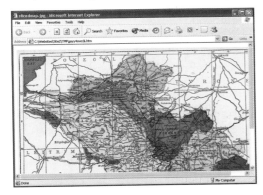

⑤ View the Files

Open your site's **images** folder in the Site panel to see all the separate image files that Fireworks created from the slices.

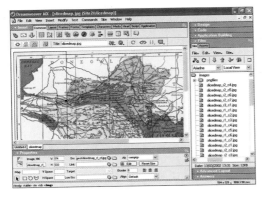

How to-Hint

Table Properties

By default, Fireworks creates a `shim.gif` file, which is a very small image file used to ensure that your tables and images align correctly. If you want Fireworks to create nested tables to achieve this alignment instead, open the HTML Properties dialog box. Choose **File**, **HTML Properties**. Note that any changes you make here become the default for future exports.

Be Careful Using Nested Tables

If you choose to use the **Nested Tables** option for your sliced images, beware! Using nested tables can increase download time for your rebuilt file.

How to Create a Text Slice

A text slice is a great way to add HTML text to a section of your image. When you slice the image, Fireworks creates a separate table cell that contains only text, no images. The cell is completely editable in Dreamweaver, so you can change the text without having to launch Fireworks or change the image in any way.

❶ Open Fireworks

Open Fireworks and load the image to which you want to add a text slice.

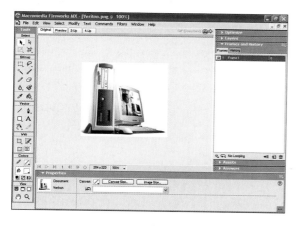

❷ Draw a Slice

In the Tools panel, click the **Slice** tool to select it. Drag out a slice rectangle where you want the text to appear on the image.

❸ Set the Slice Type

Be sure the slice is selected. In the Property Inspector, choose **HTML** from the slice **Type** drop-down menu.

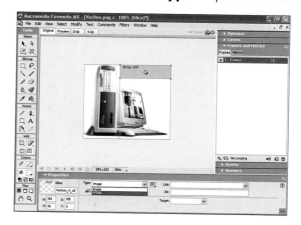

④ Type the Text

Click the **Edit** button to open the Edit HTML Slice dialog box. Simply type in the content you want to appear. You can add HTML tags for formatting here, or you can format the text when the image is in Dreamweaver. Click **OK** to close the dialog box and continue.

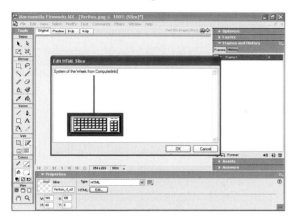

⑤ Export the File

Select the image (not the slice) and use the Optimize panel's settings menu to select your file type. I chose a JPG file because the base image is a photograph with many colors. The slice remains as HTML. Click the **Quick Export** button at the top of the document window and select **Dreamweaver**, **Export HTML**.

⑥ Export Slices

Select the **Export Slices** option in the **Slices** box of the Export dialog box to ensure that the text slice is correctly exported with the HTML. Fireworks creates a complete HTML file containing the image and text slice. As always, be sure you save a copy of the Fireworks PNG file in case you need it later.

⑦ Edit the Text

Because the text is not actually part of the image (it is located in a single cell within the Fireworks table), you can format the text in Dreamweaver just as you do any other text on the page. Open the HTML file Fireworks created into Dreamweaver. You can then use the Properties Inspector to format the text to match your site.

How to Insert Fireworks HTML into Dreamweaver

Fireworks creates a complete HTML page for you that contains not only your sliced graphic, but also any HTML code or JavaScript needed to display your image correctly in the browser window. In the preceding tasks, we have worked on these HTML pages only as complete entities. In this task, we look at what happens when you want to use the image and code in an existing HTML page. You also can copy the Fireworks-created code from Dreamweaver and use it in a different application. The code is well commented, as you will see.

1 Open Dreamweaver

From Fireworks, follow the steps in Task 1 to export an image containing slices into your Web site's directory. Notice that the single image file you started with has multiplied: Now there are several image files (one for each slice) as well as an HTML file. Open the HTML file directly into Dreamweaver as a separate page.

2 Copy and Paste If Needed!

Click the **Show Code View** button on the toolbar to see the Fireworks-created HTML. It's clearly marked within the code. If you want to use the HTML outside of Dreamweaver—in another Web design application, for example—you can simply copy and paste this code into another document. Dreamweaver, however, has a much better way of doing this—read on!

3 Open an Existing Page

Dreamweaver has a built-in facility that inserts HTML code generated by Fireworks into an existing Dreamweaver page. In Dreamweaver, open the file you want to contain the exported Fireworks HTML, and click where you want the file to appear.

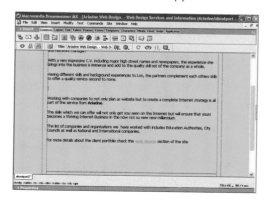

④ Use the Insert Panel

From the **Common** tab of the Insert panel, select the **Fireworks** logo to open the Insert Fireworks HTML dialog box.

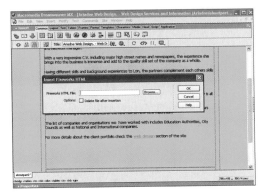

⑤ Locate the File

Click the **Browse** button and use the Select the Fireworks HTML File dialog box to locate the Fireworks-generated HTML file you want to insert into the current document. Select the file, and click **Open**. Back in the Insert Fireworks HTML dialog box, click **OK** to insert the selected file into the document window.

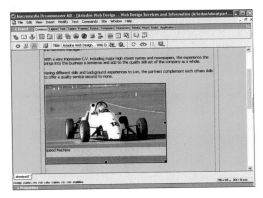

⑥ Edit the Properties

The HTML file you inserted into the current Dreamweaver document is called a *Fireworks Table* by the Properties Inspector. You can change the properties (size, alignment, and so on) for this table just as you would for any other table you create in Dreamweaver. After the file is inserted it has no connection with the original file, so changes made here leave the original intact.

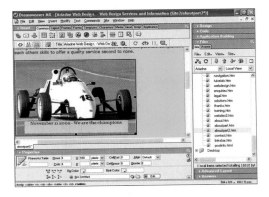

Copying and Pasting the HTML

In Step 2 of this task, I mentioned how to copy the HTML, a really quick way of moving the information from Fireworks into any HTML editor. (Many people use more than one editor; just because most people who use Fireworks also have Dreamweaver doesn't mean they are always using Dreamweaver as their editor.)

If you select **Edit**, **Copy HTML Code**, a wizard opens that will guide you through exporting the image files to a specified location and copying the HTML code to the Clipboard. When you paste the code into your editor, the links to the graphics are updated.

Task

Optimizing Images

The main idea with Web graphics is to create something that looks great in a browser and that site visitors will wait around long enough to see. There's no point in creating the perfect graphic if it takes forever to download—quite simply, no one will wait to see it. Fireworks has a lot of helpful tools to make your life easier in this regard. You can establish your own optimization settings to ensure that the graphics you create not only look good, but also download quickly and wow the visitor with speed and quality.

One of the main features that sets Fireworks apart from other imaging applications is that various parts of the same image can be optimized in different ways. As you know, various types of images have different attributes. Photographs have millions of colors and should be saved as JPEG files. Small graphics, such as bullets, lines, and buttons, contain very few colors; are usually small; might be transparent in parts; and should be exported as GIF files. What happens if your graphic is a composition that uses different object and image types? In most applications, you must select the best compromise you can find. In Fireworks, however, you can use slices to optimize the different parts of the image to best suit those parts.

How to Use the Optimize Panel

In Fireworks, you can optimize your image files as you work in the main window. You also can optimize the image when you finish manipulating it or during the export process. In this task, you get acquainted with the Optimize panel.

1 Open an Image

Select an image you want to optimize and open it in Fireworks. Choose **Window**, **Optimize** to open the Optimize panel. If the panel is already visible, expand it using the drop-down arrow in the panel's title bar. Familiarize yourself with this panel before we start to use it.

2 View the Information

The Optimize panel contains options that you can set to make the image appear the way you like. Among other things, the panel shows the default type of file, the number of colors used, and any transparency in the file.

3 Preset Choices

Fireworks comes with some built-in optimization settings that you can choose for the current image. These presets vary based on the type of file you are creating. From the **Settings** drop-down menu, choose the appropriate option for your file. The default setting is GIF WebSnap 128, which results in a file with a maximum of 128 colors, as close to Web-safe colors as possible. The word *snap* means that the exported image uses colors that are snapped as closely as possible to Web-safe colors. If you're working with a photographic image, choose one of the JPEG options. I'm working with a logo that has few colors, so I choose the default option.

4 Use the Export File Format Options

Use the **Export File Format** options to select the type of file you are creating. Each available file type has some unique optimization settings. For example, you can't have transparency in a JPEG file. The choice you make here should follow the selection you made in Step 3. Recall that GIF files can be up to only 8-bit color and PNG files can be up to 32-bit color. The next task looks at JPEG files in more detail.

5 Understand Transparency Options

PNG and GIF images can contain transparency when they're exported, meaning your Web page background can appear through parts of your image. Transparency doesn't affect the actual graphic file: The effect is visible only when the page displays in a browser. You can choose the color or colors to be transparent in the browser. See the "Transparency Issues" hint at the end of this task.

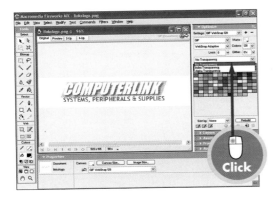

6 Set Number of Colors

The **Colors** option lets you set the maximum number of colors used in the file. By keeping this number to a minimum, you can keep the file size down. Dithering colors is the process used when a color in the image is not in the current panel. Fireworks uses two Web-safe colors and alternates between them to create the closest match possible. The amount of dithering in the file is set using the slider.

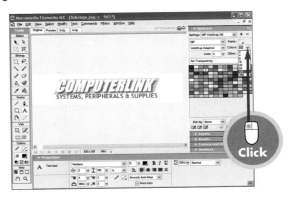

How-to Hint

File Type Confusion?

In this task, we merely introduced the Optimize panel, so it's possible that you're still a little confused. Don't worry too much, because the following tasks will help you understand the various file types—and the optimization methods that work best with each.

Transparency Issues

Index Transparency is used when optimizing 8-bit (256-color) images—you can set individual color pixels to be transparent. The effect is that set colors are "turned off" and don't show against a Web background.

Alpha Transparency can be used only with PNG and PSD (Photoshop) file formats. The main difference is that you can display semi-opaque pixels rather the straight on/off choice in Index transparency.

How to Optimize JPEG Files

JPEG is a compression format designed particularly for graphics with noncontinuous colors, such as photographs. Images in the JPEG format cannot have transparency. You can adjust the amount by which the JPEG file is compressed by changing the quality value in the Optimize panel. Note that this option is visible only when you're working with a JPG file. Remember that the more the file is compressed, the smaller the file is—and the lower the quality of the image. This task looks at the optimization settings available for a JPEG file.

① Preview a JPEG file

Open a JPEG file in Fireworks. Click the **4-Up** tab to preview the image in four panes. Click a preview to select it; all changes are applied to this preview. Select another preview and apply different options, and then check the differences in the download time and file size. Start optimizing by dragging the **Quality** slider on the Optimize panel to **75** percent. This example shows a different quality for each image.

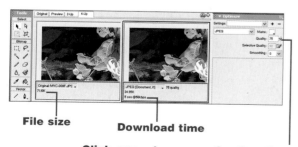

File size

Download time

Click arrow to access Quality slider

② Balance Quality with Time

Reducing the quality reduced the download time and file size, but the previews show that the image quality is diminished. Adjust the **Quality** slider until you reach a compromise between file size and image quality.

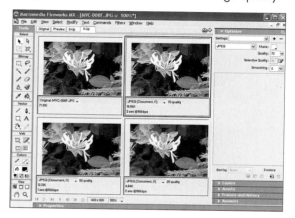

③ Smooth Edges

Reduce the size of a JPEG file by smoothing the hard edges in your file. Smoothing blurs the hard edges in JPG files that don't compress very well. Do this by adjusting the **Smoothing** setting in the Optimize panel. However, you might decide that smoothing the edges blurs your picture too much, even on a low setting.

Click

④ Sharpen Edges

Rather than smoothing edges, you can preserve the edges between color and text or two colors. Sharpening edges is useful if you have text within your JPEG file. (Note that sharpening edges can bloat the file size.) To sharpen edges, select **Sharpen JPEG Edges** from the Optimize panel options menu.

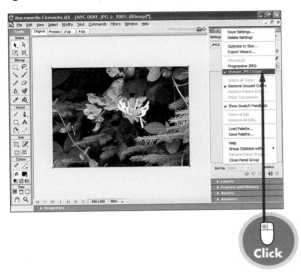

⑥ Match a Background Color

When exporting a JPEG for use on a page that has a color background, it's handy to set a Matte color in the Optimize panel. Choose a color from the Matte color picker that is as close as possible to the background color. This attempts to blend the edges of the image with the background, giving a smoother visual transition.

⑤ Progressive JPEGs

Progressive JPEGs load into the browser at a low resolution and then progressively increase in quality until the image is fully displayed in the browser. Some older browsers (version 3 and below) can't display progressive JPEGs. To export your file as a progressive JPEG, select **Progressive JPEG** from the Optimize panel options menu.

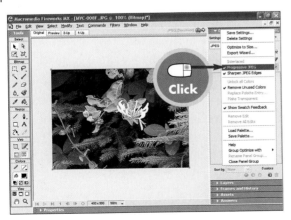

How to Optimize GIF and PNG Files

GIF and PNG files have similar properties, except that GIF files are limited to 256 colors and PNG files can contain more. You will generally find that GIF and PNG file formats are more effective at compressing files with large areas of solid color (those images without the graduating colors common to JPEG files). This task explains how to optimize GIF and PNG files for Web use.

1 Select an Image

Find an image that's appropriate to export as a GIF, and open it in Fireworks. Show the Optimize panel (**Window**, **Optimize**) if it's not already visible.

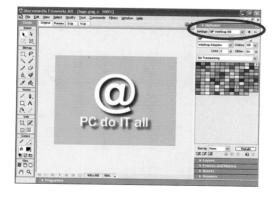

2 Set Color Depth

The color depth of an image is the number of colors available for the image. You can change the number of colors used by a GIF image; the fewer the colors, the smaller the file size. Note, however, that you might lose image quality by deleting too many colors. A GIF file can use a maximum of 256 colors, but you can choose a different number from the drop-down menu.

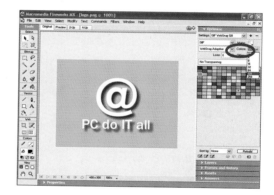

3 Set Dither

Adjust the **Dither** slider to determine the extent to which the browser can dither colors it can't display. The greater the percentage of dither, the closer the end result will be to the original. If the browser can't display a particular color in the image, it dithers (that is, it tries to reproduce the color using alternating pixels of two other colors).

Dither slider

④ Set Loss

Drag the **Loss** slider to reduce file size and quality. The higher the loss value, the smaller the file is and the greater the reduction in image quality. Any value over 20 is likely to result in a serious loss of quality, but a value less than 5 probably won't show much difference in image quality. Here you can see how much the image is affected by a loss of 100.

⑤ Remove Unused Colors

From the Optimize panel options menu, choose **Remove Unused Colors** to create the smallest image file size. All the colors left in the panel after reducing the color depth (Step 2) that the image does not use are removed.

⑥ Create Interlaced Images

Interlaced images appear in the browser bit by bit, the quality improving as each part of picture appears. An interlaced GIF file is always larger than a file that's not interlaced, but being able to display a complex graphic and then update the image as the file continues to download might be worth the additional file size. To create an interlaced GIF file, select **Interlaced** from the Optimize panel options menu.

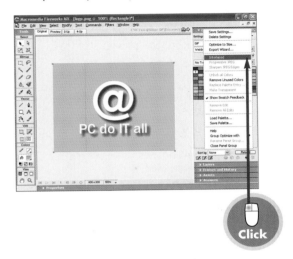

How-to Hint

Optimize a PNG File

When working with 8-bit color images, the options for GIF and PNG files are very similar; however, PNG files can be exported with greater color depth. The greater the depth of color selected, the greater the resulting file size, so use 24-bit or 32-bit PNG files only when you need to to retain image quality. PNG and GIF images both support the use of transparency and interlacing.

How to Optimize Colors

When you export either a GIF or a PNG file in 8-bit color or less, the file uses a color panel that contains the required information for the colors used and referenced in the image. This color panel is optimized using the color table. You are able to lock colors (so that even if you switch palettes they are not deleted), set the maximum number of colors, or even edit colors.

❶ Open a File

Open a GIF or PNG file for which you want to optimize the color panel. Choose **Window**, **Optimize** to open the Optimize panel. The default color panels listed in the Indexed panel drop-down menu are explained in the How-To Hints at the end of this task.

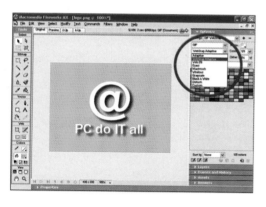

❷ Specify Color Depth

Use the **Colors** option to specify the color depth (the maximum number of colors) for the image file. The smaller the number of colors, the smaller the file size, but the more you might degrade the quality of the image. These changes affect only the image you export, not the original, so don't expect to see changes in the editing window. Click the **Preview** tab to view changes as you work.

❸ Examine the Color Table

The color table is visible so you can see all the colors in the panel. Change the Indexed panel option in the Optimize panel to change the display in the color table. Step 1 shows the WebSnap Adaptive panel's color table; here you see the Windows panel's color table. This changes other options, such as color depth, automatically. Refer to the How-To Hints at the end of this task for information about each panel.

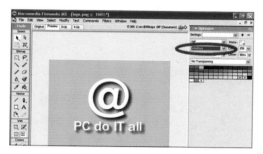

④ Lock and Unlock Colors

Locking colors into a panel ensures that even if you change panels, specific colors will be retained by the image. You might want to lock specific colors for an image if the image uses specific Pantone colors (as is true with many logos). Select the color you want to lock, and then click the **Lock** icon at the bottom of the panel. Select the color and click the **Lock** icon again to unlock this color.

⑤ Sort the Colors

By default, the colors in the table are unsorted; however, you can sort them by either **Popularity** or **Luminance**. Use the **Sort by** drop-down menu to change the display.

Color Panel Options

Fireworks ships with nine preset color panels and an option to create custom color panels. Each preset can be selected and optimized to suit your requirements:

The Adaptive panel is self-created based on the colors that Fireworks detects within your file. In most circumstances, an Adaptive panel produces excellent results—a high-quality image with a small file size.

The WebSnap Adaptive panel detects colors that are close to Web-safe colors and converts them in the exported file to the nearest Web-safe color.

The Web 216 panel uses the 216 colors available on both Macintosh and Windows computers. It's commonly known as a Web-safe panel and produces results that are usually consistent in all browsers. This panel differs from the Windows and Macintosh panels, which use the 256 colors available on each operating system.

The Grayscale panel uses a maximum of 256 shades of gray. Any image using this panel converts the exported image into shades of gray.

The Black and White panel uses only two colors: black and white. There are no shades of gray at all.

The Uniform panel is made up of the red, green, and blue (RGB) values of pixels in the image.

The Custom panel has been either imported from an external location or saved from a previous GIF image.

How to Optimize Using Different Compression Levels

One of the most appealing features of Fireworks is the fact that not only do you have total control over how to optimize images, but you can optimize the same image using different settings. In this task we'll take a photograph saved as a JPEG and save different parts of the same image with different compression settings. Why would you want to do this? When you take a photograph there is usually an area around the main focus of the picture that is less important, so it does not need to be so clear. This lets the visitor focus on the main subject of your picture.

1 Open a Photograph

Open or create a graphic that contains elements to be optimized in different ways.

2 Create a Marquee

Select the **Lasso** tool from the Tools panel to create a marquee that is going to be compressed. This will be the area away from the actual focus of the photograph.

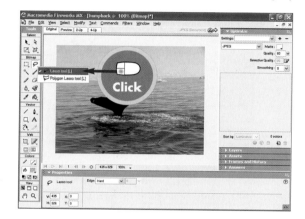

3 Draw the Marquee

Draw the area to be compressed on the photograph. You can see here that I have drawn around the humpback whale, making a marquee of all that really exciting sea, which we will compress!

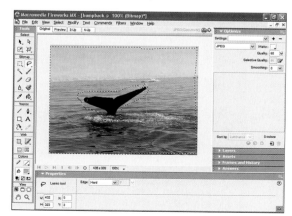

④ Create a Selective Mask

From the **Modify** menu, choose **Selective JPEG**, **Save Selection as JPEG Mask**. The selected area becomes highlighted onscreen, making the selection obvious.

⑤ See What's New

The Optimize panel is slightly different from when we have looked at it before. Below the **Quality** setting is now a new option called **Selective Quality**, which we'll use to optimize our masked area (the sea).

⑥ Open the Dialog Box

Click the **Selective Quality** icon to open the **Selective JPEG Settings** dialog box.

⑦ Edit the Settings

Change the number in the dialog box to reduce the quality of the area. Play with this setting until you're satisfied with the look of the image—you can go quite low on the quality here because this isn't the focal part of your photo. You can change the Overlay Color, if you like. The **Preserve Text Quality** and **Preserve Button Quality** options are selected by default, which is fine; although they aren't needed here, they're useful when optimizing images that are part of a navigation system or that have text on them. Click **OK** when you're finished.

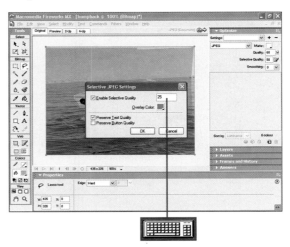

8 Preview the Image

As you are changing the settings, you need to preview the results in your browser window to see the effects. Either select **File**, **Preview in Browser** or press the **F12** key to see the image.

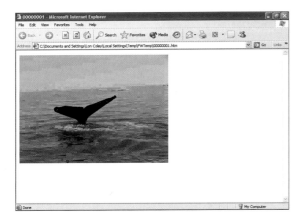

9 Making Changes

With the image still open for editing, you can modify your Selective JPEG settings by going to **Modify**, **Selective JPEG**, **Restore JPEG Mask as Selection**. Your masked selection will be highlighted again. You can now make changes to the size or shape of the selection.

10 Remove the Mask

If you decide you don't want to mask any of the area, and optimize it separately, select **Modify**, **Selective JPEG**, **Remove JPEG Mask**. The lassoed area will still be selected while in Bitmap mode, but clicking the stop icon at the bottom of the document window returns you to the original photo intact.

Export the Image

When you're satisfied with the compression settings and how they look in the browser, export the file to your Web site folder in the normal way.

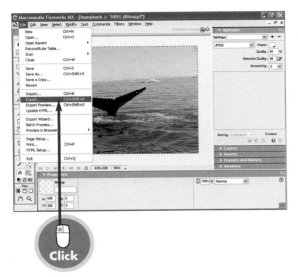

Task

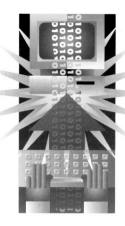

17

Working with Forms in Dreamweaver

Forms let you, the site owner, receive information from your site visitors. This information can take many different formats. From simple feedback forms to complete surveys, a form lets you find out your visitors' thoughts and feelings on any subject you choose to ask them about. The first Tasks in this part of the book look at the different options you have when creating a form in Dreamweaver; then you'll learn how to make a complete form using different form fields and layouts.

Before you get too carried away with forms, check with your hosting company about what it allows you to use. Although any type of form is usually acceptable, most hosting companies are a little more restrictive when it comes to scripts. Some companies give you lots of freedom, whereas others supply standard scripts with your hosting package. Be sure, for example, that if you want your form results to do anything other than come to you by email, you have permission from the host for the form to do so.

All forms need a handling script that tells the form what to do and where to go. Get this information from your service provider before you try anything too complicated.

All hosts accept forms in one format or another; the most basic form handlers accept user input and email the results back to you—you can do whatever is appropriate with the results when you get them. If you want the results of the form to go straight into a database, you will have to learn about Active Server Pages (ASP), the technology commonly used for database interaction. There are other options available for database interaction, such as JSP or PHP, both of which are supported in Dreamweaver but are outside the scope of this book. To find out more about ASP, go to your favorite Internet search engine and look up ASP.

Forms are contained within normal Web pages and are made up of form fields into which the user types information or chooses from selections you offer. You can use form validation combined with behaviors to make sure the user inputs the correct type of information. Behaviors are a combination of events and actions; in the case of a form, the act of submitting the form (an event) causes the script to check that the information is correct (an action).

How to Create a Form in Dreamweaver

Inserting a form on a page is incredibly simple, mainly because the form itself is merely a container. All the clever stuff is done when you start inserting form elements in the following task. However, before you can have form elements, you must have the form! This task explains how to get the basic form on a page.

① Open a Page for the Form

Open Dreamweaver and choose **File**, **New** to open a blank document window, or open an existing page to which you want to add a form. Here, I'm using an existing page that has my layout in place.

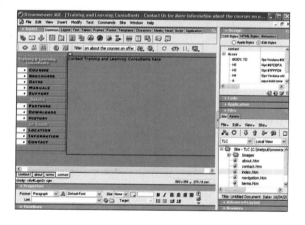

② Insert a Form Using the Menu

You can insert a form into the page by using the menu system or the Insert bar. To insert a form using the menu commands, choose **Insert**, **Form**. A default, blank form is inserted at the insertion point.

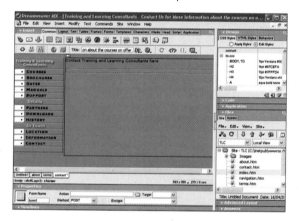

③ Use the Insert Bar

To insert a form using the Insert bar, you must first click the **Forms** tab of the Insert bar.

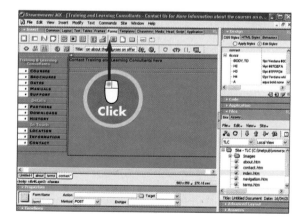

④ Insert a Form Using the Insert Bar

Click **Insert Form** on the **Forms** tab of the Insert bar. A default, blank form is inserted at the top of the page (or at the insertion point on an existing page).

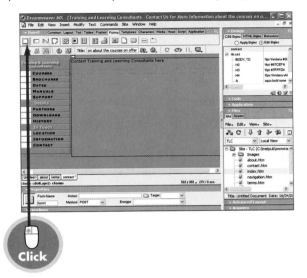

Click

⑤ Identify the Form

No matter which method you used to insert the form, the form appears in the document window as a series of dashed red lines and the form tag is added to the bottom of the document window.

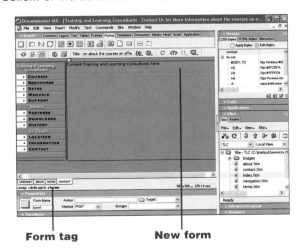

Form tag   **New form**

How-to Hint

Not Seeing Red?

If you can't see the red dashed lines that represent the form, open the **View** menu and be sure the **Invisible Elements** option has a check mark next to it. When this option is turned on, not only is the form visible, but any other "invisible" elements on the page are as well. These other elements include markers for named anchors, comments, and layers.

Place Your Form

In Task 1, we inserted a form into a blank page so the form appears at the top; however, when working with existing pages, forms can go inside tables or layers, or simply at another location on the page. Simply click in the location you want the form to appear and insert a form using one of the methods already outlined. The form appears wherever the insertion point was.

How to Insert Form Elements

*F*orm elements are the parts of a form—the text fields, check boxes, and radio buttons—that the visitor fills in or selects. Each element you can insert into a form looks and acts differently. This task looks at the different types of form elements and how to insert them into an existing form. Tasks 3–5 explain how to format the elements after you've inserted them into the form.

1 Insert a Text Field

Click inside the form area to position the cursor. On the **Forms** tab of the Insert bar, click **Insert Text Field**. A text box appears inside the form. These text boxes let visitors type free-form responses. Add a text label (by clicking the **Label** button on the **Forms** tab) to tell the visitor what type of information to add.

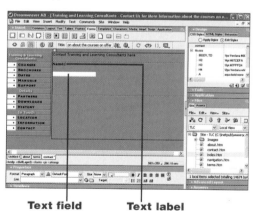

Text field   **Text label**

2 Insert a Check Box

Click inside the form box to position the cursor (press **Enter** to insert additional space between elements). Click **Insert Check box** on the Insert bar. A small square appears in the form. Forms typically use multiple check boxes when more than one answer is acceptable; a single check box is often used to sign up for a newsletter or sales materials. Add a text label to be sure visitors know what they need to do.

Insert Check box button

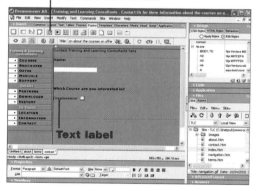

Text label

3 Insert Radio Buttons

Click in the form box to position the cursor. Click **Insert Radio Button** in the **Forms** tab of the Insert bar to insert a single radio button into the form. Radio buttons (sometimes called option buttons) are used when the visitor must choose only one of several options. You must group associated radio buttons together, as explained in Task 5, "How to Format Radio Buttons." Don't forget to add text labels to identify the radio buttons.

Insert Radio Button button

4 Insert a List or Menu Field

Click in the form box to position the cursor. On the **Forms** tab of the Insert bar, click **Insert List/Menu** to insert a menu or list field in the form. Whether the element you insert becomes a menu or a list depends on the settings you make in the Property Inspector, as explained in Task 4.

Insert List/Menu button

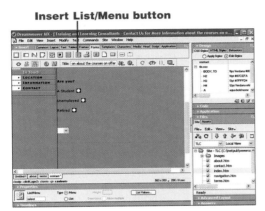

5 Insert a File Field

With the cursor inside the form, click the **Insert File Field** button. A file field is a specific kind of text box that accepts the pathname to a file or folder. It has a browse button with which the user can locate files or folders on the local machine. Forms use file fields so that users can specify the location from which they want to upload files. Before you use a file field, check with your hosting company to be sure your server accepts files attached to forms.

Insert File Field button

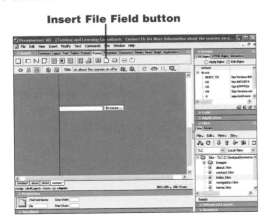

6 Insert a Button

With the cursor inside the form, click the **Insert** button on the Insert bar. Buttons perform actions such as submitting the completed form to the server or resetting the form. Edit the text on the button face to make it clear what the button action is. By default, the inserted button is a Submit button. The button properties determine what happens when the button is clicked.

Insert Button button

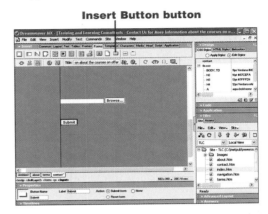

7 Insert an Image Field

Instead of Dreamweaver's standard gray buttons, you can use any appropriate graphic as a button for your form. On the Insert bar, click **Insert Image Field**. Use the dialog box to browse to the image file you want to use. You can attach behaviors to image fields and use them to perform other events; you learn about behaviors in Part 12, "Using Scripts and Behaviors in Dreamweaver."

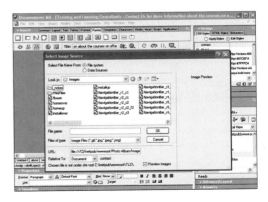

⑧ Insert a Hidden Field

Hidden fields usually contain information used by or saved by the server when it processes the form. The user can't see or change this information. To insert a hidden field, click **Insert Hidden Field** in the **Forms** tab. We'll look at hidden fields further in Task 7, "How to Collect Data from a Form."

Insert Hidden Field button

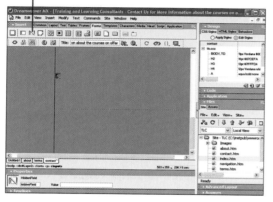

⑨ Insert a Jump Menu

A *jump menu* is a list of hyperlinks presented on the form as a drop-down menu. When the user makes a choice from the drop-down menu, a hyperlink is activated. Click **Insert Jump Menu** in the Insert bar to open the Insert Jump Menu dialog box.

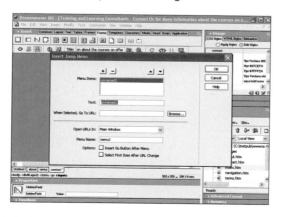

⑩ Specify the Menu Options

In the **Text** box in the Insert Jump Menu dialog box, type a description for the first link to be created. The items you place in the jump menu can be links to files within your own site or to external pages elsewhere on the Internet.

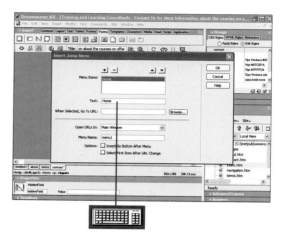

⑪ Browse to the Linked File

Use the **Browse** button to navigate to a file in the current Web site to which you want this menu item to link. Alternatively, type a complete Web site address in the **When Selected, Go to URL** text box.

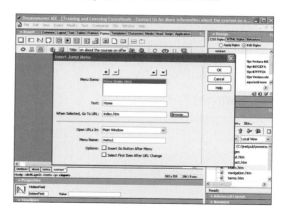

12 Add More Items

Click the **+** button to add the item you have just defined to the list of jump menu options. (Alternatively, select an option in the **Menu Items** list and click the **–** button to remove that option from the menu.) Repeat Steps 10 through 12 to add all the options and their links to the jump menu.

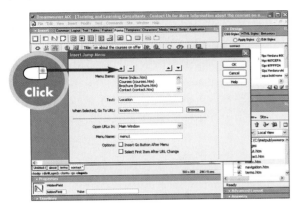

13 Put the Menu Items in Order

You can change the order in which the items appear in the jump menu. In the **Menu Items** list, select the entry you want to reposition. Click the up or down arrow button to move that entry in the list.

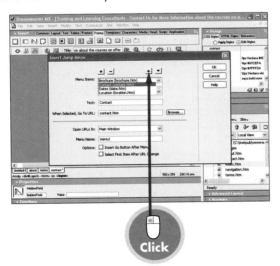

14 Target the Items

Use the **Open URLs In** list to choose where you want the linked pages to open. This option is handy if the page on which your form appears uses frames and framesets (as described in Part 6, "Frames and Framesets").

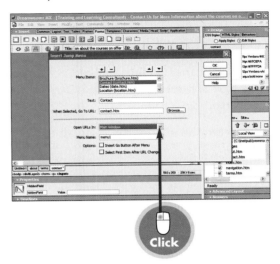

15 Set Other Jump Menu Options

The dialog box offers two other options: You can insert a **Go** button on the form that the user clicks to trigger the selected link. The **Select First Item After URL Change** option means that the menu reverts to the first item in the list after a hyperlink has been activated. If you use this feature, make the first item something like **Please Select One**. Click **OK** to close the dialog box and insert the jump menu.

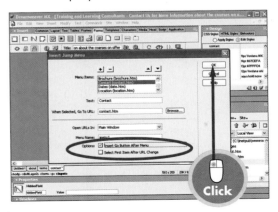

How to Format a Text Field

All the form elements you learned to insert in the preceding task have their own properties and features that should be formatted. You can control many properties of the form elements you've inserted, from the size of the element to the type of data allowed in the element. This task focuses on the Properties Inspector options for the text field element; other form elements have similar property options.

1 Format Text Fields

Click the form element you want to format. In this example, click the text box you inserted in the last task. The properties of the selected element appear in the Property Inspector. (If the Property Inspector isn't displayed, choose **Window, Properties** to access it.)

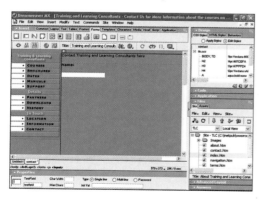

2 Edit the Properties

The **Char Width** field controls how wide the text box is in the browser; the **Max Char** field determines how many characters the visitor can type into the text field (regardless of the **Char Width** value). If the user types more than 15 characters, the text scrolls inside the text box.

3 Change to a Multiline Scrolling Box

Select the **Multiline** radio button to change the text field into a multiline box, which appears larger onscreen and lets the user enter multiple lines of information. Use the **Num Lines** field to specify the number of lines deep the box will be. (This value specifies only the number of lines shown onscreen, not the actual number of lines the user can enter.)

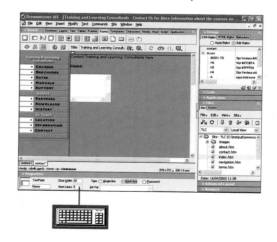

④ Change to a Password Field

If you enable the **Password** radio button in the Properties Inspector, anything the visitor types in this text field will appear as hidden characters when the form is viewed in a browser.

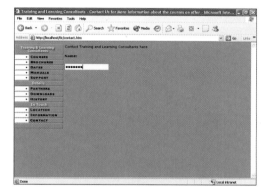

⑤ Set an Initial Value

The **Init Val** option lets you specify some text or a message that will appear in the text field when the page first displays. The text you specify in this field can act as a prompt for information, as it does in this example. Visitors can select and delete the text before typing their own response.

How-to Hint

Text Fields Galore

Although this task used only one text field to demonstrate the concept of text fields, your forms can use as many text fields as you like. Most forms have many text fields, each designed to contain specific information such as first name, last name, and the numerous fields typically used to accept different parts of an address. Splitting information in this way makes it much easier to use the information after you receive it.

Looking Good

Don't forget to use the skills you just learned. Not all text fields have to be the same size: If you have only a little space to display the field, make the width smaller—the text will scroll inside the field if it has to.

How to Format a Menu or List

Menus and lists have similar physical appearances, so let's first establish the differences between them. A menu appears as a drop-down list from which only one option can be selected. A list does not have a drop-down arrow and can be set to allow the visitor to select more than one item. Although this task focuses on the creation of a menu, you can follow the same steps to create a list if you first select the **List** option in the Properties Inspector.

❶ Look at the Properties

Click to select the menu or list element you want to format. The properties of the selected menu are displayed in the Properties Inspector. Give the element a unique name by typing it in the **Menu/List** box.

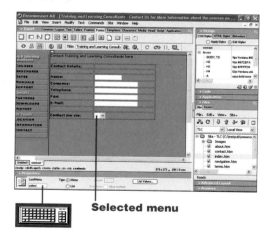

Selected menu

❷ Decide on the Type

The two **Type** radio buttons determine whether you are creating a list or a menu. For this task, we create a menu, so click the **Menu** button.

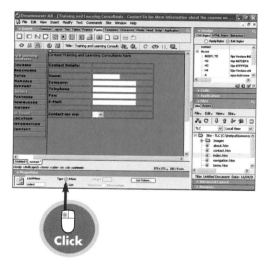

Click

❸ Open the List Values Dialog Box

Any list or menu needs items for the user to choose from. In the Property Inspector, click the **List Values** button.

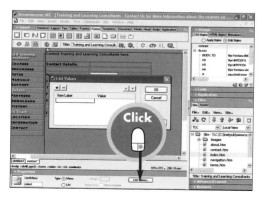

Click

4 Add List Items

In the dialog box, click in the **Item Label** column and type the text for the first entry in the list. Press **Tab** to move to the **Value** column and type a label for that entry. (The Value can be abbreviated but must remain relevant to the Item Label.) **Item Label** column entries appear in the list box displayed to the visitor; Value column entries are submitted with the form.

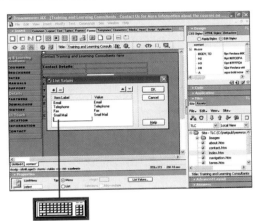

5 Change the List

You can use the **+** and **–** buttons in the List Values dialog box to delete and add the items in the list. The up and down arrows let you change the order of the list items. When you are done adding items, click **OK** to close the List Values dialog box.

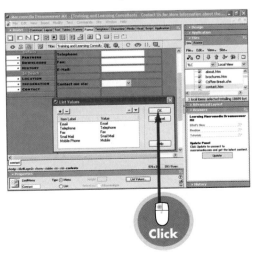

6 Preview the Menu

Preview the page in your browser to see the menu working. You can check that the items are in the order you want. Notice that the menu expands to the width of the longest item.

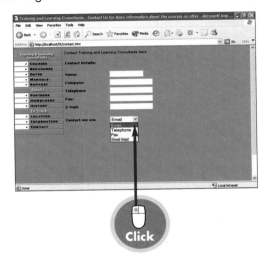

How-to Hint

Give the Visitor Instructions

When creating lists, you can choose to allow multiple selections; however, it isn't always obvious to site visitors that they can make more than one selection from this type of list. Be sure your page clearly explains that visitors can make more than one selection and that they can Shift+click or Ctrl+click to select multiple options.

Not Wide Enough?

When you insert a menu, it automatically resizes to the width of the longest item so that the item labels you entered are always visible. Unfortunately, when you use a list, this doesn't happen, and the edge of the text disappears. You can cheat a little: In the List Values dialog box, select the longest item (in terms of characters) and hold down the spacebar until you reach the end of the typing area. Then press the period (.) key. The result is that the list box expands by about three characters, and the end of the text is visible!

How to Format Radio Buttons

Task 5

Radio buttons are unique among form elements in that they come in groups of which only one at a time can be selected. In Task 2, you learned how to insert radio buttons into a form. In this task, you learn to format radio buttons and group them correctly so that only one can be selected at a time.

1 Space Out the Radio Buttons

In Task 2, you inserted a single radio button. As an alternative you can insert all your radio buttons at once using the **Radio Group** button on the Insert bar. Click the Radio Group button to open the dialog box.

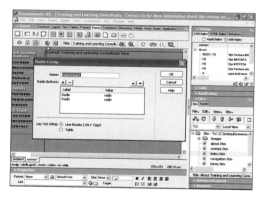

2 Name the Group and Add an Option

In the dialog box, type a **Name** for the group of radio buttons. Then click in the **Label** column and type the first option for the visitor to see.

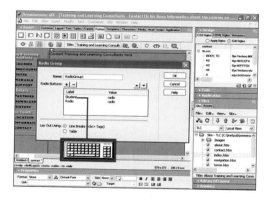

3 Give Each Button a Value

The value of the radio button is submitted with the form. Each button within the group must have a unique value. Click in the **Value** column and add a value for the option. This is the value that will be submitted with the form.

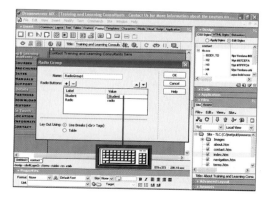

4. Add More Buttons

Use the **+** (plus) button in the dialog box to add more radio buttons and values until you have the complete list. Choose the layout option you want, and click **OK** to continue.

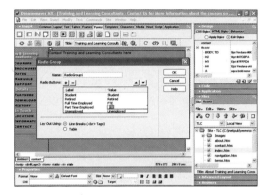

5. Decide on the Default Button

Only one radio button can be selected when the form loads (by default, Dreamweaver loads the form with all the buttons deselected). If you want a particular button to appear selected when the form loads, select that radio button in the form and enable the **Checked** option in the Property Inspector.

Click

6. Preview and Test the Form

Load the form page into a browser and click the different radio buttons in the group to make sure that only one can be selected at a time. If you can select more than one radio button, go back to Dreamweaver and check that the **RadioButton** text box has exactly the same name for each radio button in the group.

How to Use Behaviors with Forms

A behavior can be set up with a form to check that the visitor has entered the right kind of information in each field and to ensure that necessary information has not been missed. This process is called *form field validation*. The form is checked when the visitor clicks the **Submit** button. If the site visitor attempts to submit a validated form without first entering the correct type of information, an error message displays. He must correctly complete the validation fields before the form can be submitted successfully.

1 Select the Form

Suppose you want to make sure a text field on your form that asks for an email address is correctly filled out (the response must contain an @ symbol). When you work with behaviors in forms, you must first select the entire form. Click the `<form>` tag at the bottom of the document window to select the entire form.

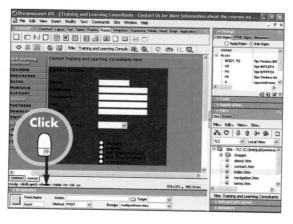

2 Open the Behaviors Panel

Choose **Window**, **Behaviors** to open the Behaviors panel.

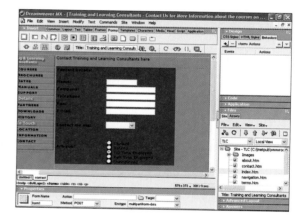

3 Choose Validate

Click the + button on the Behaviors panel and choose **Validate Form** from the menu. The Validate Form dialog box opens.

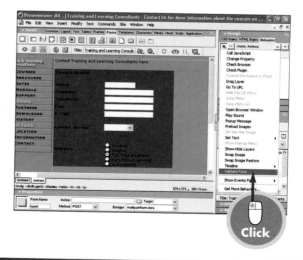

4 Pick the Fields to Validate

The **Named Fields** list contains a list of all the named form elements in your form. Click to select the field you want to validate (in this example, it's a text field with the name Email). Enable the **Value: Required** check box if you don't want the form to be submitted unless the visitor has typed some information in this field.

5 Make It an Email Field

After you have made the field required, be sure the form handler looks for the required @ symbol in the response the visitor types into the field by clicking the **Email Address** radio button in the **Accept:** section of the dialog box. Now the visitor's browser will not submit the form until the text in this field includes an @ symbol.

6 Validate a Telephone Field

Using the same Validate Form dialog box, you can validate other form elements. Select the name of the field you want to require the visitor to complete and enable the **Value: Required** check box for that field. For a field that asks the visitor to type a number (such as for a telephone number field), you can make sure that what the visitor types is indeed a number (and not text or other characters) by enabling the **Number** radio button.

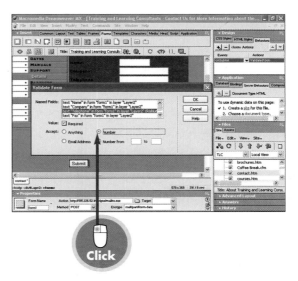

How-to Hint

Don't Go Mad with Validation!

It's all well and good to make sure that visitors provide the information you want in your form, but don't force them to tell you too much or most people will simply ignore the form completely! Don't validate fields that might not be relevant to everyone (not everyone has a cell phone or a fax machine, for example, so don't make these required fields). Validate only the information that's vital to the success of the form.

How to Collect Data from a Form

When a visitor to your form clicks the **Submit** button, what happens to the data? To receive results from your form, you need a form handler. A *form handler* is a program (usually a CGI script) that tells the server what to do with the information when a visitor submits the form. The program runs on the server and is not part of an HTML page. Fortunately, if you're not a CGI script programmer (and don't want to learn), you can download some basic form handlers that will get the form data from the visitor to you.

❶ Check with Your Service Provider

Most Internet service providers supply form-handling scripts that come with instructions on how to use them. Check the home page for your ISP to see what your hosting company says about forms. This figure shows some information about forms from the ISP I use.

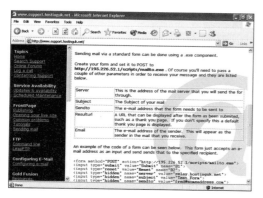

❷ Download a Form Handler

Although form handlers can be complicated, don't worry. Many places on the Internet, including most ISPs, offer free scripts you can download to use with your Dreamweaver forms. Make sure your ISP allows you to add these scripts to your server; many ISPs restrict you to using their own scripts. Here you can see a search results page offering many alternatives.

❸ Configure the Script

To configure the script to work with your form, start by opening the form in Dreamweaver. Click the `<form>` tag at the bottom of the screen to select the entire form. From the **Method** drop-down menu in the Property Inspector, choose the form method, which states what you want the form to do when the **Submit** button is clicked. Typically, you select **POST** (the documentation that came with your form handler script will clarify what you should select).

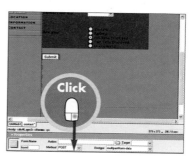

4 Set the Action

When the **Method** field is set to **POST**, the **Action** field typically contains the URL to which the form should be sent (usually the location of the handling script). The URL is usually supplied with the script. Type this URL in the **Action** field in the Property Inspector so that the form knows where to look for the script.

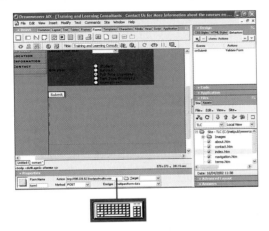

5 Customize the Form

Normally, you must customize the script to add the email address that the handling script uses to send the form results back to you. To do this, click **Insert Hidden Fields** from the Insert bar and complete these fields with the information required by the script (the documentation that came with your form-handler script will specify the information you must include).

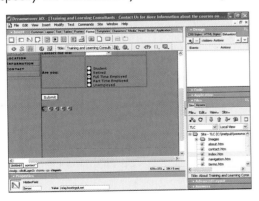

How-to Hint

Test It Yourself

Be sure you follow the instructions that came with your form-handling script; otherwise, you might never see results from your form and might think that no one is filling it out. Test your form fully before you tell others it even exists.

Capitalization Is Important

When you add hidden fields that contain email addresses and specify URLs in the **Action** field of the Property Inspector, be sure you use uppercase and lowercase letters very carefully. If you mistype one letter, your form probably won't work.

Form Buttons

Every form must have a **Submit** button that the user can click to send the contents of the form to you. By default, clicking **Insert Button** on the Insert bar inserts a **Submit** button. You might want your form to contain a **Reset Form** button that the user can click to clear the form and start again. Insert a second button and use the Property Inspector to format the button accordingly.

Task

Using External Media in Dreamweaver

By now, you have a pretty solid understanding of working with both Dreamweaver and Fireworks, but what if you need that movie file or sound file, sitting nicely inside your Web site? The simple answer is that you can use all those things right here inside Dreamweaver. The great thing about Dreamweaver is that it supports all the common media types—Java applets, QuickTime movies, and Flash movies, to name just three.

Inserting media objects has never been easier. The Media category of the Insert bar makes it as simple as a couple of clicks on a page. In many cases, not only is it easy to add, but Dreamweaver gets you right in there to add the code you need to show the element or placeholder onscreen.

You can even use Dreamweaver to create a Web photo album using the images you select to show off your family or demonstrate your photographic skills. You can see just how easy this is in Task 1. Starting with a folder that contains the images you want to display, Dreamweaver automatically creates thumbnails (small versions of your images) that automatically link to the full-sized image files.

How to Create a Web Photo Album

Dreamweaver makes it straightforward to create a Web photo album and guides you nicely through the process. Before you start, be sure the images you want to use are all within a single folder in the structure of your Web site. The Web photo album requires both Dreamweaver and Fireworks.

① Open the Dialog Box

From the Dreamweaver **Commands** menu, choose **Create Web Photo Album** to open the photo album dialog box.

② Add a Title and Headings

In the **Photo Album Title** field of the dialog box, type a title for your photo album. This title will display in a gray rectangle at the top of the album. Optionally, you can add a subheading and other information to display below your title.

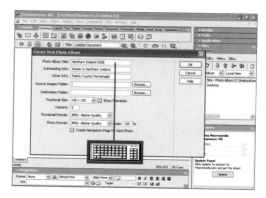

③ Locate the Images

Use the **Browse** button to the right of the **Source Images Folder** text box to locate the folder containing all the images you want to use in the album. These images should ideally be JPG files. Click **Select** when you have located the folder.

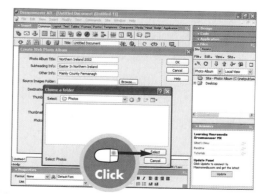

4 Choose a Destination Folder

Click the **Browse** button to the right of the **Destination Folder** text box to choose a second folder in the site structure to hold the images, JavaScript, and HTML that Fireworks will generate for you. If necessary, create a new folder for this information by clicking the **New Folder** icon and typing a name. Click **Select** when you're done.

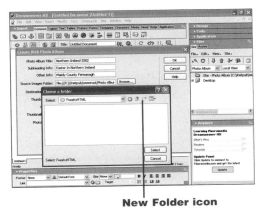

New Folder icon

5 Set Thumbnail Options

Choose a **Thumbnail Size** for the small images to be displayed—the default is usually fine. You can show the filenames on the Web page by checking the box. The images display in a table, so set the **Columns** box to the number of columns you want to use.

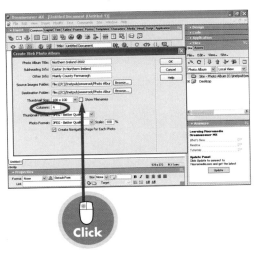

Click

6 Choose File Formats

In the **Thumbnail Format** and **Photo Format** boxes, set the file formats for the images. I recommend JPEG files for both options because this displays photos better, even though the file sizes might be larger.

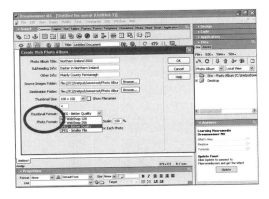

7 Choose a Scale

Set the **Scale** option for the larger images. Setting the scaling to 100% means that the large images will be the same size as the originals. Note that the scaling applies to *all* images in the album. If your originals are not all the same size, scaling can cause problems.

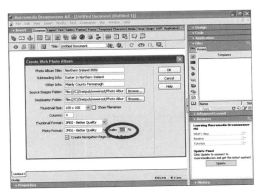

⑧ Set Navigation Options

Checking the **Create Navigation Page for Each Photo** option will create a Web page with navigation options for each large picture. Leave it unchecked and the user will have to use the Forward and Back buttons built into the browser.

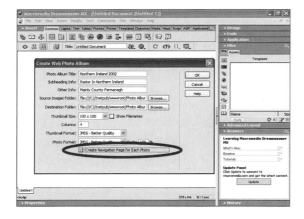

⑨ Processing Time

Click **OK** in the dialog box to continue. Fireworks launches and automatically starts processing the images from the locations you specified.

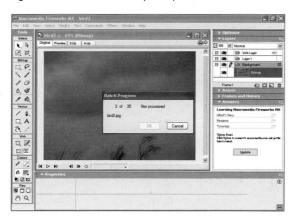

⑩ Album Created

After Fireworks processes the images, Dreamweaver automatically becomes active again, displaying an **Album created** message. Click **OK** in the message box, and Dreamweaver will create your album page.

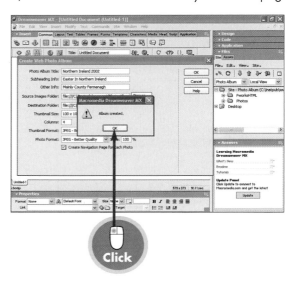

Click

⑪ View the Page

The album page displays all the thumbnail images. They are displayed in alphabetical order regardless of whether you chose to display the filenames.

⑫ Edit and Save

You can edit or format the heading text in the normal way to make it fit with the rest of your site. Don't mess with the images as this will cause JavaScript problems. Save and test the page. You have a complete Web photo album.

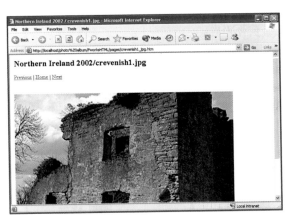

Task

4 Select with WHERE

You can put steps 2 and 3 together to create this query: SELECT FirstName, LastName FROM tlbstudents WHERE City=Leicester. Note that you do not have to show the City field to use it in a query.

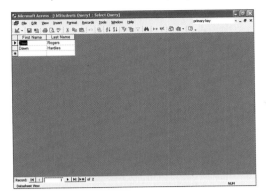

5 SQL Statements

A SQL statement always begins with a SQL verb. The following keywords are commonly used SQL verbs:

Keyword	Description
SELECT	Retrieves the specified records
INSERT	Adds a new row
UPDATE	Changes values in the specified rows
DELETE	Removes the specified rows

6 Statement Clauses

Use the following keywords to refine SQL statements:

Keyword	Description
FROM	Names the data tables for the operation
WHERE	Sets one or more conditions for the operation
ORDER BY	Sorts the result set in the specified order
GROUP BY	Groups the result set by the specified select list items

7 Operators

The following basic operators specify conditions and perform logical and numeric functions:

Operator	Description
AND	Both conditions must be met
OR	At least one condition must be met
NOT	Excludes the condition following
LIKE	Matches with a pattern
IN	Matches with a list of values
BETWEEN	Matches with a range of values
=	Equal to
<>	Not equal to
<	Less than
>	Greater than
<=	Less than or equal to
>=	Greater than or equal to
+	Addition
-	Subtraction
/	Division
*	Multiplication

How to Connect to Your Database in Dreamweaver

The steps in this task show you how to set up a database connection in Dreamweaver. To achieve this, you must have access to a server and have a Web site set up to connect to the server. We looked at setting up a site to use a server in Part 2 of the book. Servers are covered in more detail in the next part of the book as well. Here, we'll set up a connection to the ColdFusion MX server.

1 Open a Site

In Dreamweaver, open a site that has been set up to work with a server, and then display the Bindings panel. The Bindings panel shows the Document Type for your selected server—in this case, ColdFusion.

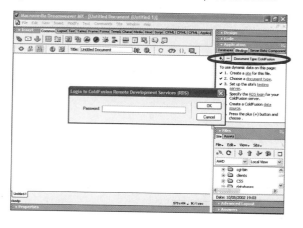

2 Enter the Password

For the ColdFusion Server, you need to enter the password you chose when you installed the server. Type your password and click **OK** to continue.

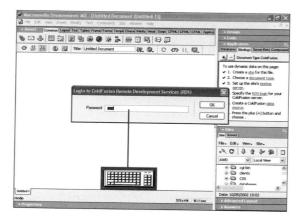

3 Log In to the Server

Click the **Create a ColdFusion Data Source** link in the Bindings panel to open the ColdFusion login screen. Enter your password, and click **Login** to continue.

4 Create a Data Source

In the Add New Data Source dialog box, type a name for the new data source. This can be a friendly name; I'm using **Students**.

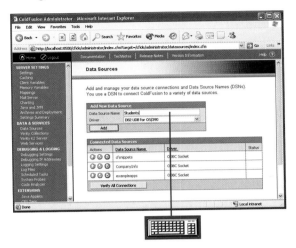

5 Select a Driver

Use the **Driver** drop-down menu to select the correct driver for your database. In my case, this is Microsoft Access. A driver enables your Web server to connect with your database and read the information from it.

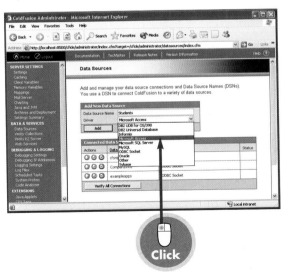

6 Add the Data Source

Click the **Add** button to open the Data Source dialog box. Click the **Browse Server** button to locate your database file. Select it and click the **Apply** button to continue.

7 Submit the Information

Click the **Submit** button. The screen will refresh and display a message saying, "Datasource updated successfully." The Connected Data Sources dialog box now displays your new database in the list of connections, and you're ready to use the database in Dreamweaver.

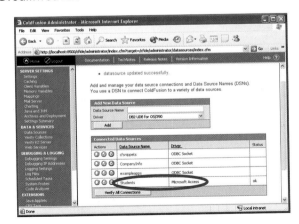

Dynamic Pages: Getting Started

In Part 19 we looked at the basics of databases, including making a connection to your database. Before attempting the tasks in this part you must be sure you are able to make a connection to your database (this was detailed in the final task of Part 19). Now we consider how a database can be used within your Web site to create dynamic content. Dynamic content is the ability to generate the content of your pages directly from a database. You create the skeleton of the page and the actual data is written only when the page is displayed in a browser. We'll look at the basics of extracting data from your database and making it visible to the world!

One of the great things about Dreamweaver MX is how easy it makes this process. When you add dynamic content into your pages, Dreamweaver writes all the code you need to store or display the information. In this part I'm creating ColdFusion (.cfm) pages; however, you can modify the instructions to work with your personal set up.

How to Get Started with Dynamic Pages

We looked at Dreamweaver behaviors earlier in the book, and now it's time to move on and look at server behaviors. These are prewritten pieces of code that apply the required logic to your pages. The server behaviors in Dreamweaver are designed to work with ColdFusion, ASP, ASP.NET, JSP, and PHP document types. Server behaviors can be added to your page either through the Insert bar's **Application** tab or the **Server Behaviors** panel. Let's look at the server behaviors available and learn what they do.

1 Create a Document

Dynamic pages must have the correct file extension. From the **File** menu, choose **New**. In the New Document dialog box, choose **Dynamic Page** from the **Category** list.

2 Choose the Page Type

From the **Dynamic Page** list, choose the appropriate page type for your server. (If necessary, check with your server administrator about this.) I have selected ColdFusion. Click **Create** when you have made your selection.

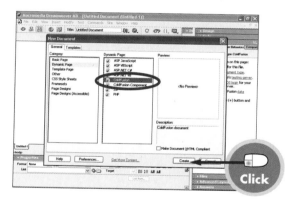

3 Save the Page

Save your page now. Choose **Save As** from the **File** menu. The **Save as type** drop-down at the bottom of the dialog box should display the page type you chose in Step 2. Type a name for the page in the **File name** box, and click **Save**.

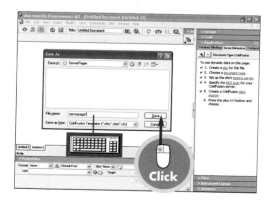

④ Add Page Elements

Add a background, title, and other standard elements to your page. Leave the area blank where you want your database information to be displayed.

⑤ Show the Server Behaviors Panel

In the Application panel group, select the **Server Behaviors** tab. It displays the information you created in the last task of Part 19.

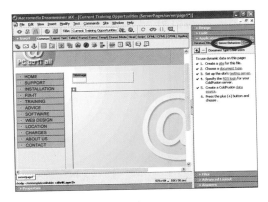

⑥ View the Server Behaviors

Click the **+** button at the top of the panel to display a list of the available server behaviors. The server behaviors are preconstructed pieces of code that allow you to make pages dynamic without writing the code yourself.

Click

How-to Hint

Definitions

The complete list of server behaviors is way beyond the scope of this book, but in the next few tasks we'll look at the most common ones. This will get you started in using dynamic elements in your pages.

How to Create and Use a Recordset

When using a database, the most important server behavior is the recordset. A *recordset* is data pulled from your database, stored temporarily in the memory of the server, and then displayed on the page. A recordset can contain all the information from your database or, more commonly, selected information that is relevant to a particular page. Dreamweaver allows you to create a recordset quickly and easily.

1 Open the Recordset Dialog Box

From the menu in Step 6 of the preceding task, choose **Recordset**. The Recordset dialog box opens.

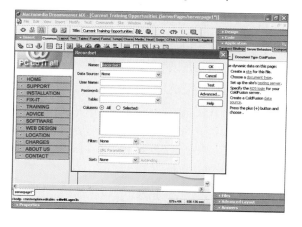

2 Name the Recordset

In the **Name** field of the dialog box, type a name for the recordset. This needs to reflect the data you are selecting. I am calling mine **Courses**.

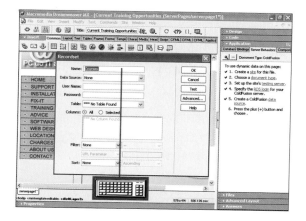

3 Choose a Data Source

From the **Data Source** menu, choose a data source to work from. This can be the data source created in the Part 19 or another data source you have.

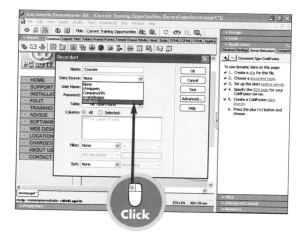

Click

4 Choose a Table

If you have more than one table in your database, use the **Table** menu to choose the one that holds the data you require.

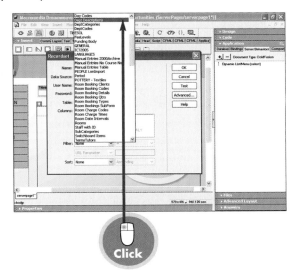

5 Choose Columns

Use the **Columns** radio buttons to choose whether you want all columns in the database to be used or to select only the ones you want. Ctrl+click (or Shift+click) to select multiple columns.

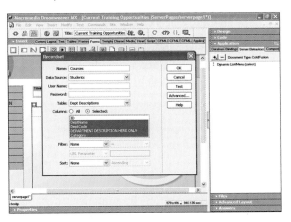

6 Sort the Records

You can use the **Sort** option to control how the records are displayed. Sorting can be set on any column in the table, even if it is not being selected.

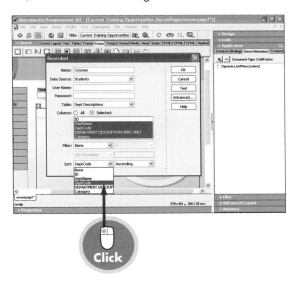

7 Test the Recordset

Click the **Test** button to view your selected data. You should see only the columns you chose in the order you selected them. The results should also be sorted according to your selection in Step 6. Click **OK** twice to close the Test box and dialog box.

How to Bind the Recordset

Now you have a recordset, but there's nothing on your page. Add a menu to your page that enables users to choose from a single column in the database. You'll let them filter the results that are returned. In this example, each course has a department ID, and that's the column in which you'll allow the user to make a selection.

❶ Add a Form to Your Page

Add a blank form to your page by clicking the **Insert Form** button on the Insert bar's **Forms** tab. A box appears with a dotted red line indicating it is a form.

Click

❷ Add a Table

Using the **Insert Table** button on the **Tables** tab of the Insert bar, add a table to the form. The table should have three columns and a single row, and can be formatted to suit your page.

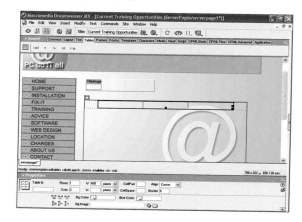

❸ Add Some Text

In the left column, add some text telling the visitor what to do. I am adding **Select a Department**.

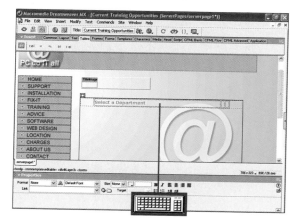

④ Add a Menu

In the middle column, click the **Insert List/Menu** button on the Forms tab of the Insert bar. In the Property Inspector, be sure that **Menu** is selected.

⑤ Make It Dynamic

In the Property Inspector, click the **Dynamic** button to open the Dynamic List/Menu dialog box.

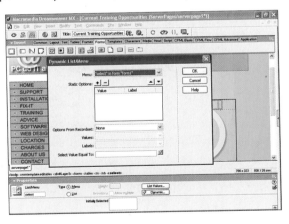

⑥ Choose a Recordset

In the **Options From Recordset** menu, choose the recordset you created in Task 2.

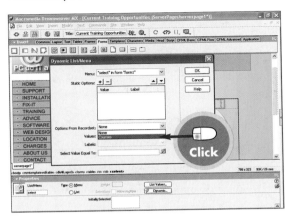

⑦ Select a Value

From the **Values** menu, choose a column from your table that you want visitors to use as selection options. This is the information that will be passed to the database as a query.

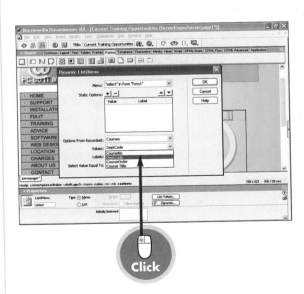

⑧ Select Labels

Use the **Labels** menu to choose the information that the visitor will see in the menu—this must be the same as the column you selected in Step 7. Click **OK** to close the dialog box.

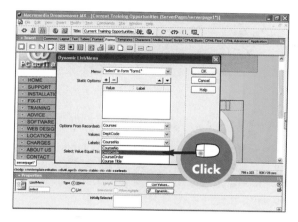

⑨ Notice the Changes

Now you are back on your page. Notice the menu is now dynamic. This is indicated onscreen by the menu changing to a blue color.

Blue indicates that the menu is dynamic

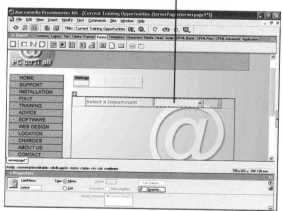

⑩ Add a Go Button

Click in the last table cell and add a button by clicking the **Insert Button** button on the Insert bar's **Forms** tab. Use the Property Inspector to change the button label to **Go** or **Select**; the button type remains **Submit**.

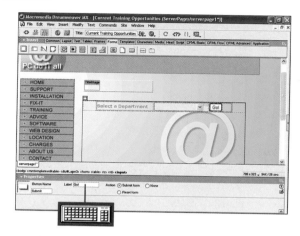

⑪ Save and Preview

Save your page, and then choose **File**, **Preview in Browser**. Click the down arrow to open the menu. The menu should now show the information from your database column for the visitor to choose from.

View the Code

Dreamweaver has added the required code to your page. Switch to **Code View** by choosing **Code**, **View**, and then scroll to the top of the page. You will clearly see the **<cfquery>** tag that has been added.

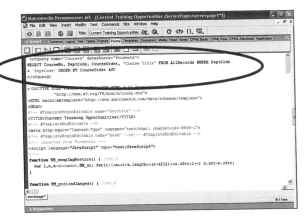

How-to Hint

Bindings and Sources

In this book we are only looking at the basics of dynamic Web sites and, hopefully, opening your eyes and minds to the possibilities they offer.

It's worth noting that the options available in the panels dealing with dynamic content change depending on the type of pages you are working with. Here, all the pages are .cfm; however, .asp and .jsp pages offer the facility to link to a related page. This is useful when working with search pages and you want to retain the search terms entered by a user between pages. Also note that when working with ASP.NET, the term used is *dataset*, not *recordset*—this can be confusing when you are used to using recordsets.

How to Create a Form to Display the Results

Now you have a page that lets the visitor make a selection from an automatically populated menu, but where do the results go? The answer is quite simple—wherever you want—although you need to create a page to hold them. This task shows you how to bind form text boxes to the recordset to see the result of the selection made previously. You'll use the page from Task 3 to send the selection to a second page, which will display the selected results. Start by creating a new page with the correct server type. Add standard formatting that you require.

1 Add a Form and Table

Click in the new page, and then click **Insert Form** in the Insert bar. Add a table with enough rows and columns to hold the data you selected in the recordset you created in Task 2, Step 5.

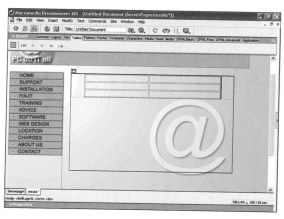

2 Add Text Descriptions

In the left-hand column, add text descriptions for the data that will be displayed.

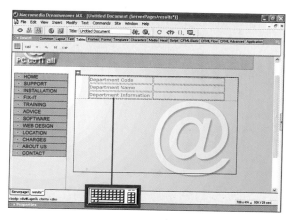

3 Add Text Fields

In the right-hand column add text fields or text areas from the **Forms** tab of the Insert bar. These will hold the information. For database columns with a large amount of data, use text areas.

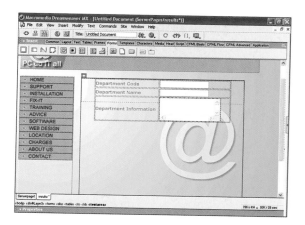

④ Name the Fields

Name each of the text fields or text areas to match a column name from the database.

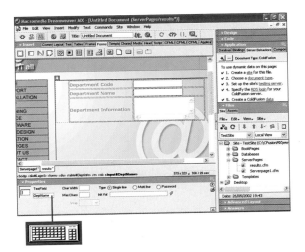

⑤ Create a Recordset

Select the **Binding** tab in the Application panel group. Click the **+** and choose **Recordset (Query)** from the list. The Recordset dialog box opens.

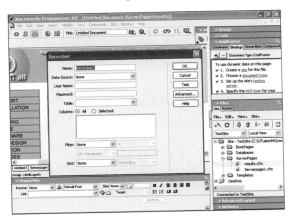

⑥ Name the Recordset

Give the recordset a unique name; I've named mine **CoursesRes** to indicate that it's used on the results page. Choose the **Data Source**, **Table**, and **Columns** used in Task 3. Click **OK** to continue.

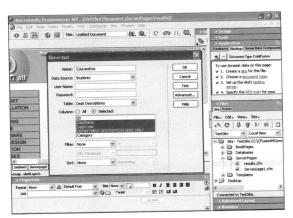

How to Link the Pages

You now have two pages that should work together; however, at the moment, they are not connected. In this task you will add the required information to use the original selection as a filter in the database and show the results in the second page.

① Open the First Page

Open the page you created in Task 1 and show the Tag Inspector by choosing **Tag Inspector** from the **Window** menu.

② Select the Form Tag

In the status bar of the document window, click the **<form>** tag. The Tag Inspector immediately jumps to the **<FORM>** tag (you can see it selected in the top pane of the Tag Inspector).

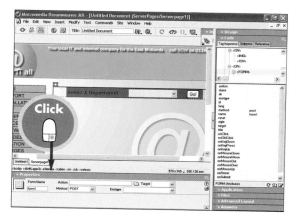

③ Add an Action

Locate the cell named **action** in the bottom pane of the Tag Inspector. In the cell, type the name of your second page (the one you created in Task 4).

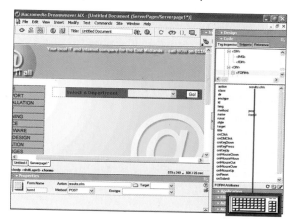

4 Change the Method

In the **method** cell change the value to **get** to tell the form to get the required information from the database.

5 Change the Name

In the **name** cell, change the name to match the column name used in the dynamic menu—in my case, this is **DeptCode**.

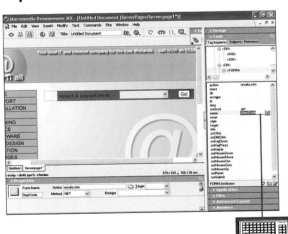

6 Rename the Menu

Click on the dynamic menu in the document window. The **<SELECT>** tag should now be selected (look in top pane of Tag Inspector). Change the name for the menu in the **Name** field of the Property Inspector to **DeptCode** (or whatever column you are using), and then save the page.

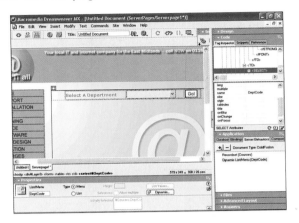

7 Open the Results Page

Open the page that will hold your results and double-click the recordset name in the Bindings panel. The Recordset dialog box opens.

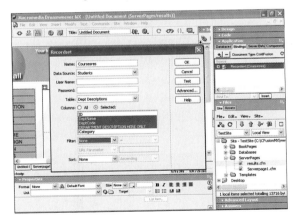

⑧ Add the Filter Information

In the **Filter** menu at the bottom of the dialog box, select the column name from the first page. The dialog box then completes the **URL Parameter** field for you.

Click

⑨ Bind a Column to a Text Box

Select the first text box; then in the Bindings panel, choose the matching column name and click the **Bind** button (the button is **Bind** or **Unbind**, as appropriate). The text field becomes blue with the recordset and column name in place.

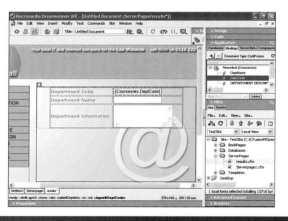

⑩ Bind the Rest

Repeat the previous step for the remaining text boxes, making sure that you select the correct column for each text box or text area.

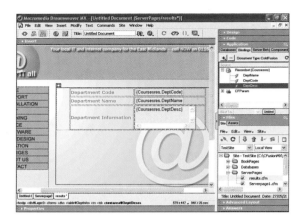

⑪ Test in a Browser

Choose **File**, **Preview in Browser** to open your first page in a Web browser. Make a selection from the menu and click **Go**.

Click

View the Results

The information based on the selection you made in the first page is now displayed in the text boxes and areas on the second page.

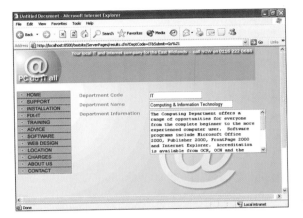

Making Changes

You can make edits to a server behavior's properties by double-clicking your selection in the panel. This opens the original dialog box you used to select the data. Simply change your options to update the page.

Moving On

These pages work together to filter the result from a database and are quite simple in terms of what can be done. I selected these tasks as an introduction, to give you some idea of what can be done. These pages could easily form the foundation of allowing users to edit records based on a username filter and so forth. Unfortunately, this book can't go that far, but it really is only a small leap to that level of user interaction.

Dreamweaver server behaviors offer many options for using dynamic data and user interaction. Spend a little time looking through the options, including building a search interface and building forms that allow users to add records to a database, edit them, and even delete them—all based on the permissions you offer! Time spent checking these options is well worth it for your development.

How to Create a Master/Detail Set

This task teaches you to create a master and detail set of pages, but first I'll explain what that is! A *master page* lists records from a database with only a limited amount of information. Each record displayed has a hyperlink on it, which takes the user to the detail page. The *detail page* contains more information about the same record. Dreamweaver makes creating a master/detail set straightforward—it even makes one of the pages for you. In this example, we'll display a code number for a course (which is unique) and the course title on the master page. The detail page will display the rest of the information.

1 Create a Master Page

Create a new page to hold the master records. Add page formatting to suit your site, and save the page.

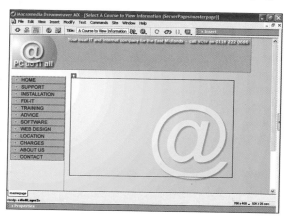

2 Create a Recordset

From the Bindings panel in the Application panel group, click the **+** button and choose **Recordset (Query)**.

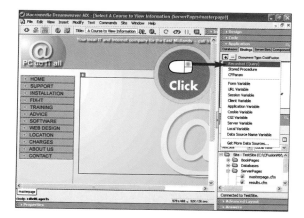

3 Complete the Dialog Box

Name the recordset, choose the **Data Source**, and select a table that contains all the information to be displayed for both the master and detail pages.

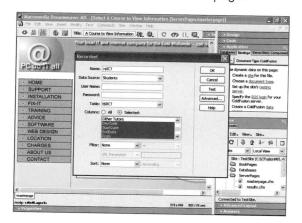

4 Add the Master Detail Page Set

With the master page open, choose **Application Objects** from the **Insert** menu, and then select **Master Detail Page Set** from the flyout menu.

5 Complete the Dialog Box

In the **Master Page Fields** part of the dialog box, select the fields from the recordset that you want to be displayed initially. In this example, I have chosen the fields **CourseNo** and **Course Title**. From this information the user will choose which record to view the details of. By default, all fields are displayed, so use the – button to remove unwanted fields.

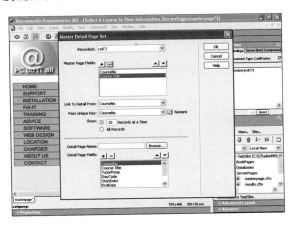

6 Choose the Link Field

In the **Link To Detail From** field, choose the field that will act as a hyperlink on the master page. This must be a field that contains unique values. If the field contains text, remove the **Numeric** check. Choose the same field in the **Pass Unique Key** field.

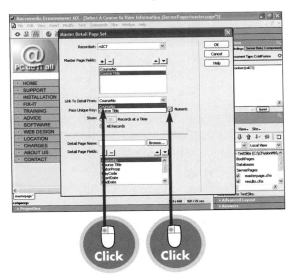

7 Choose the Number of Records

The **Show** radio buttons allow you to display either all records at once or any number of your choice. I'm choosing to display five records on the master page at a time.

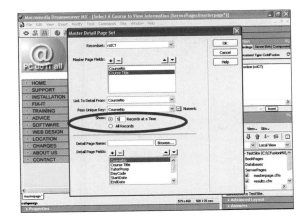

8 Set the Detail Page

In the **Detail Page Name** field you can either browse to a page that will hold the details or type a filename and let Dreamweaver create it for you. Be sure the detail page has the correct file extension; in my example, this is .cfm, indicating a ColdFusion page.

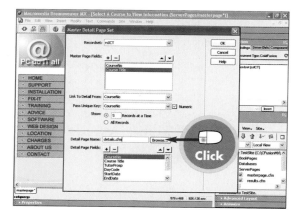

9 Select the Detail Fields

In the **Detail Page Fields**, choose which information is to be displayed. By default, this is all columns from the recordset, but you can use the − button to remove any unwanted fields. Click **OK** to continue.

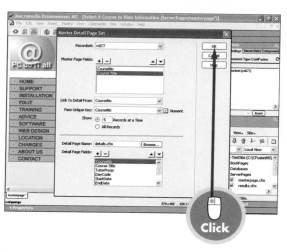

10 See the Result

The dialog box closes, and your master page now contains all the code to display your chosen fields. The page also contains recordset navigation controls to show more records. Save the master page and the results (details) page, which is created and opened automatically.

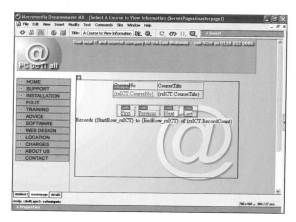

11 Preview the Pages

Choose **File**, **Preview in Browser** to preview the master page. Click on any of the links. You should be sent straight to the details for the selected record, as shown in the figure.

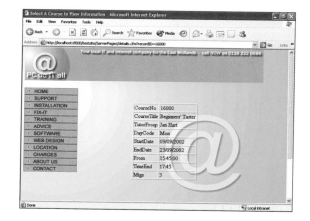

Format the Pages

Finally, format the generated fields and table cells to match your site. If you use style sheets, they can be attached to the pages to control the look and feel of the text. Once formatted, the pages are complete and ready to go.

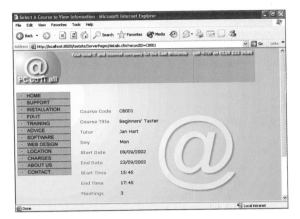

How-to Hint

Formatting Content

In previous parts of the book we looked at how to format your text, tables, and other page elements, and these formatting techniques still apply when working with dynamic data! Simply apply the formatting to a table or placeholder in your dynamic page and let Dreamweaver do the rest. When the page is displayed in a browser, your style sheet or other formatting kicks in and the page looks how you want—this makes the dynamic data fit in nicely with the rest of your site.

Formatting Data

Besides displaying the data from your recordset, Dreamweaver has built-in formatting options for different data types, such as dates and currencies. In the document window, select the placeholder where the dynamic data will display, open the **Bindings** panel, and locate the **Format** column. Expand the column using the down arrow, and then select the correct format for your data. It's easy!

Task

21

All About CSS

We've looked at using Cascading Style Sheets to set and maintain the look and feel of text on your pages—a nice easy way to control and update the entire text of a Web site quickly and easily. In this part, we look at ways that CSS can be used with other elements within your pages, such as tables, cells, and lists.

Many people don't realize that CSS can be very powerful in other ways as well. This release of Dreamweaver has significantly improved on the previous versions with much greater support for the use of CSS within your sites.

The most important thing to mention at this point is that although Dreamweaver lets you create CSS that controls things like page breaks and cursors in your files, they might not be visible to your site visitors. Many new developments with the standards of CSS have not yet been implemented into browsers. Be sure before you decide to change your cursor, or assume that a page will print correctly because you added a page break, that the page will work correctly in older browsers.

The final tasks in this part move on to using CSS-P, now integrated into CSS2, the latest developments in CSS that let you forget about tables in your layout and control the whole site using CSS! This section will not delve too deeply into what is a complex area of design, but hopefully it will get you started, and possibly encourage you to learn more.

How to Create a Prebuilt Style Sheet

The New Document dialog box in Dreamweaver lets you create a new CSS file to link to your site or document. You can create a blank file with a `.css` extension or use one of the inbuilt style sheets that ship with Dreamweaver. This task looks at the premade style sheets and how to use them.

❶ Open the New Document Dialog Box

From the **File** menu, choose **New** to open the New Document dialog box.

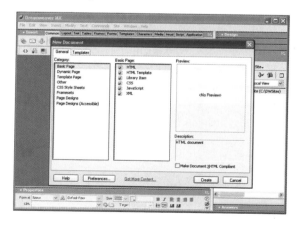

❷ Choose a CSS Page

From the **Category** list, choose **CSS Style Sheets**. The CSS Style Sheets list displays the names of the pre-built style sheets.

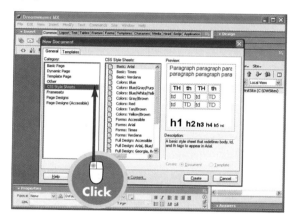

❸ Choose a Style to Use

From the CSS Style Sheets list, choose one you want to use. Click any of the styles to display a preview in the pane on the right. I've selected **Full Design Verdana Yellow/Green**.

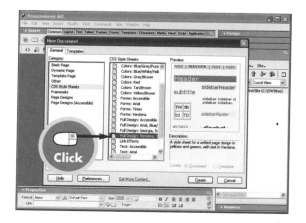

④ Create the File

Click the **Create** button at the bottom of the New Document dialog box. Dreamweaver creates the file and opens it in code view in the document window.

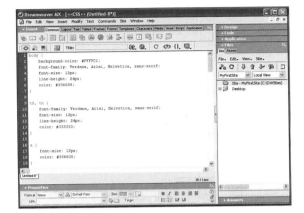

⑤ Save the File

The file opens in code view showing you the styles that are included. These styles cover the text, links, tables, and numerous other settings. From the **File** menu choose **Save As** to open the **Save As** dialog box.

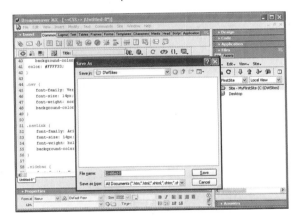

⑥ Name the File

Browse to a location inside your Web site folder, and then type a name for the file. From the **Save as type** drop-down menu choose **Style Sheets**. Click **Save** to continue and save the file.

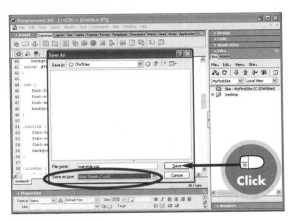

Choosing a Style Sheet

When you click a style sheet name in the New Document dialog box, a preview is visible as well as a small text description. These descriptions tell you a little about what each style sheet contains.

In this task, I chose a full style sheet, which has many elements and attributes defined. You can choose whichever style sheet suits you best. For the other tasks in this part, we'll use and then edit the style created in the Task 1.

How to Attach and Use the Style Sheet

After you've completed Task 1, you have a CSS file containing all the prebuilt design elements that Macromedia has added. Now it's time to use and edit the file to suit your layout, color scheme, and other needs. Start by creating a blank new document and saving it.

❶ Show the CSS Styles Panel

If it's not already visible, show the **CSS Styles** panel (in the Design panel group) by choosing **Window**, **CSS Styles**.

❷ Attach the Style Sheet

Click the **Attach Style Sheet** button at the bottom of the panel. This opens the Link External Style Sheet dialog box.

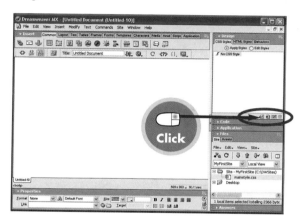

❸ Find the File

Choose the **Link** radio button, and click **Browse** to locate the style sheet file you saved in Task 1. Select the file and click **OK** to continue. Click **OK** in the alert box that appears. The file details are then completed in the Link External Style Sheet dialog box.

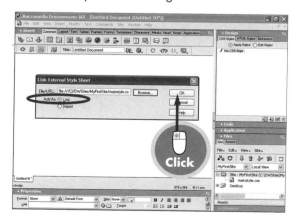

4 See the Effect

Click **OK** to close the dialog box. The document window refreshes with the style sheet now attached. Note that the background is cream, as set in the style sheet. The CSS Styles panel lists the styles from the sheet as well.

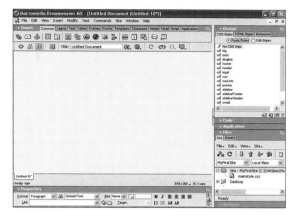

5 Add Some Text

The CSS Styles panel has two radio buttons at the top, **Apply Styles** and **Edit Styles**. The **Apply Styles** button lets you quickly and easily apply styles to selected items onscreen. Start by typing some simple text on the screen. The text appears in the color, font, and size set in the style sheet.

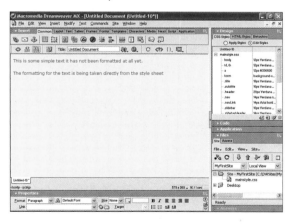

6 Change the Formatting

To change the formatting, select some text onscreen, then with the **Apply Styles** button selected in the CSS Styles panel, click a style to apply to the text. The display updates immediately. Here I've applied the **box1** style to a line of text. The status bar shows the style that has been used.

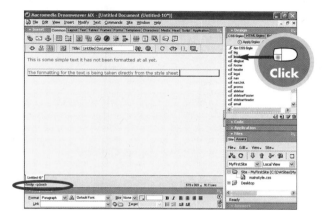

7 View the Styles

Changing any part of the Dreamweaver style sheet is easy. We'll start by changing the background color. Click the **Edit Styles** radio button in the CSS Styles panel. The display updates to show a list of the styles and their attributes. I've expanded the panel to make it more legible.

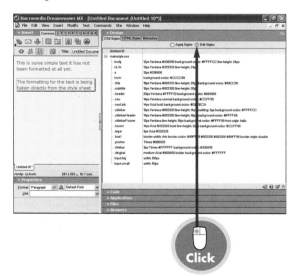

⑧ Choose the Style to Edit

The background tag is controlled within the body definition, so double-click **body** in the **CSS Styles** panel to open the CSS Style Definition dialog box. (The dialog box's title bar specifies that this is the definition for the body tag.)

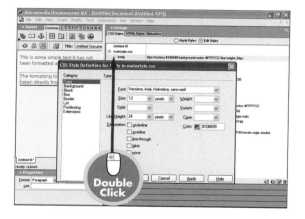

⑨ Edit the Background

From the **Category** list choose **Background**. The right side of the dialog box updates to show the background color currently in use. Use the color picker to choose a color that suits your site. If you want to use a background image, use the Browse button to locate it.

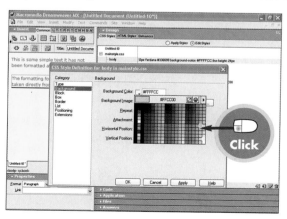

⑩ Edit Box Settings

Click **Apply** and then **OK** to close the dialog box. Now let's change the outline for the box style. Double-click **box1** in the CSS Styles panel to reopen the CSS Style Definition dialog box. Click **Border** in the **Category** list to see the current settings.

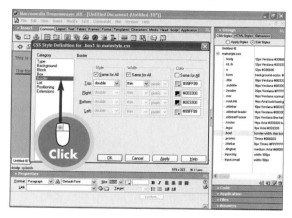

⑪ Make Edits

The Border style adds a box around selected page elements, basically putting a border around all edges to create a box. The initial settings for Style and Width are for the border to be the same all around with two colors alternating. You can edit these to match your site. Remove the **Same for All** check to set Style and Width individually.

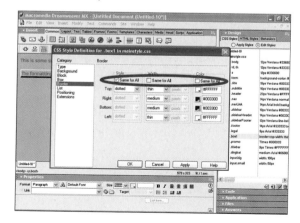

See the Changes

Some CSS Style options are not visible in the document window. If your file does not appear to display the way you expected, preview the file in a browser to see the effect. Here we see dotted lines.

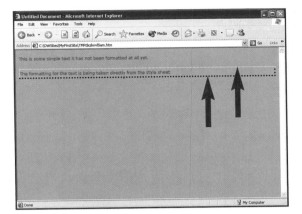

Boxes, Borders, and Blocks

The whole area of CSS is full of definitions, elements, and attributes—at times, it can become confusing, so let's try to sort out some of that confusion now. In Task 2 we put a box around an element using the **Border** category. That in itself might seem odd, so let's explain the uses of other categories here.

Block settings are used for defining the spacing and alignment settings for page elements and their attributes. You can set the space between words or letters in words using this category, as well as text alignment and indents.

Border settings, as in Task 2, enable you to set borders around any or all edges of an element, and to set color, size, and style of the borders.

Box settings are used to set definitions for tags that affect and control how and where elements are placed on a page, including the width and height of an element and the margins around it, as well as padding.

How to Format Bullets and Lists

We've looked at text and adding boxes around elements, but what about a simple list? Although Dreamweaver lets you change numbering options using standard HTML, what about the font, size, and shape? Let's look at those now by adding styles our sheet to cover these options.

1 Open the Definition Dialog Box

In the **CSS Styles** panel, click the **Edit Styles** radio button and double-click the style sheet name at the top of the panel to open the dialog box for the style sheet.

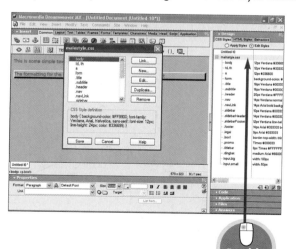

2 Choose the Tag to Redefine

Click **New** in the dialog box, and then choose **Redefine HTML Tag**. From the drop-down menu choose **ul** (unordered list) and click **OK**.

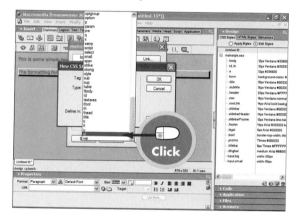

3 Add the Settings

Choose a font family, size, and color for the text in your bulleted list.

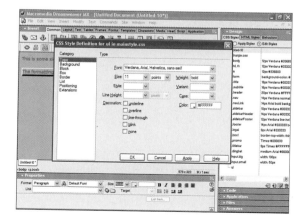

4 Choose a Bullet Style

Click **List** in the Category list, and choose a bullet style from the **Type** drop-down menu or browse to an image file that you want to use for your bullets. Then choose either **inside** or **outside** for Position (see the hint at the end of this task). Click **OK**, and click **Save** to continue.

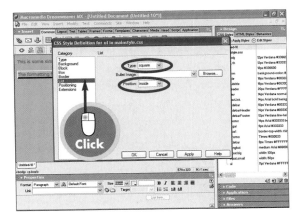

6 Numbered Lists

Set the formatting for a numbered list by repeating the previous steps but choosing the **ol** (ordered list) tag to redefine. Set the numbering style by selecting your choice from the **Type** drop-down menu. Use the style the same way you did for a bulleted list.

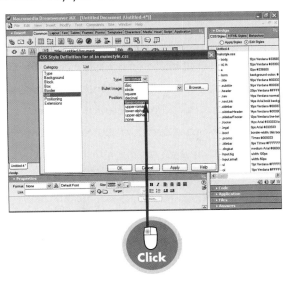

5 Format a List

Add some text to be formatted as a list, and then select the text in the document window. Click the **Bulleted List** button in the Property Inspector. The document window updates to show the formatting from your style sheet.

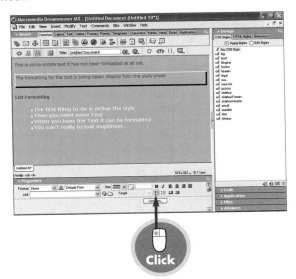

How-to Hint

Inside Out?

You saw the position options for the bulleted and numbered lists to be inside or outside. What do these mean? The difference has to do with an indent. When you choose **outside**, the text wraps in a hanging indent so that the bullet stands out from the text. When you choose **inside**, the text wraps to the left margin of the page, under the bullet.

How to Create a Layout with CSS

Formatting elements is easy with CSS, but what if you want to do away with tables and create a complete layout? The next few tasks look at how to achieve a two-column layout doing just that. There'll be a sidebar on the left to hold navigation information, content on the right, space for a page title, and a footer area. You'll need an image to use for the background. I'm using an image that's 140 pixels wide and 20 pixels deep. The width of your image must be the width you want for the sidebar. Start with an empty page, with no content or background.

1 Start with the Body

From the **Text** menu, choose **CSS Styles**, **New CSS Style** to open the New CSS Style dialog box.

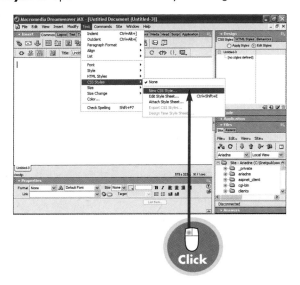

2 Define the Body

Select the **Redefine HTML Tag** radio button and choose **body** from the **Tag** drop-down menu.

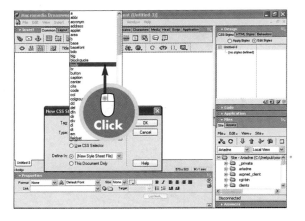

3 Save and Name the File

In the Save Style Sheet As dialog box, name the file and save it in a location within your Web site structure. Click **Save** to continue to the CSS Style Definition dialog box.

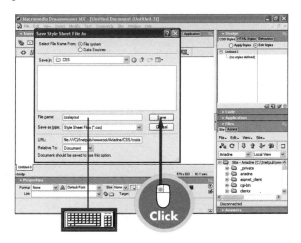

④ Choose Font Settings

Select **Type** from the Category list, and choose a font family, size, and color for text.

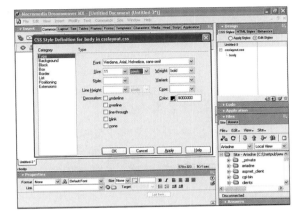

⑤ Set the Background

Click **Background** in the Category list, and set a background color for the page—this will be the area not covered by your background image. Use the **Browse** button to locate the image you want to use.

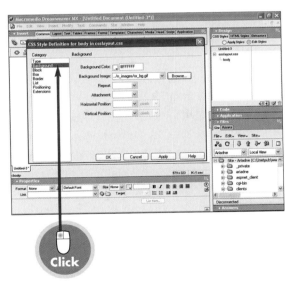

⑥ Set the Repeat Options

Because we want the image to appear on the left only, choose the **repeat-y** option. This sets the background to repeat on the y axis (up and down).

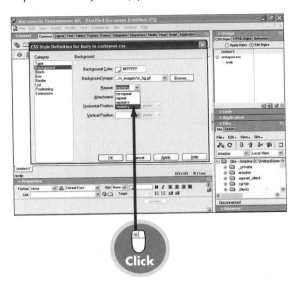

⑦ Apply the Styles

Click **OK** to close the dialog box. Your background should now appear as a sidebar on the left of the screen. Save the file before you continue.

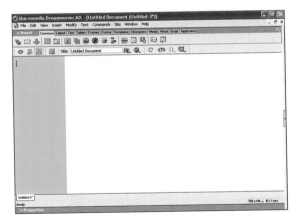

How to Create the Navigation Area

Before we continue to add to our style sheet, we need to ensure that the page displays correctly (there are known issues with Netscape, which I'll address). Then we'll create a style for the navigation area in our page and add that to the existing style sheet.

1 Add the Resize Fix

From the **Commands** menu, choose **Add/Remove Netscape Resize Fix**. This command adds JavaScript into the **<head>** of your file to ensure that it displays correctly in Netscape even if the user resizes his browser. Check out **Code View** to see what Dreamweaver has added.

2 Open the Style Sheet Dialog Box

In the **CSS Styles** panel, click the **Edit Styles** radio button, and double-click the filename for your style sheet. (Mine is **csslayout.css**.) The dialog box for the style sheet opens.

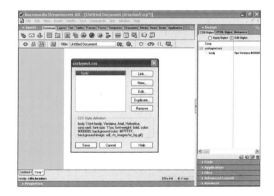

3 Add a Style

Click the **New** button, and choose **Make Custom Style (class)**. Be sure the **Define In** box names the existing **.css** file. Type a name for the class—something like **.navclass** is a good idea (note that the name must begin with a period).

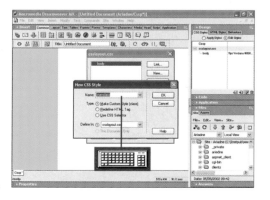

4 Define the Style

Click **OK** to continue and define the style. Select **Type** options for text in the navigation area. I am also choosing to set the line height at 115%, to make sure the text looks neatly spread out.

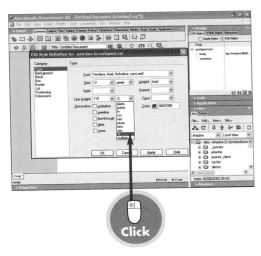

Click

5 Set the Position

Because the navigation area needs to be located where the background appears, we'll set positioning to be absolute. Click **Positioning** in the Category list, and then choose **absolute** from the Type drop-down menu.

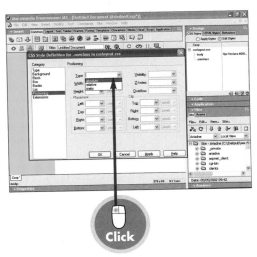

Click

6 Set Width and Height

The width of the navigation area must be less than the width of the colored area on the background. Type a value for **Width** and choose pixels. Set the **Height** to **auto** so that it expands to hold all required text.

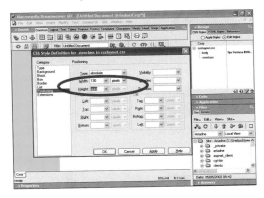

7 Set the Location

We want the navigation area to start just in from the left, so in the **Placement** section of the dialog box, set Left to **5 pixels**. Set Top to **20 pixels**; this starts the area 20 pixels down from the top of the page. Click **OK** and then **Save** to return to your document.

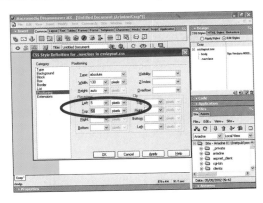

Continued **5**

8 Add a New Tag

Show the **Tag Inspector** inside the Code panel group. You will see the HTML tags for the page so far. Select the **<BODY>** tag, and then from the options menu, choose **New Tag Inside**, **New Tag**.

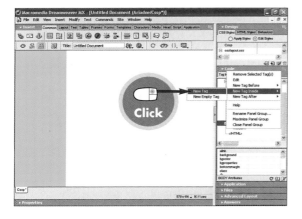

9 Add the DIV Tag

Type **DIV** in the box provided. Then, in the lower part of the Tag Inspector, find the class attribute for the tag and, on the right, type **navclass** (or whatever you named your navigation style).

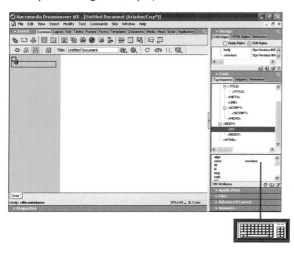

10 Add Some Content

In the document window, there is now an area representing the navigation class. Add some content here to see that it works correctly and does not spread into the main content area.

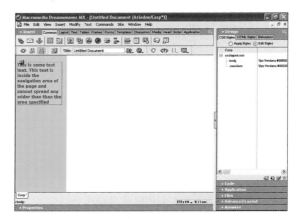

11 Show the Style Definition

I intend to add a logo in my layout, so the navigation area needs to be relocated. This is best done via the style sheet. Select the **Edit Styles** radio button, and then double-click the **.navclass** style to open the CSS Style Definition dialog box.

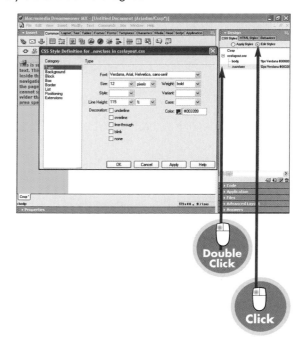

⑫ Change the Position

Select **Positioning** from the Category list, and change the values for **Top** and **Left**. Click the **Apply** button to see the dummy content update. Keep playing with the value until the location suits you. Now we're ready to add the main content.

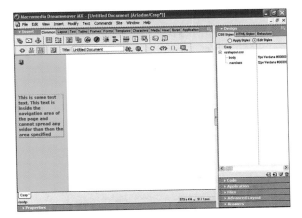

How-to Hint

Moving Content

Because this whole part is about styles and positioning, I deliberately used the CSS Style Definition dialog box to make changes to the position in Task 5. However, you can actually move and resize **Div** classes just as you would normal layers.

In reality, the **Positioning** category in the CSS Style Definition dialog box is used to take your block of text and turn it into a new layer. You could achieve a layered layout simply by drawing the layers onscreen, then moving them to your desired position and adding the content of your choice. Notice that the options in the **Positioning** category are the same as the settings available in the Property Inspector when a layer is selected onscreen.

Closing Tag

Notice that we did not type an end tag for the **Div** on the page. This is not a problem because Dreamweaver adds it automatically. Check the code at any time to see how Dreamweaver handles this.

How to Add the Main Page Content

So, we have a page with a background in place and space to add our links, but what about the actual content? That's coming next. Using another style, we'll position the main content away from the navigation area. Start by repeating steps 2, 3, and 4 of the previous task, only this time name the class **mainarea** or something similar. You can spread the text out or leave the line height as normal.

① Set Box Options

The main content area will be defined as a box, so click the **Box** category. Set a width for the content area. This can be a % or fixed width. I am setting mine to be **550 pixels**. Again, I'm leaving **Height** set to **auto** to allow for variable content.

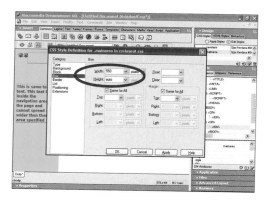

② Set Padding Options

Set options in the **Padding** section to keep content away from any border. I'm setting **Top** to **5** and leaving the **Same for All** check box checked to keep 5 pixels all the way around.

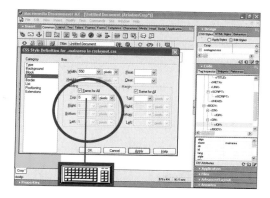

③ Set Left Margin

We want our content to appear to the right of the navigation area, so use the **Margin** options to set the left-hand position within the mainarea. Remove the **Same for All** check, and in the **Left** box, type an amount that's 10 pixels greater than the width of the navigation area (I'm using **150**).

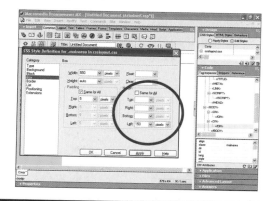

4 Set the Top Placement

Select the **Positioning** category and, in the **Placement** section, add a value in the **Top** field. This value sets the position of the content in relation to the top of the page. I'll be adding a page title, so I'm setting this at **100**. In this case, the content begins 100 pixels down from the top of the page.

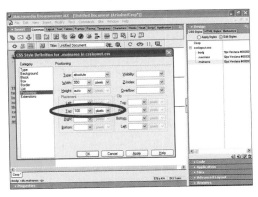

5 Add a Border

To add a border around your content, click the **Border** category on the left. Choose a style, width, and color for any border. Again, these can be the same on all sides or variable. I've chosen a solid thin border, but have varied the color.

6 Add Some Content

Add the **Div** tag and class name as in the previous task. Then add some content. For now, just add some dummy content as you did for the navigation area. This can be as much or as little as you want.

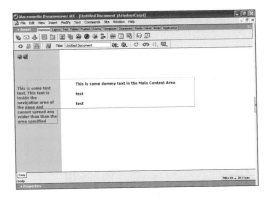

7 Preview the Page

Preview the file in a browser window to see how it looks. You should see the page as intended, even allowing for some of the box settings that might not look as expected in the document window.

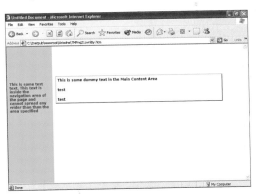

How to Add Headers and Links

Although there's no right or wrong way to add headers and links, some thought is required. The navigation area has a different background than the body text, so links must be different colors. We also need to add normal styles to our style sheet for lists and paragraph text. You can create custom classes or redefine tags for the normal elements, but you must create classes to hold any headings and footer text that you want. The final style sheet will be quite full, but you'll have a layout with no tables and with the elements exactly where you want them.

1 Add a Logo

Create a class style to hold your logo or welcome image. This element won't have text, so you only need to define size and position for it. After the **Div** tags are inserted, place an image inside the tags.

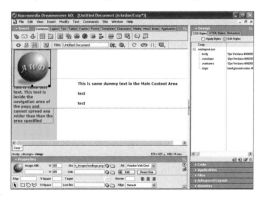

2 Add Some Heading Text

Create a class style containing font, size, and color information for your heading text. Because we want to position this heading, we cannot simply redefine an **H** tag. Set the **Positioning** to be where you want the heading to appear.

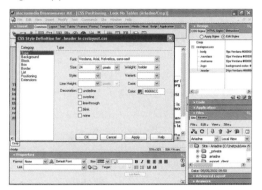

3 Define Link Styles

Create class styles for links. You will need to create **Link**, **Active**, and **Hover** classes for links in the mainarea and also the navigation area. For the links in the mainarea, you can use the **Selector** from the New CSS Style dialog box.

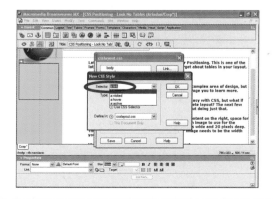

4️⃣ Define Navigation Links

Defining navigation links is a little more complicated. The link styles must have the states of **Link**, **Hover**, and **Visited** included, as well as a tag to indicate that they are links. Dreamweaver does not cope well with this, so we will add them manually. From the **File** menu, choose **Open** and locate your **.css** file.

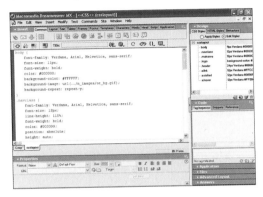

5️⃣ Copy the Link Info

In the style sheet file opened in the previous step, scroll to locate the **a: link**, **hover**, and **visited** definitions. Copy this part of the file, and then paste it into the bottom of the document. Then for each one, type **.navigation** after the **a** and before the **:**, as shown here.

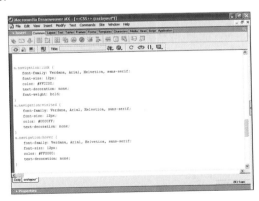

6️⃣ Save and Edit

Save the CSS file and return to the HTML file you've been working on. The new styles show in the CSS Styles panel. Although Dreamweaver doesn't let you create multiple definitions for links styles, you can now double-click each one in turn to edit the font, size, and color that you want in the navigation bar.

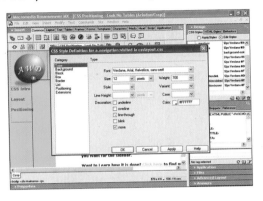

7️⃣ Apply the Styles

Add some links into the navigation area, click the **Apply Styles** radio button, and choose the navigation class. The navigation links will appear as you defined them. Save and preview the page. A complete page with no tables and two sets of link colors!

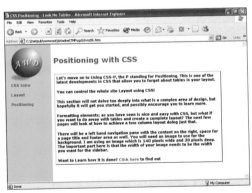

Task

Project Management

Managing your Web site or project is just as important as all the time and effort you put into the creation and design of the site. A well-managed Web site with easy-to-follow links and up-to-date information can often be the difference between a successful Web site and one that just bumbles along.

Making sure that your site is how it should be, checking links, solving any problems on the site, and uploading changes when required are all tasks that Dreamweaver can help with—but you have to know how to achieve these goals, and you need to remember to do them.

We've looked at the Site window in various parts of the book for different reasons, defining a site and creating files specifically, but now it's time to take that information and use it in the bigger picture. It's time to take the leap and use the site properly.

In this part, I'm working with a real Web site that starts with no files in the directory and ends up not only with files but live on the Internet. From testing a site to setting up the remote location to upload the files—it's all in this part. I'm deliberately using an incomplete site with broken links, missing files, and code that doesn't work in older browsers to show you all the error screens; I hope you will never see most of them!

When you signed up with your Internet service provider or Web host, it will have given you the necessary information to connect to its server for uploading your files, and usually a recommendation as to which FTP software to use. Using Dreamweaver, which has a built-in file transfer system, you don't need any other software.

Be sure you're connected to the Internet before you start this part; without an Internet connection you will not get very far!

How to Use the Site Window

Initially, the Site window is used only to show the files on your local machine—simply because until you create a remote site there is nothing to show. Earlier in the book we looked at some shots of a remote site already in use, but let's now look at the process of creating a remote site and making sure that Dreamweaver can connect properly.

1 Open the Site Window

Open the Site panel in Dreamweaver. Initially, all that's visible are the files within your site on your local computer. Click the **Expand** button in the Files panel to show the Site window, as shown in this figure. (Clicking the Expand button a second time returns you to the normal document view.)

Expand button

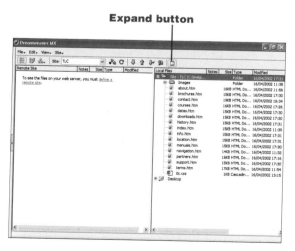

2 Define the Site Information

In the left panel of the Site window, click **Define a remote site** to open the Site Definition dialog box for the current site.

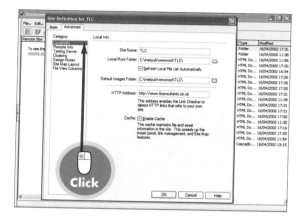

3 Edit the Site Information

Click the **Advanced** tab in the dialog box, and select **Remote Info** in the Category list to start setting up the remote information. Initially, the screen shows that you have no remote connection set up.

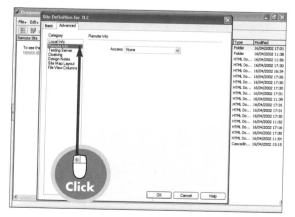

4 Specify the Connection Type

Use the drop-down menu and select the option for how you will connect the information. In most cases, this will probably be FTP. If you are connecting in any other way, check with your ISP or network administrator for information.

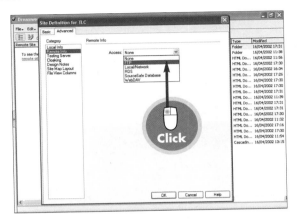

5 Complete the Dialog Box

Your ISP will have given you your username (login) and password, as well as the address for its FTP server. Complete the appropriate boxes with this information. Click **OK** to continue.

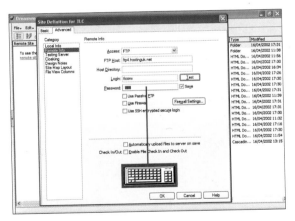

6 Connect to the Remote Server

Check that the connection is working by clicking the **Connect to Remote Server** button on the toolbar. The screen will refresh, and the left panel shows any files and directories on the remote server.

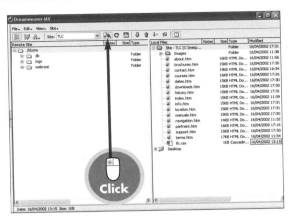

How-to Hint

Connection Problems?

Numerous things can affect Dreamweaver's capability to connect successfully to the remote server. Some of the common ones involve firewalls and speed of connection (FTP timeouts). If you're struggling to connect, check with your service provider or network administrator.

Dreamweaver has an FTP log file that can be accessed from the Window menu in the Site screen. The log tells you about any transfer errors, so it's a good place to start problem solving!

How to Test Browser Compatibility

Testing and checking your pages and links is a major part of managing any Web site. Throughout this book we've checked our pages, so you can be pretty certain that your pages look the way you want on the browsers that you have installed on your system. Dreamweaver lets you check compatibility on other browsers as well. The **Check Target Browsers** command in Dreamweaver checks your documents or whole site against the browsers you specify, finds any problems, and lets you decide what to do about them. It doesn't check any scripts in your sites, however.

1 Show Your Local Files

Open the Files panel group to the **Site** tab to show your local files. On a Mac, you will need to open the Site window.

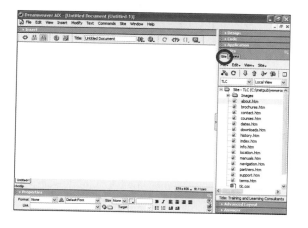

2 Select the Files to Check

In the Site panel, select the files or directories to check. (To select multiple files, use **Shift+click**.)

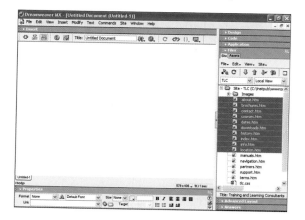

3 Check the Browsers

From the **File** menu, choose **Check Page**, **Check Target Browsers**. The Check Target Browsers dialog box opens.

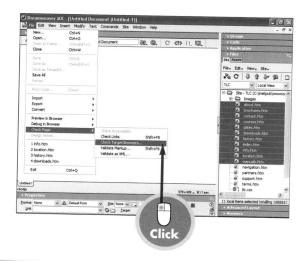

Click

④ Select the Browsers to Check

A complete list of available browsers appears. Select the browser that you want to check your files against. I'm deliberately choosing an older browser, which will throw up errors. Click **Check** to continue.

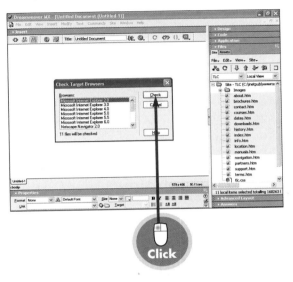

⑤ View the Results

Dreamweaver displays a list of results—the browser you checked against, and errors and warnings with the pages in which they were found—in the Results panel at the bottom of the screen.

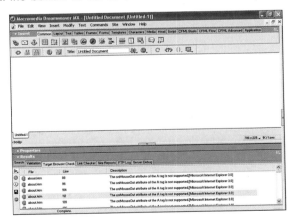

⑥ View a Page

The checked pages are displayed in the Results panel. Double-click a page name to open the Page View; the file opens with errors highlighted. Click the **Information** button to see the report about each error found in a new window.

How-to Hint

What to Do?

So now you have a huge report telling you about all of these problems. What do you do about them? The decision is never totally simple but is yours and yours alone to make.

If the errors only show as relating to much older browsers, you can decide that they won't affect enough of your site visitors to be a real problem. However, if the problems appear in reports for newer browsers, you really need to address the issue and make appropriate changes to your files.

How to Test Links

Testing links in a site to make sure they point to the right files and open in the correct window or frame is absolutely vital, as is keeping track of links to external files over which you have no real control. Site visitors expect your links to work, so be sure all internal and external links are working. Dreamweaver has a facility to check the links across your whole site and give you a list of any broken links it finds. In this process, Dreamweaver creates a list of external links but can't check them—this is something you must do manually.

① Check All Links in the Site

In the Results panel, choose the **Link Checker** tab. Use the drop-down to choose which links to check, and click the play arrow on the left of the panel.

② Choose a Report to View

Choose which links the checker is to look at; you can choose an open document, the whole site, or within selected files or folders in the site. As soon as you choose, the checker runs; its output is displayed in the Results panel.

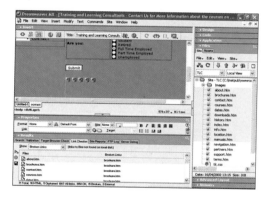

③ Fix Broken Links

In the Broken Links list, clicking any filename opens it for editing so that you can correct or delete any of the broken links. Here the link is pointing to a file named `brochure.htm`, when the file actually has an **s** at the end.

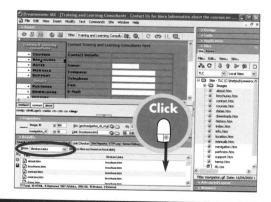

4 See External Links

The Link Checker screen can also display a list of the external links in your site. Although Dreamweaver can't check these for you, it's great to get a complete list. Use the **Show** drop-down menu in the Link Checker to see the list.

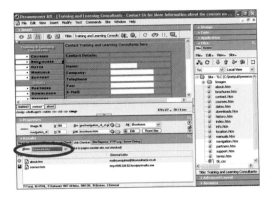

5 Save the List

You can save the list of external links for checking at your leisure—or to check that you haven't missed anything! On the Link Checker panel, click the **Save** icon to name and save the file.

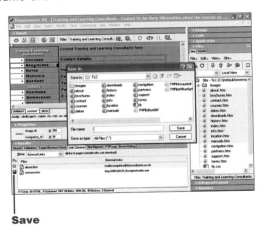

Save

6 View the File

The file is saved as a text file, which can be opened and viewed in any text editor, such as Notepad.

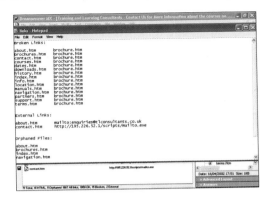

Orphaned Files

Dreamweaver has a facility to check the links across your whole site and give you a list of any broken links or orphaned files that it finds. (Orphaned files appear in your site but have no links to them from anywhere else.)

How to Upload Files

Uploading files to the remote server is usually a straightforward process of selecting files on the local machine and transferring them to the remote server so that they become visible on the Internet. Initially, you might want to transfer all local files, and subsequently only transfer files that have been modified since you last uploaded.

Although it's not a requirement of Dreamweaver, I recommend that you close any open files, or at least save them, before uploading. This ensures that the files you upload are the most recent versions.

1 Show the Site Files

Expand the Site panel to full screen by clicking the **Expand** button on the right of the panel.

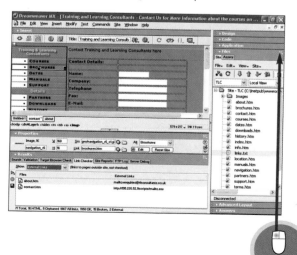

2 Connect to the Remote Server

In the Site screen, click the **Connect to Remote Host** button. You should be connected to the Internet before attempting to connect to the remote host.

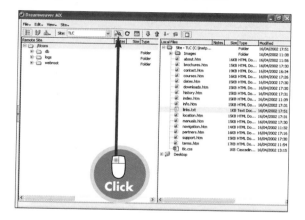

3 Select the Remote Directory

If the connection does not automatically show the remote folder you want to put the files in, select it by double-clicking the folder icon in the Remote Site pane.

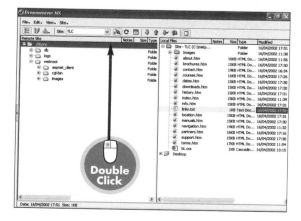

④ Select the Files to Upload

In the Local Files pane, select the files and directories to upload to the remote server. You can use **Shift+click** to select multiple files.

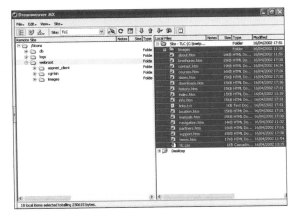

⑤ Put the Files onto the Internet

Click the **Put** button on the toolbar to begin the process of uploading the files. If you are uploading a large number of files—which is entirely possible when uploading for the first time—this could easily be a good time for a coffee break.

⑥ Watch the Status Dialog

The status dialog box shows the running progress of each file being transferred, including the filename, size, and progress. Dreamweaver continues until all files are transferred (the status bar stops being active) and your pages are live on the Internet. We'll look at the live site in the next task.

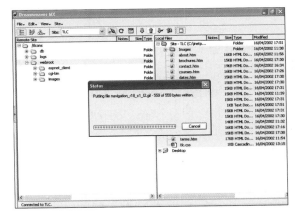

How-to Hint

Need to Stop the Transfer?

Click the **Cancel** button in the status dialog box at any time to stop the transfer of files to the remote server. Remember that stopping the transfer might lead to files becoming corrupt, so you should do this only if absolutely necessary.

Dependent Files

One thing worth noting is the concept of dependent files. Dreamweaver is able to understand from your pages which elements are required to make the page complete—for example, the HTML file alone would be a little empty without the images. These images or other external page elements are classed as *dependent files*. If Dreamweaver detects that you are uploading pages with dependent files, you will be asked if you want to upload these as well. In most cases you can say No—unless you have changed the actual image as well as the page.

How to Test the Site Online

Before you tell everyone that your Web site is on the Internet, go to the site yourself and check that everything is working as you intended. (In theory, your pages should be visible as soon as you upload them; in some cases, however, the service provider might have a caching system, which means your files won't be available until its server refreshes.) Note any errors that you find so that you can make the changes in Dreamweaver. The next task in this part deals with making those changes and reuploading as required.

① Open Your Home Page

After all your hard work, now is the moment of truth. Open your home page live on the Internet and just check that it's there! You should know your home page address, so type it into the address bar in the browser and away you go.

② View the Page in Another Browser

Open the page in a second browser and compare the output. The page should look the same in both. If it doesn't, you need to identify why and think about the page content and what could cause the differences. It's always best to check your site in more than one browser.

③ Check Titles and Alt Text

Work through the pages on your site and be sure that Alt text is visible for your images (be sure there are no spelling mistakes in the Alt text as well). Check that all your pages have an appropriate title in the title bar and that any rollovers on buttons work correctly.

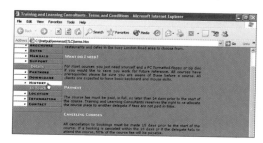

4   Locate Any Errors

Notice that there's at least one spelling mistake on this page. Make a note of any pages with errors so that you can edit them. Spelling mistakes are among the most common errors because even if you have run a spell check it will only have found incorrect words, not just ones "wear ewe have made a miss steak."

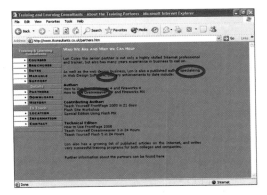

5   Locate Any Broken Links

Check all the external links on your site. Make a note of any that can't be found and, more importantly, why. You might have mistyped the link in the first place, so if you get an Object Not Found message, check that the URL in the address bar is the one you intended. Again, note any problems for editing.

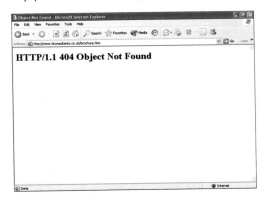

6   Check Download Time

Using a standard Internet connection (most likely a 56K modem), see how long your pages take to load; if any of them seem to take too long, check the estimated download time in Dreamweaver, and see how you can improve the situation—maybe delete some graphics. Remember that not everyone has super-fast Internet connections.

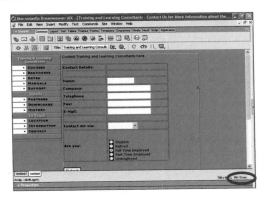

7   Check for Scrollbars

Ideally, your pages should not have any horizontal scrollbars (unless you planned it that way). Check the pages in the site and if scrollbars appear, identify the content that is causing it—it could be an oversized image or a table specified to be too wide. Here you see the effect of a table set to 600% instead of pixels!

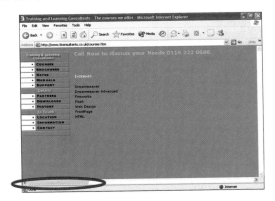

How to Change Pages and Synchronize

This task is about uploading your corrections to the Internet, so before you go further, work through the notes you made about errors during the previous task and make the required changes to your pages in Dreamweaver. Whenever you edit or create a file in Dreamweaver, the file is timestamped (the exact time and date the file is created or modified is saved to the system). The timestamp can be compared against the remote server, so you can make sure that you always upload the most recent version of files.

❶ Open the Site Files View

Open your local site in Dreamweaver and view the site files, making sure that you can see the Modified column. Notice that the time for the files you just edited is later than when you uploaded the files to the remote server.

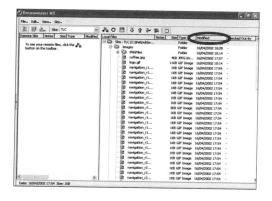

❷ Connect to the Remote Server

Be sure you're connected to the Internet, and click the **Connect to Remote Server** button to view the remote files as well. Here you can see that the time for some local files is later (more recent) than some of the remote files. In this figure, I scrolled the left pane so you could see the timestamps.

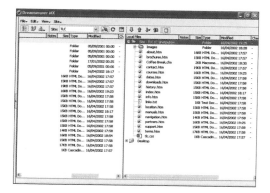

❸ Select Synchronize

From the **Site** menu, choose **Synchronize** to open the Synchronize Files dialog box. Synchronizing files enables you to make sure that the most recent versions of your files match on both the local and remote machines.

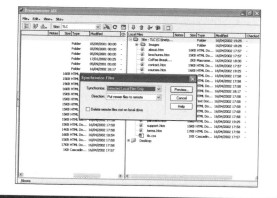

4 Choose What to Synchronize

From the **Synchronize** drop-down menu in the dialog box, you can choose to synchronize either the entire site or simply selected files. I'm going to synchronize the entire site.

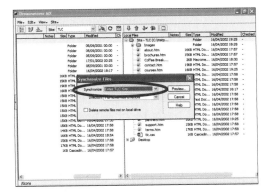

5 Choose the Direction

Using the **Direction** drop-down menu, choose to put newer files onto the remote server (upload your changes). Other options are to get newer files from the remote server or to put and get newer files, although neither is likely to be used when an individual creates the site.

6 Preview the Synchronization

Click the **Preview** button. Dreamweaver checks the files on the local system against those on the remote server, and a preview screen displays a list of files that are newer on the local server. Tick the **Action** box next to each filename to ensure it is uploaded. Click **OK** to start the synchronization.

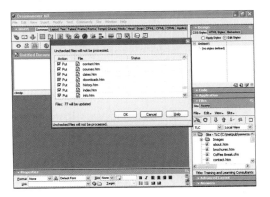

7 Save or Close the Log

Dreamweaver displays a dialog box telling you that the synchronization process is complete. You can choose to save a log file telling you which files were synchronized, or simply close the dialog box.

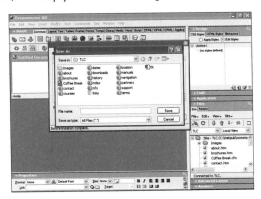

How to Use Check In/Out and Design Notes

Dreamweaver's Check In/Out facility is designed for when more than one person is working on your site. You check a file out to work on it and to ensure that no one else can open or edit the file until you check it back in. The options for Check In/Out must be set up before you implement it; we'll address that in the first part of this task.

Design Notes, saved with your Web pages, can contain any information—from reminder notes to a complete Web site plan to instructions for a team member—and integrate with Flash and Fireworks.

❶ Open the Define Site Window

From the Site panel's **Site** menu, choose **Define Site**. The Edit Sites dialog box opens; choose the site you are working on, and click **Edit** to open the Site Definition dialog box.

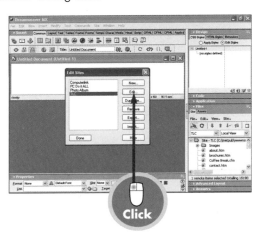

❷ Select the Remote Panel

On the Advanced page, select **Remote Info** in the Category list. In the Check In/Out section, put a tick in the **Enable File Check In and Check Out** box.

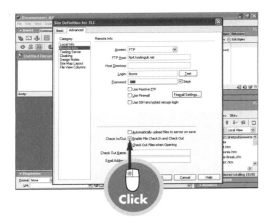

❸ Complete the Information

Insert a name and email address in the appropriate fields to identify yourself when checking files in and out. This information is required before you can continue. Putting a tick in the **Check Out Files when Opening** box means that the checkout process is automatic. Click **OK** and then **Done** to continue.

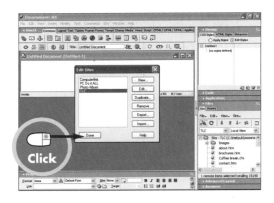

4   Check the Site Files View

The expanded Site panel now has two additional active buttons on the toolbar: Check In and Check Out. In the file list, any checked-out file has a tick next to it as well as the name of the person who's editing it. Clicking the **Check In** button checks the file back in so others can edit it.

Check In ——————————— Check Out

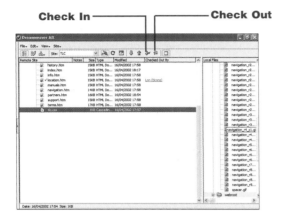

5   Enable Design Notes

Enabling Design Notes lets you share information about files with your co-workers. Open the Site Definition box and select **Design Notes** in the Category list. Check the **Maintain Design Notes** box. To provide co-workers with access to your notes from the remote server, check the **Upload Design Notes for Sharing** box. Click **OK** to continue.

Click

6   Add Notes to a Page

Open a file into the document window. From the **File** menu choose **Design Notes** to open the Design Notes dialog box. Type as much information as you want into the Notes field on the Basic Info page.

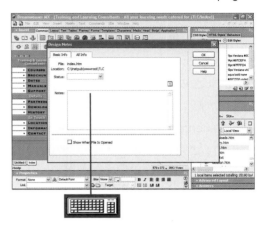

7   Complete the Dialog Box

Use the Status drop-down to define the development stage of your page. Check the **Show When File Is Opened** box to have the Design Notes display each time you open the file. The **All Info** tab shows you all the notes that have been added to the page. Click **OK** to save the information with the file.

Click   Click

Task

Applications and Beyond

By now, you should have a reasonable understanding of Dreamweaver MX and Fireworks MX, and a Web site that's ready for public consumption. So let's move on, learning more about Dreamweaver, Fireworks, and other applications that can help you develop and maintain your Web site in the future.

In addition to all Dreamweaver's built-in functionality within your control—from working with the different views available and changing them, to moving panels—and all the other topics we've covered so far in this book, Dreamweaver lets you manipulate the generated HTML code. You can change the colors of different sections of the code, making them more obvious if you're looking for something specific. You also can get add-ons (extensions) for the software from the Macromedia Web site. The new Reference feature lets you view the information for a specific tag or scroll through a complete alphabetical list and choose the tags about which you want more information.

The tasks in this part of the book show you how to make the code that Dreamweaver creates for your Web pages look the way you want it to when you view it onscreen. You also learn how to assign editors to non-HTML documents that you might want to open in Dreamweaver, and how to download and install new behaviors, or extensions, from the Macromedia Web site for both Dreamweaver and Fireworks. This book proves that you don't have to be an HTML programmer to make great Web pages.

You have, of course, seen references to Code View throughout the book. Learning a little about the code will help you understand what's happening in your pages and prepare you for the time when you decide that you want to manipulate the code on your own. A great thing about creating and maintaining Web sites is that they're never really complete—there's always something new to add, or new skills to use to implement changes and enhancements. The more you know, the more you want to learn.

How to Change the Code Layout

Dreamweaver MX makes it easier than ever before to check the HTML code and work with it as you create your pages. You can even work in a split-screen environment so that you can see the design and code at the same time. Keeping an eye on the code might not seem important to start with, but the more code you learn, the greater your understanding will be. Let Dreamweaver's built-in facilities help as you go—after all, that's what they're there for.

1 Open the Page in Code and Design View

Open Dreamweaver and open one of your pages. With the page open in the document window, click the **Show Code and Design View** button on the toolbar.

2 Adjust the Split Screen

By default, the screen splits in half, with the code at the top and the design at the bottom. Click and drag the middle bar up or down to change the screen division to suit your needs.

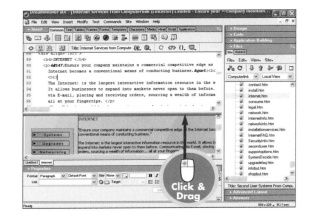

3 Open the Options for Code View

Click the **Options** button on the toolbar. The **Options** menu that appears lists several handy features you can use to arrange the code the way you want it.

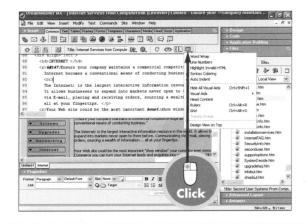

④ Set the Code to Wrap

If it's not already selected, choose **Word Wrap** from the **Options** menu to ensure that the code is visible at all times without the annoyance of a horizontal scrollbar.

⑤ Show or Hide the Line Numbers

Choose **Line Numbers** from the **Options** menu to show (or hide) the line numbers in the Code View. The line numbers appear on the left of the Code View window. This is a great feature when you're trying to deal with problem scripts that always refer to a line number.

⑥ Swap the Windows

By default, the code window appears at the top of the split screen; Choose **Design View on Top** from the **Options** menu to change the option; the windows are rearranged.

⑦ Set Syntax Coloring

By default, the **Syntax Coloring** option should be selected. Syntax Coloring highlights the tags and code in different colors to enable you to distinguish between them more easily. If this option is not already enabled, select it now.

⑧ Check for Invalid HTML

As I've mentioned before, Dreamweaver does not change any HTML that you have written in the Code Editor, which makes the **Highlight Invalid HTML** option such a bonus. If you enable this option in the **Options** menu, Dreamweaver will highlight any invalid HTML that you type, without actually changing it.

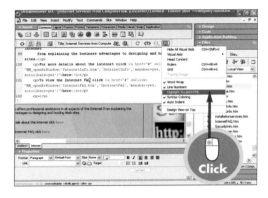

⑨ Change the Colors

You can change the colors used for different parts of the code with the Preferences dialog box. Choose **Edit**, **Preferences** to open the Preferences dialog box. From the Category list, choose **Code Coloring**, and then select **Edit Coloring Scheme** for each of the code elements presented.

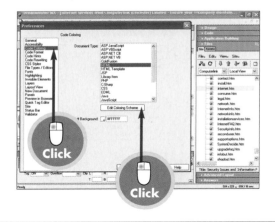

⑩ Change Code Colors

You can select the colors you want for the various page elements within the code. Use the color pickers to change the color for different tags and text in the code view. Click **OK** when you have made your changes. Your color choices are immediately reflected in the code on the screen—as you can see from this rather dramatic example!

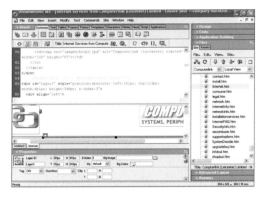

⑪ Format the HTML

You also can control the way the code is displayed onscreen. For example, it's a good idea to have the HTML tags in uppercase letters to make them stand out when you are looking at the code. Choose **Edit**, **Preferences** to open the Preferences dialog box; and choose **Code Format** from the Category list.

⑫ Make Format Changes

Change the settings for the way the code is presented onscreen to suit your preferences. For example, to make all HTML tags appear in uppercase letters, choose **<UPPERCASE>** from the **Default Tag Case** drop-down menu. Click **OK** to close the dialog box when you're done.

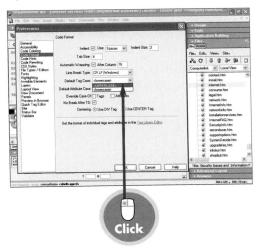

⑭ Clean Up the HTML

If you've created your Web pages entirely in Dreamweaver, there should be nothing to tidy up, but the more you work with your pages, the more likely you are to bring information in from other sources. Choose **Commands**, **Clean Up HTML** to open the Clean Up HTML dialog box.

⑬ Apply the Changes

Changing the Code Format options affects only new documents, unless you specifically tell Dreamweaver otherwise. Choose **Commands**, **Apply Source Formatting** to update the current page with the changes you made to the Code Format page of the Preferences dialog box.

⑮ View the Report

Until you're more confident about working with the code, leave the default check boxes enabled. Notice that you can actually insert specific tags to remove comments from the code. For now, click **OK** to close the Clean Up HTML dialog box and view the report of how Dreamweaver cleaned up your code. The ideal result is shown here.

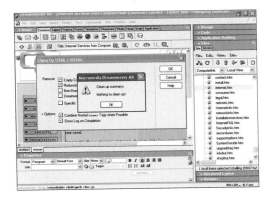

How to Use the Code Inspector

In Task 1, you learned how to view the HTML code for a page by opening the code window from the toolbar. Instead of splitting the screen as you did in the last task, you can access the code in a separate panel, called the Code Inspector. When you display the code for a page in a separate window, you can have the complete design view visible in the background and move the Code Inspector window around to whichever part of the screen you choose to display it.

① Show the Code Inspector

From the **Window** menu, choose **Others**, **Code Inspector**, or press the **F10** key on your keyboard.

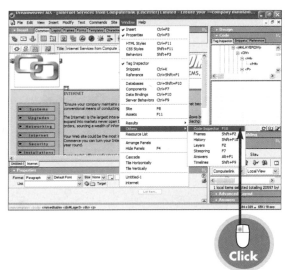

② Resize the Code Inspector

The Code Inspector opens onscreen. You can change its size by dragging the bottom-right corner.

③ Move the Code Inspector

You can move the Code Inspector to any convenient location on the screen simply by dragging its title bar.

④ Check a Tag Reference

Dreamweaver MX enables you to check the meaning of specific tags in your pages. In the Code Inspector (or in the Code View you opened in Task 1), select the tag you want information about. In this example, I have selected the **<IMG>** tag.

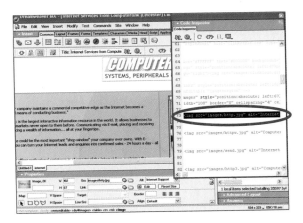

⑤ Open the Reference Panel

On the toolbar in the Code Inspector, click the **Reference** button. The Reference panel immediately displays the information about the tag. Read through the information in this panel to learn more about the selected tag.

⑥ Use the Code Inspector

The Code Inspector's menu includes options such as **Find and Replace**, **Insert Tag**, a link to work on templates, and **Create New Snippet**. You can open the menu at any time by clicking the options menu button at the top of the panel.

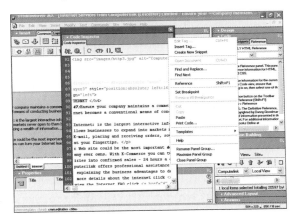

How-to Hint

What's the Difference?

If the Code Inspector introduced in this task and the Code View explained in Task 1 seem to do a lot of the same things, it's because they do. Having different ways of viewing the code is just part of the Dreamweaver way of making sure that you have control over how the code and screen look.

More References?

Task 3, "How to Use the Reference Panel," explains how to check more and different references. Never again will you struggle to know what a tag is or does. As a bonus, the Reference panel contains help not only for HTML, but also for CSS and JavaScript.

How to Use the Reference Panel

The Reference panel, introduced in Dreamweaver 4, has been enhanced in Dreamweaver MX. It enables you to get definitions of tags, Cascading Style Sheets (CSS), JavaScript, ASP, Sitespring, ColdFusion, and many other terms. This great built-in facility will save you hours of time scouring books and Web sites to find out exactly what something means. You can view the Reference panel at any time by selecting the Reference tab within the Code panel group.

① View the Reference Panel

With a document open in the document window, expand the Code group panel and select the **Reference** tab.

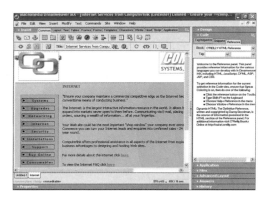

② Select a Tag to Learn About

Use the **Tag** drop-down menu to select a tag that you want more information about. As soon as you make your selection, the information is displayed in the bottom part of the panel.

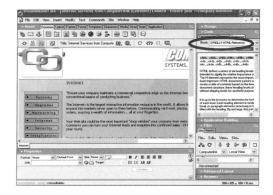

③ Learn About CSS

The options in the **Book** drop-down menu let you choose the reference source you want to use. You can choose from numerous options. To open the reference source for CSS terms, for example, choose **O'REILLY CSS Reference** from the **Book** menu.

Click

4 Choose a CSS Tag

After you've opened the O'REILLY CSS Reference book, the tag options change automatically to display an alphabetic list of all CSS styles. To learn about a specific one, select it from the **Style** drop-down menu. The description appears in the lower part of the panel.

5 Select a Tag in Code View

With the code showing either in the split screen or the Code Inspector, highlight a tag or click the **Reference** button in the toolbar. The Reference panel opens to display the reference for the tag you have highlighted.

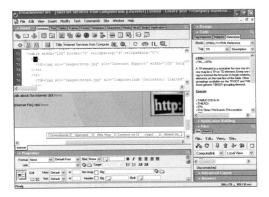

Click

How-to Hint

Attribute Information

Many tags are not standalone tags; they have attributes and values as well. For example, the `<FONT>` tag can have attributes such as face, color, and size. You can see the attributes for a selected tag by using the **Description** drop-down menu in the Reference panel. After you have displayed the information in the Reference panel for a given tag, you can use the **Attributes** drop-down menu to look at each the attribute used by that tag.

Don't Want to Scroll?

Instead of having to scroll through all the tags in the drop-down list, you can type one or more letters into the **Tag** field. The index jumps straight to the first item in the list that starts with the letter you typed, making it easy to find what you want.

How-to Hint

Other Applications

Besides Dreamweaver and Fireworks, Macromedia is probably most well known for Flash. It's almost impossible to use the Internet these days without coming across a Flash Web site. Such is the dominance of Flash in the industry that I'm almost certain you will want to learn about it in the future. Besides being an industry leader in itself, Flash can be integrated with both Dreamweaver and Fireworks, as you've already seen, so learning Flash is a natural progression from here.

Macromedia (http://www.macromedia.com) lets you download evaluation versions of its software and use them as fully functional trials for 30 days. If you want the application after that, simply purchase online and carry on using it.

How to Assign Editors to Non-HTML Documents

Although Dreamweaver is primarily an HTML editor, it has the capabilities to open and edit other types of code file types, such as JavaScript files (.js). Foreign files that you open in Dreamweaver automatically open in Code View (Design View is actually disabled for non-HTML files). After you have edited the file, you can resave it with the original extension or as an HTML file.

❶ Set the Preferences

If you're planning to work with non-HTML files in Dreamweaver, you should set up your preferences for working with these foreign file types. Choose **Edit**, **Preferences** to open the Preferences dialog box. From the Category list, select **File Types/Editors**.

❷ Add a File Type

In the **Open in Code View** field, you can add the extensions for any new file types you want to open in code view. In this example, I've added the .asp file type to the existing list. Use a space to separate extensions in the list. Click **OK** when you're done.

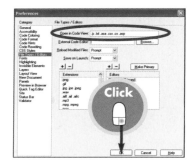

❸ Launch an External Editor

Dreamweaver also lets you edit files in their native environment (the application you used to create the file). When you install Dreamweaver, a large number of editors are already configured. Open the Site window and double-click any file to open it into its associated program. In this example, I selected a Flash movie that will open into Flash for editing.

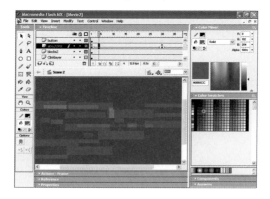

4 Add an Editor for a File Type

In this example, we tell Dreamweaver that .xls files should be opened in Microsoft Excel. To add new file types into the Preferences listings, open the **Preferences** dialog box and choose **File Types/Editors** from the **Category** list. Click the **+** button above the **Extensions** list to open a text box.

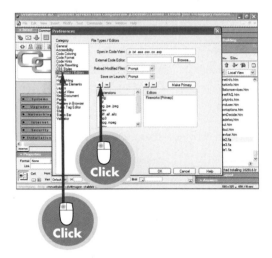

5 Add a File Extension

In the text box, type the file extension that you are adding to the list. Be sure to include the period (.) with the extension, or the file type will not be recognized.

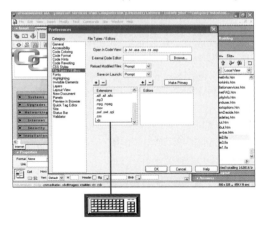

6 Add the Editor

Select the file type you just added and click the **+** button. In the dialog box that opens, browse to the application file you want to use to edit the file type. I selected the .xls file extension and then selected Excel as the editor. Click **Open** to continue.

7 Remove a File Type

You can easily remove a file type from the Extensions list at any time. Choose the file type you want to delete and click the **–** button above the **Extensions** list.

How-to Hint

Caution About Removing File Types

Be sure you really want to delete a file type because Dreamweaver displays no confirmation dialog box before deleting the entry from the list. You might want to delete an extension if you uninstall the associated application from your computer.

How to Download New Extensions for Dreamweaver and Fireworks

The Macromedia Web site is home to some great help files and also the Macromedia Exchange, a great place for getting new behaviors and extensions for the software. The behaviors and extensions are written by other Dreamweaver and Fireworks users who post the files to the site for free download. There is no limit to the number of extensions you can download. Visit the site to discover what timesaving extensions are available. The steps here relate to Dreamweaver; however, they work in the same way if you access the Exchange from Fireworks.

1 Open the Exchange

Jump right to the Macromedia Exchange Web site by choosing **Help**, **Dreamweaver Exchange**. Click the **Browse Extensions** drop-down menu to display a list of Dreamweaver extensions that you can search the site for. Select the type of file you are looking for; select **All Categories** to see the complete listing of available files.

2 Select an Extension

The extensions that satisfy your selection in Step 1 are displayed onscreen. You can see the name of the extension along with other relevant information. Click the name of any extension to learn more about it. (The Macromedia logo indicates that Macromedia has approved the extension and found it to be stable in the working environment.)

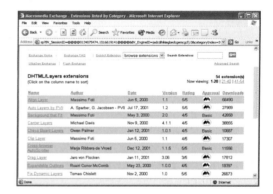

3 Read All About It

The information page for the extension you selected contains details about the purpose of the extension and download information. To download the file to your computer, click the **download** link for the appropriate version of the file. When prompted, choose to save the file, and choose the location on the disk to which you want to save the file.

Click

④ Install the Extension

Back in Dreamweaver, choose **Commands**, **Manage Extensions** to open the Extension Manager. Click the **Install Extension** button on the toolbar to open the Select Extension to Install dialog box. Browse to the file you downloaded, select it, and click **Install** to continue.

⑤ Accept the Disclaimer

You are presented with a disclaimer screen informing you that you are about to install a third-party product. To continue, you must click **Accept** or the extension will not be installed. When the installation is complete, you'll see a confirmation screen telling you what to do next.

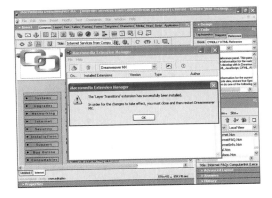

How-to Hint

Remove an Extension

If you decide that you don't want an extension you have downloaded (for example, if it doesn't work the way you expected), choose **Commands**, **Manage Extensions** to open the Extension Manger. Choose the extension you want to delete and click the **trash can** to remove it.

⑥ Read the Information Screen

The next screen tells you more about the extension you have installed, such as the name, author, and a little more detail.

⑦ Close and Reopen Dreamweaver

Most extensions require you to shut down and reopen Dreamweaver before the installation takes effect. Be sure you have saved all your work before you close the program. Immediately reopen the application to continue your work. The extension appears in the location specified in the Extension Manager screen.

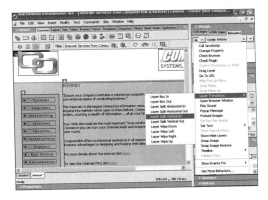

Index

Symbols

3D images (Fireworks), 212
circles, 213-215
effects, 220-225
gradient fill in circles, 213
layers, 218-219
objects, 215-216
special effects, 217
text effects, 218-225

4-Up tab, 264

A

Active Area tab, 157

Adding button states, 158-159, 162-165

Advanced settings, pop-up menus, 174

Appearance tab, 172

Appearances, pop-up menus, 172

actions
behaviors, 194
recordsets, 330

activating layers, 181-182
Fireworks, 229

Add to Favorites icon, 61

adding
assets to groups, 64
behaviors to pages, 198-201
frames, Fireworks, 232-233
layers, Fireworks, 228-229
Library items, 66-67
template items, Assets panel, 72

Advanced tab, 25, 32

Align Center button, 39

Align Left button, 39

Align Right button, 39

aligning
images, Property Inspector, 134
text, 38-39
Fireworks, 211-212

anchors, 84
creating, 85-87
linking to, 85-86
menus, 86-87
naming, 85-87

Animate dialog box, 231

animating layers, 177

animations
Dreamweaver, inserting into pages, 236-237
Fireworks, 146-147, 230
creating, 231
editing, 238-242
exporting to Dreamweaver, 235
exporting to Flash, 237
Frame Delay, 249
frames, 231-233
layers, 238-242
looping, 234, 244-245
multi-frame editing, 249
onion skinning, 248-249
saving as Flash files, 246-247
settings, 234
symbols, 242-247
testing, 234
text, 230
text as symbols, 233

timeline, 190-191
transformations, 244-245
viewing, 232-233

Answers panel (Fireworks), 122

anti-aliased text (Fireworks), 212

Application tab, 15, 318

applications, code, 373
Code Inspector, 379-383
colors, 377
formatting, 377
modifying, 374-376
split screens, 375
syntax coloring, 376
viewing, 378

Apply Styles button, 341

assets
adding to groups, 64
colors, applying to text, 60-61
copying, 58-59
defined, 55
deleting, 62-63
embedded, 58
inserting, 59
libraries, 66-68
links, 58-61
naming, 62-63
removing from Favorites list, 64
subgroups, 63
templates, 59-61
adding content, 72
creating, 70-71
opening, 75
saving content, 73-74
setting preferences, 74-75

How can we make this index more useful? Email us at indexes@quepublishing.com

How can we make this index more useful? Email us at indexes@quepublishing.com

Frames panel group
(Fireworks), 121
Frames tab, 13, 94, 104-105
framesets, 93. *See also*
frames
borders, 94-95, 99-100
columns, 100
creating, 94-95
deleting, 96
horizontal splits, 95
links, 108-109
nested, 104-105
overview, 97-99
properties, 98
borders, 100-102
margins, 102
Nested Frameset option,
103-105
NoFrames option,
103-104
scrolling, 102
selecting, 99
setting, 101-105
viewing, 99-101
titles, 100

G

GIF image files (Graphics
Interchange Format
images), 126
opening in Fireworks,
144-145
optimizing files, 266-267
gradient fill (Fireworks)
circles, 213
objects, 216-217
graphics
buttons, editing, 160-165
Fireworks overview, 111
Graphics Interchange
Format. *See* GIF image files
grids, snapping layers to,
186
groups, assets, 64

H

Head tab, 14
headings
text, 39
Web photo albums, 294
Help menu (Dreamweaver),
9
hiding panel groups
(Dreamweaver), 17
History panel group
(Fireworks), 121-122
home pages, setting, 30
horizontal splits, framesets,
95
Hotspot tool, 171
Hotspots, defined, 171
HTML
document lists, 45
creating, 45
deleting styles, 50
editing properties, 47-49
removing formatting, 46
Fireworks, inserting into
Dreamweaver, 258-259
formatting text, 37
importing documents from
Word, 42-43
non-HTML documents, edi-
tors, 383-385
text slices, 257
drawing, 257-258
editing, 258
exporting, 258
text styles, 47
deleting, 50
fonts, 48
text, 49
HTML code, 374
Code Inspector, 379
tag references, 380-383
formatting, 377
modifying, 375-376
colors, 377
split screens, 375
syntax coloring, 376
viewing, 378

HTML editor, 45
HTML source code, hyper-
links, 82
HTML Styles panel, 48-50
HTML tag styles, 37
HTML tags, redefining in CSS,
52-53
hyperlinks. *See also* links
creating, 78-79
deleting, 80-81
editing, 80-81
email
anchors, 84-87
colors, 88-89
creating, 82
form elements, 90
Insert bar, 84
testing, 86
text, 83-84
thumbnails, 84-86
external, 77-79
files, 82
Find and Replace option,
81-82
frames, 109
HTML source code, 82
images, 79
internal, 77
locating, 80-81
overview, 77
text, 78, 83-84
URLs, 82
hypermedia, 77

I

icons
Add to Favorites, 61
Colors category, 60, 63
Draw Layer, 179-180
Fireworks, 166
Flash, 298
Image, 132
Image Placeholder, 136
Library, 68

How can we make this index more useful? Email us at indexes@quepublishing.com

How can we make this index more useful? Email us at indexes@quepublishing.com

How can we make this index more useful? Email us at indexes@quepublishing.com